Cultivating Freud's Garden in France

Cultivating Freud's Garden in France

Marion Michel Oliner, Ph.D.

Jason Aronson Inc.
Northvale, New Jersey
London

10 9 8 7 6 5 4 3 2 1

Library of Congress Cataloging-in-Publication Data

Oliner, Marion Michel.

Cultivating Freud's garden in France / Marion Michel Oliner.
p. cm.
Bibliography: p.
Includes index.
ISBN 0-87668-995-0

1. Psychoanalysis—France—History. 2. Freud, Sigmund, 1856–1939. 3. France—Intellectual life—20th century. I. Title.
BF175.039 1988
150.19'52'0944—dc19 87-31908

Manufactured in the United States of America.

To Alan, who helped me
cultivate my garden.

Contents

Preface

This book relates the fate of Freud's heritage in France where fascination with the unconscious prompted its acceptance and led to its evolution. I came upon this relatively uncharted territory, surrounded by language and cultural barriers, in search of insight into clinical problems. What I found were studies couched in Freud's early terminology on sexuality and its relation to narcissism; on the nature and structure of the unconscious—the hub of internal conflicts between French analysts—and on the complex issues of mind and body.

In exploring this material, I have tried to act as a guide, not merely a translator, and to show that the French contribution to psychoanalysis, despite its diversity and controversy, is characterized chiefly by the endeavor to further, deepen, and integrate the study of the unconscious. Mine was not an easy task. The existing literature does not guide the uninitiated, and the French themselves are happily unconcerned, or unaware, that their communications are relatively inaccessible to colleagues in other countries. They expect to be understood because they assume that everyone thinks as they do; therefore they do not offer any assistance to those who would map out the territory called *French psychoanalysis*. This book is the result of my wish to bring the work of the French to others in order to demonstrate the fertility of their approach to Freud.

I discovered that the French study Freud's work as if Columbus's voyage were relevant only to geographers and as if progress in psychoanalysis could be achieved without reference to the ever-growing array of new concepts that have so encumbered the field. I became aware that the French act tacitly as if France were the center of the psychoanalytic world and as if the task of maintaining and defining the true nature of psychoanalysis rested entirely on their shoulders. Pierre Nora has referred to this as the French attitude of stewardship in matters intellectual.

Only one man, Jacques Lacan, went so far as to proclaim himself alone vis-à-vis Freud. The other French analysts watch over the purity of psychoanalysis more discreetly and with greater humility. Their insistence that the current generation of analysts remember that the psyche is grounded in mortal flesh and their admonitions against flights of speculation and metaphysics reminded me of Voltaire's caution against excesses of philosophical speculations, illusory optimism from abroad, and verbal pyrotechnics, which are so dear to his countrymen. Voltaire's words: "That's well said . . . , but we must cultivate our garden" are a plea to resist the attraction of philosophy and the lure of its brilliant discourse. By choosing the title *Cultivating Freud's Garden in France*, I intend to stress the similarity between Voltaire's appeal and the French attempts to keep Freud's heritage grounded in material reality.

The text will show the specific way in which the French have studied Freud's entire legacy; how they plowed Freud's garden but reaped a harvest bearing the imprint of the cultivators. They have enriched it, corrupted it, attempted to purify it, tried to sanctify it, and used it to revolt against the establishment. They have watched over it in order to guard it against decay and old age. Their success in this is undisputed: psychoanalysis is more alive in France than anywhere else in the world.

The French have kept Freud's ideas alive by showing respect for them without embalming them. His theories have been exposed to many currents of thought that stimulate and influence each other and that reflect "the immoderate taste of the Gallic people for discussions and for quarrels, but also for intellectual analysis and exactness" (Laplanche 1987).

The first third of this book might interest any student of French culture, since it covers intellectual trends, the history of psychoanalysis in France, and comments about psychoanalysis in general as well as about its transmission by established psychoanalytic organizations. The second part concerns the field of classical analysis: clinical problems interpreted by means of relatively uncommon theoretical formulations and studies of some of the implications of Freud's theory on sexuality. In this section, it is shown how close adherence to interpretations based on psychosexual phases has yielded a wealth of insights beyond those discovered by the pioneers of psychoanalysis, including interpretations of problems around separation–individuation and narcissism. The third section covers nonverbalized reactions to stress with an excursion into some fascinating theories of the birth of mental life itself. This last part discusses another aspect of the mind–body problem: the treatment of psychosomatic illness. It describes the theory of the cause of somatic reaction to stress and ends with some interesting speculative hypotheses about the foundations of mental life.

Because I lacked a map of this territory I was traversing, I needed, asked for, and obtained the assistance of many French colleagues. Madame Janine Chasseguet-Smirgel and Dr. Béla Grunberger were unstinting with their time and friendship. From them I received all the help I needed to assure me that my interpretation of their work was in keeping with their ideas.

They also supplied me with material pertaining to the history of psychoanalysis in France and its philosophical underpinnings. My good friend Dr. Régine Herzberg-Poloniecka opened the world of psychosomatic medicine to me and introduced me to Dr. Pierre Marty, who graciously permitted me to attend numerous case conferences at the Institut de Psychosomatique de Paris and who supplied me with background material (as well as a T-shirt marked IPSO). Dr. Joyce McDougall generously provided me with reprints and books, and Dr. Denise Braunschweig devoted all the time I needed to verify and clarify my ideas concerning her work and that of Dr. Michel Fain, himself unavailable. Other colleagues, Drs. P.-C. Racamier, J. Laplanche, D. Anzieu, A. de Mijolla, C. Chiland, J.-B. Pontalis, C. Girard, F. Pasche, and S. Schneiderman answered my questions fully, and all helped with reprints and reference to other pertinent material. I am responsible for the translation of the French and German texts. Where this is not the case, the reference indicates the source of the text.

Here at home, Dr. Otto Kernberg laid the cornerstone for this project and generously made suggestions for improving it. Dr. Edith Schwartz was always open to the ideas I found stimulating and refreshing. She discussed them with me and reinforced my belief that the French approach is sufficiently different and valid to merit the attention I was giving it. Dr. Edith Kurzweil, whose sociological study of psychoanalysis in four countries parallels mine with regard to France, acted as a welcome sounding board. We were able to compare our observations informally, and I felt less of the pain of the writer's isolation because of my contact with her. For that reason, I am also indebted to my students and supervisees whose interest stimulated my own effort.

Mrs. Natalie Altman and Carolyn S. Oliner, my daughter, helped me over rough spots of style and organization; Andrew J. Oliner, my son, and Mr. Sol Goodman stood by me as I struggled with the mysteries of that great invention, the computer. My thanks go to Mrs. Marthe Eidelberg for her interest in the manuscript and to the staff of Jason Aronson, in particular Elena LePera, whose cooperation and respect I appreciate.

My husband, Alan, never waivered in his belief in this book and its potential interest for others. He took the backseat cheerfully and without question any time it concerned the book. Without his encouragement this endeavor would have been unthinkable.

Marion Michel Oliner

PART I

THE FREUDIAN HERITAGE IN FRANCE

1

Psychoanalysis with a French Accent

Psychoanalysis in France is unlike psychoanalysis in other countries. The French have given it their own imprint so that their approach, their emphasis, and their techniques differ from those of any other country. The unique character of French psychoanalysis is related to the nation's cultural milieu: its erudition, its reverence for tradition, and its intellectuals' capacity for incisive logic and passion for independence. Psychoanalysis in France began relatively late in comparison to the rest of the Western world, and it had a rather unorthodox introduction. Enthusiasm for the new science initially came from literary figures, led by the surrealist poet, André Breton, rather than from members of psychiatric circles who responded to the theories imported from Vienna with considerable reticence. Although since that time a proper French psychoanalytic organization has been founded, the imprint of the discipline's unusual origins persists.

This book concentrates on those contributions by French

psychoanalysts that are different from and challenging of most commonly held notions. The main topics covered are the history of psychoanalysis in France, the reflections of French analysts on the influence of Freud, the man, on psychoanalytic thinking, and the attempts of French analysts to find a purer way of transmitting psychoanalysis, to apply psychoanalytic knowledge to the understanding of cultural or political events, to construct their own versions of how Freud's theory should evolve, to return to some very early issues, such as the relation between mind and body, and finally to question the nature of psychic reality.

I selected material based on its clinical usefulness, its challenging aspects, and, in some cases, for its entertainment value. My wish to be fair and representative was sometimes frustrated by my own limitations: the subjects of child analysis, group analysis, and psychosis are not included, nor did I convey the literature that is so convoluted and intellectualized that its sense escaped me. I admit to having given short shrift to analysts whose ideas are similar to those prevalent elsewhere, but I also found such writers to be in the minority of those who publish in France.

I have acted as an interpreter as well as a translator, attempting to clarify many of the complexities and convolutions in the texts I present, though these very characteristics are what make the French rewarding, charming, and exasperating. Thus in bridging two quite different worlds, I endeavored to retain the flavor of the original French so that Anglicizing it does not completely flatten its character.

Because of the publicity he has received and the notoriety attached to his name, many Americans have the mistaken impression that Jacques Lacan represents the views of most French psychoanalysts. He does not, but writing about French psychoanalysis without paying attention to him is almost like looking at the painting of a pipe by René Magritte entitled "This is not a pipe." Lacan's presence has been pervasive, even to those who rejected him from the start, because these analysts defended vigorously and often brilliantly their continued adherence to psychoanalytic tradition. I decided that the soul-searching he engendered among the orthodox analysts was too valuable to be ignored and should be included even though this book is not about Lacan.

His impact was both political and theoretical. A detailed rendering of his theories has been given by others who know that his texts are essentially unreadable and need to be interpreted, something that I have rarely attempted to do. However, I shall discuss Lacan's extensive contribution to the psychoanalytic political scene in Chapter 3 and some of his thinking in Chapter 7.

He and his many followers are also responsible for the great proliferation and popularization of psychoanalysis in France, even though it is questionable whether his method deserves that designation. Lacan called his organization École Freudienne; attaching the name of the founder of psychoanalysis to the name of his group is, in my opinion, an illustration of Freud's caustic comment that there were "those who would warm their soup at our fire."

In order to do justice to the current intellectual climate in Paris, it was necessary to consider the writings of some analysts whose questioning of psychoanalytic theories seems undeterred by the possibility that it might undermine some idea or organization they basically cherish. To my mind, these individuals, like Michel Fain, for example, whose work will be extensively discussed throughout the book, occasionally threaten to take that wonderful French capacity for logical examination one step too far, but this is something for the reader to judge. What looks to one person like sawing off the branch upon which one is sitting may look to another like a much-needed housecleaning.

I have stated that the French analysts tend to think differently. In order to learn from this difference, one must accept, at least partly, the premises on which their thinking is based. Their most important assumption is that French analysts are intellectuals. Nora (1978) compared them with their American counterparts in the following manner: "American intellectuals are invested with a function, not a ministry; they exercise a trade, not a stewardship" (p. 335). What especially commands the interest and attention of the French are the nature and essence of the psychoanalytic process, and their attitude often suggests that they think of themselves as the guardians of Freud's heritage. They watch that it remains pure, and therefore they tend to go back to Freud and the other founders of psychoanalysis rather than quote one another as American analysts frequently do.

With their preference for elaborating Freud's theories rather than discarding or revising them, the French analysts have kept Freud's heritage alive and have attempted to give new life to concepts that have fallen into disuse elsewhere. For many of them, Freud's initial formulation of the death instinct is a fertile field for updating earlier ideas because Freud never integrated his later thoughts about instincts with his previous understanding of the unconscious. Typically, many French analysts have remained with the original formulation of Thanatos and have not settled for its later, more generally accepted, version: aggression.

Freud, however, is not their sole mentor; Abraham and Ferenczi rank high among the theorists the French are fond of, and Klein's works are studied seriously. The majority of the French are not Kleinians, however, although they have not hesitated to adopt those of Klein's ideas that they regard as useful. "After all, without being Kleinian, how can we not keep something of that which Klein taught us about the early roots of the Oedipus?" Chiland (1974, p. 45) queries.

Another important difference is inherent in the French language. Mavis Gallant (1985) compared it to English: "English and French are not negative-positive images of each other, but entirely different instruments. The two languages cannot be made to work in the same way. A French sentence, transcribed exactly as it stands, means an English sentence with five words too many. The poise and tension of French, translated word for word, turns into a length of frayed elastic" (p. 24). Many French analysts seem to cherish a style that tries to reflect the multiple determinants of psychoanalytic concepts. They are not striving for scientific conciseness. Quite the contrary. The French prefer a style that will express the amorphous, open-ended, even ambiguous character of the unconscious, a style that does not use expressions borrowed from the natural sciences but strives for poetic evocativeness.

Such titles as "*Fantasme originaire, fantasmes des origines, origine du fantasme*" abound. When this particular one was translated into English for publication, it became *Fantasy and Sexuality* (1968). Interesting enough but extraordinarily flat and in no way evoking the richness of "Original fantasy, fantasies of origins [otherwise known as family romance], and origin of fantasy." The authors of this particular article, Laplanche and Pontalis, are responsible for the carefully researched and extremely practical *The Language of Psychoanalysis* (1973). André Green, who like many of his compatriots, cannot resist the sound of words, entitled one of his articles "L'objet dans l'analyse, l'analyse de l'objet, l'objet de l'analyse" ("The object in analysis, the analysis of the object, the object of analysis").

Although the French analysts seem to be united in trying to make psychoanalytic theory yield more explanations, they often come up with very different answers. When they disagree, they analyze the problem down to its very foundations; in the course of doing so, however, they draw attention to issues that might otherwise not be considered. It is important to remember that the French are accustomed to judging an argument by its elegance rather than its usefulness. And if they are inordinately eager to challenge all assumptions, the outcome of their analyses is often, as will be seen, impressive.

This emphasis naturally leads the French toward abstraction in their writings. Their failure to consider the practical applications of their pronouncements can sometimes be frustrating, especially if one wishes to find out how they actually conduct themselves technically. French psychoanalytic literature is notorious for its sparsity of case material. Moore (1984) put it well in his review of a recent collection of French analytic essays: "One will look in vain for practical approaches to better technique in these essays, but should read them with an appreciation of esthetics; they do not provide solutions, but an enlightened perspective on the human condition which will make enjoyable reading in an intellectual excursion abroad" (p. 199). For who but a Frenchman could have said, "The answer is the misfortune of the question"?

By the same token, the French are undeterred by certain incompatibilities in Freud's theories. Rather than throw out the theory, they find some element in it that will accommodate the incompatibilities. For example, let us consider the problem of the ego and the introduction of the concept of the self. Left with the legacy of Freud's "Ich," Hartmann devised a theory from which three concepts emerged: the biological and innate autonomous ego, the ego born out of conflict with external reality and in identification with it, and the self as the object of libido. Laplanche also tackled Freud's problematic legacy, but with different results. Nothing, he says, is biological. Freud never meant psychoanalysis to be the equivalent of biology, although he was frequently seduced by the possibility of an equation between what is innate and what is psychic. We can say that the ego is both subject and object if we assume that it is self-love that makes us function. Laplanche consistently maintains that if Freud was ambiguous when he used "Ich" as both object and subject, then that ambiguity should be retained and its meaning explicated.

Another important difference between French and American psychoanalysts is that the broad background of the French in the humanities takes precedence over their adherence to medicine or psychology. They are not specialists in the vocational sense. They are intellectuals and don't hesitate to show their erudition. Hence, in France the line of demarcation between psychoanalysis and the worlds of religion, philosophy, politics, and art is simply not as hermetic as it tends to be here, where the emphasis is on the connection between psychoanalysis and medicine. The French psychoanalytic literature is studded with references to the culture at large, making for a much livelier exchange of ideas between psychoanalysis and these other worlds than exists elsewhere. This is not surprising to anyone acquainted with the humanistic tradition in French education. Because of this link between psychoanalysis and the broader French culture, the still unresolved issue of how Freud's work is to be translated into French was debated in *Le Monde*, a daily newspaper, by two specialists who expounded their opposing views.

As a corollary to this mingling of disciplines is, or was until recently, the fervent involvement with politics on the part of French intellectuals. They feel a much greater need to define themselves politically than do most of their non-French colleagues, a tendency best illustrated by Malraux and Sartre. It is a historical fact that alongside those who quietly studied psychoanalysis in an effort to understand mental illness were those more vociferous types who responded with equal enthusiasm to Freud and Marx. Fired by revolutionary zeal, they studied the ideas of both, thinking that they provided the cure for the ills of mankind. Nowhere else do we find this peculiar combination of ideas. Indeed, this parallel interest reflects the tendency of twentieth-century French intellectuals toward a militant and revolutionary leftism. The French kind of political involvement in the postwar era is different from the benign liberalism of American psychoanalysts. The latter have tended to vote, at least until recently, mildly left of center, but they generally do not consider that their political position has anything to do with the structure of the psychoanalytic institutes or with the private practice of psychoanalysis. But "Politics and tradition, even when not explicit, are in the air French intellectuals breathe," Edith Kurzweil observes (1980, p. x).[1]

The French seemingly interdisciplinary approach to psychoanalysis owes more to the classical education common to French intellectuals than to an alliance between psychoanalysis and any of the established academic disciplines. The tie between psychoanalysis and the medical profession is weaker in France than in the United States, and the French prefer it that way. The Americans, in contrast, seem more committed to gaining acceptance in the scientific world, especially in the field of medicine. French intellectuals, almost from the beginning, envisioned psychoanalysis as having a wider application than the cure of mental illness. It was definitely greeted and treated more as a cultural than as a therapeutic phenomenon. According to Anzieu (1975) the poets André Breton and Louis Aragon celebrated the fiftieth anniversary of the study of hysteria as the "greatest poetic discovery of the end of the nineteenth century" (p. 131).

To this day, therefore, no alliance exists between psychoanalysis in France and medicine or any other established discipline. Barande (1975) states this position vigorously: "If theory does not convince us of it, history confirms that being outside established territories is the only status viable for analysis" (p. 238). Others have expressed similar misgivings about any possible encroachment upon the ground French psychoanalysis has mapped out for itself.

This attitude places the French at a great distance from their North American colleagues, whom they consider wedded to psychiatry. "The Americans followed their own road. As a new science, psychoanalysis was incomprehensible in America if only because Americans understood 'science' to apply only to natural sciences and to laboratory research. . . . Soon pushed out of psychology by behaviorism, [psychoanalysis] was welcomed into psychiatry" (Federn 1975, p. 66).

The French see no need to make psychoanalysis "respectable" by applying the criteria of the natural sciences to its methodology. In this respect they are closer to Freud's view of psychoanalysis as *Geisteswissenschaft*, science of the spirit. They are convinced that the instrument of psychoanalysis is interpretation; this orientation again tends to alienate them from a hard science, such as medicine. Americans are drawn to direct observation and Freud's genetic reconstructions, whereas the French tend to be more interested in symbols, metaphors, and the here and now of the analytic situation. Green (1975a) is critical of the genetic approach since he considers that it is used by those who do not wish to accept the total edifice of psychoanalysis. Pasche (1969) insists that drives belong to the realm of theoretical constructs, not observable phenomena, and warns against thinking of them as motivated behavior. However, for Brenner (1955), an American, "the division of drives . . . is based on clinical grounds" (p. 22).

Despite their erudition, most French analysts rarely refer to foreign colleagues, except for the founders. They vary in their knowledge of foreign psychoanalytic literature, but the majority seem as little concerned with what is being done anywhere abroad as their foreign colleagues are with them. The myth of the tower of Babel describes aptly the world of psychoanalytic theories.

Those French analysts who are studying psychotic and borderline pathology, like Racamier and Anzieu, may occasionally draw from the work of Americans, but for the most part, when they are not crusading against others, the French ignore those contemporaries whose ideas do not fit in with their thinking. Again, this is partly caused by a different approach to scientific writing. Until very recently the French have not provided well-documented references to the pertinent literature. Lately, however, an increase in the publication of some French articles abroad has been having an effect, and there has been a perceptible trend toward more care in citing precise references.

At a time when psychoanalysts in other parts of the world, following Freud's initiative, have turned to a study of the ego, the French have remained concerned with the study of the unconscious. In their relative neglect of the ego, one gains the impression that they are Kleinians. As already stated, the majority are not, although they have not hesitated to adopt Kleinian ideas that they regarded as useful. Colette Chiland (1981) describes the French attitude: "We are neither eclectic, nor do we wish to be confined to the viewpoint of a given school. Variety, for us, appears to be a source of richness and we attempt to combine clinical work with philosophical reflection, taking precautions at the same time, not to succumb to the power and magic of words" (p. 67). There tends to be a great variety of ideas among the French, who pride themselves on their diversity of opinions.

The French are in the habit of taking parts of theories and integrating them with their own thinking without becoming disciplines or belonging to this or that school. They are iconoclastic, yet they retain a respect for tradition. They show an independence which the Americans, who are still trying to assure themselves that they have a tradition, lack. Perhaps this is why the Europeans who came to the United States, Hartmann, Kris, and Loewenstein, for example, attained positions of such influence and leadership in American psychoanalytic thinking.

Concepts such as separation–individuation, object constancy, or self–object, and many others, are foreign to the French, even if the phenomena these terms attempt to describe are related to what they are studying. The reason these words do not appear in the French works is that the French pretty much ignore Hartmann, Jacobson, Mahler, and Kohut, and formulate their theories in the more traditional terminology. Pontalis (1977) questions whether the self is a concept that can be exported, even though the French language has the equivalent *soi*. Is it surprising, then, that there is no self-psychology in France?

By far the greatest number of criticisms of their American colleagues are aimed at Hartmann and the concept of the autonomous ego. Here the French agree among themselves, if not explicitly, at least tacitly. I have not run across any French writer who mentions American ego psychology in an accepting vein. The opinions reproduced below stem from a wide spectrum of the French psychoanalytic field.

"If Freud's work is open to multiple interpretations and as a consequence dedicated to divergent developments, we can only say that the orientation taken by Hartmann and the greatest part of North American psychoanalysis is unjustifiable," says André Green (1975a, p. 114). Robert Barande (1975) refers to ego psychology as the "deviation which rules officially and represents the positive conformism of psychoanalysis, instituted by ego psychology, which rules psychoanalysis in its highest circles since its consecration to the presidency of the International Association through the mediation of its instigator, H. Hartmann" (p. 243). Béla Grunberger (1971, 1979 ed.) says, more moderately, "In my opinion, acceptance of the notion of the 'autonomous ego,' with its denial of the conflicted genesis of the ego, would deprive psychoanalytic theory of the whole primitive instinctual dialectic, that is, the unconscious as conceived by depth psychology, and would foster a trend (which is already evident) toward superficial study of the 'ego functions' exclusively. To follow such a course would be to depart from the Freudian orientation and regress toward academic psychology" (p. 14). Michel Fain (1971), who on many issues differs from the others, says: "You know with what vigor Christian David, Pierre Marty, Michel de M'Uzan, and I have answered this hypothesis: the autonomous ego is like a skeleton when it is perceived. The introduction of such a theory appears to us even as symptomatic of a form of dementalization of psychoanalysis, of a deadly retreat from Freud's opinion" (p. 302).

Pontalis (1977) cautions that structural theory runs the risk of being mechanistic. The general suspicion with which the

French view the structural theory is evidenced by the fact that it has not even been endowed with a special French name: it is called simply the "second topography" (p. 137).

Pontalis (1979) further states that the structural hypothesis has a "localizing" impact with regard to the unconscious, where, whether in reality or in the imagination, the ego attains a central place. He contrasts this with what he calls the decentering effect of the unconscious, that is, the unconscious as "the other scene." The unconscious, he explains, is connected with the "subversion of the subject"—"a subversion that psychoanalysis has first met in its old territory, the mind, and that psychoanalysis is destined to induce, to provoke in all places, be it in the field of knowledge or social institutions" (p. 9).

It is evident that the French analysts as a whole are different in their approach to psychoanalysis for many reasons, even though there are considerable variations among them. Because they are not infatuated with novelty, they study the ideas that the pioneers left unfinished and try to find a place for them within the corpus of psychoanalytic theory. In directing their efforts in this way they have, I believe, rendered psychoanalysis an important service.

Unfortunately, some of them have tended to assume that they are continuing Freud's tradition, while others judge them to be seriously deviating from it. But French reverence for tradition ultimately saves them from their own excesses. The love for the new is a characteristic of the New World. The French like to think of themselves as the stewards of classical analysis.

Much as some, like Chasseguet-Smirgel and Roudinesco, stress the universality of psychoanalysis and imply that tying a statement to a national origin diminishes its validity, I think that there is an identifiable way in which the French solve problems. Thus, while there is no French psychoanalysis in the sense of a school to which most practitioners belong, there is nevertheless a recognizable French style of following the Freudian tradition. At a time when novelty "is in," French analysts have demonstrated the fertility and the malleability of the old by conceptualizing some of the newer concerns in terms of the language of Freud's original theories. These new theories are not just manifestitations of the well-known French intellectual inclination; rather, they are the work of people who spend most of their time in the consulting room and gather their data from clinical observations. They shed light on clinical problems and add a fresh dimension to the approach to patients. I welcome the opportunity to introduce some of these theories and observations to analysts who do not have access to this body of literature because of linguistic barriers. If this book succeeds in prescribing areas of inquiry other than those already familiar to Americans, and if it expands the horizons of those who are open to a different approach to the issues facing psychoanalysts, it will have served its purpose. If, in addition, it enlightens, challenges, and entertains, it will have conveyed my attitude toward French psychoanalysis.

Notes

[1] There were leftist analysts in the United States, but they did not participate publicly in Marxist causes as some of the leading members of the Paris Psychoanalytic Society did after World War II.

2

Psychoanalysis in France before World War II

Those Who Told the Tale

The history of psychoanalysis in France has been tumultuous. We are probably too close in time to the events to be assured of a completely reliable account, especially since many of the participants are still alive and have strong partisan feelings. The most complete account we have is Roudinesco's (1982, 1986), which is extremely well researched but reflects the author's bias. The other sources, such as Turkle's sociologically oriented account, are incomplete. Thus the total picture has to be patiently knitted together from the various writings that are available plus official letters and documents.

Turkle's 1978 account, *Psychoanalytic Politics, Freud's French Revolution*, suffers from her method of gathering data. She interviewed "nearly one hundred and fifty French psychoanalysts" of all parties, including Lacan, to whom she acknowledges her gratitude, but she deliberately avoided attributing material derived from the interviews and made short shrift of the non-Lacanians.

Roudinesco, whose story is titled *La Bataille de Cent Ans*, is herself a warrior with a pen. Her declared enemies are the International Psychoanalytic Association, with its wish to standardize psychoanalysis and, according to her, to keep it purely medical. She does broaden her crusade and through the use of guilt by association leaves only one anointed saint in the person of her mother, one of the participants in the most turbulent period of psychoanalysis in France. This bias has undoubtedly influenced her selection of the material, but she has amassed so much of it and provided so many details from original sources that her report constitutes an important source of information. It is thanks to her that the history of French psychoanalysis has been chronicled at all.

Gradually, more and more accounts of later developments are becoming available. Recently I received a 1982 account by de Mijolla, "La Psychanalyse en France (1893–1965)," which provided some much needed corroboration and elaboration of data obtained through other sources, such as the booklet by Jacques-Alain Miller, Lacan's son-in-law, clearly partisan in intent. It contains certain of the original documents and letters pertaining to the important controversy of 1953 and convinces most poignantly that neither Lacan nor his opponents had the monopoly on sainthood.

Other material, such as Freud's letters, an article by Smirnoff ("From Vienna to Paris," 1979), Ilse and Robert Barande's *Histoire de la Psychanalyse en France* (1975), Chiland's 1981 account, and a more recent account by Chasseguet-Smirgel (1984a), are complementary and provide the basis for a more reliable and trustworthy history. By checking the sources that have an obvious stake in one side of the battle against those from the other side, a reasonably cohesive and most interesting story emerges.

The Problem of Translating Freud

The best way to prepare the reader for what will be a turbulent tale is to describe the fate of the translation of Freud's work in France. To begin with the end of the story: to this day there exists no unified and consistent French translation of Freud's work comparable to the English *Standard Edition*, although many people thought that the project of translating Freud's work into French was desirable. (At the present time, a team of twenty translators directed by Jean Laplanche, Janine Altounian, André Bourguignon, Pierre Cotet, Alain Rauzy, and Francois Robert is working on a collected works of Freud.) The bilingual psychoanalyst, René Laforgue, who corresponded with Freud, mentioned his interest in the project as early as 1923, but for reasons unknown he never undertook the work, although he himself published extensively. At the present time, 85 to 90 percent of Freud's work has been translated into French. Unfortunately, both the quality and the terminology vary substantially, and many articles appeared in obscure places and are out of print. Some works have had as many as eighteen different translations.

The copyrights to these translations belong to various publishers, who showed their goodwill by signing an agreement in 1966 to permit a complete and uniform edition to appear. Immediately, problems arose around the style of translation. The issues are comparable to the questions that have been raised with increasing urgency concerning Strachey's choice of a technical vocabulary. However, in the English-speaking world the debate came long after the fact, whereas in France the issue of the style presented the first hurdle to any translation at all. Typically, this debate went as far as *Le Monde,* in which Marthe Robert, a Germanist herself, argued that the task should go to a "Germanist" whose translation would stress the colloquial and artistic aspects of Freud's vocabulary. Laplanche and Pontalis countered this view, also in the public press, insisting that one has to know Freud before translating him (Bourguignon and Bourguignon, 1983).

The group sponsoring the complete edition of Freud's work chose Pontalis and Laplanche, thus opting for the more technical approach. Questions of the relationship to the German publisher delayed the project again, and by the time there was any possibility of starting this time-consuming work, both men were committed elsewhere and had to give up their role in the translation of Freud's work. In the meantime, Laplanche and Pontalis's *The Language of Psychoanalysis* (1967) provided the first standard for the French equivalents to Freud's German. Isolated translations and retranslations, such as those of *The Ego and the Id* by Laplanche, *Beyond the Pleasure Principle* by Laplanche and Pontalis, and other works emerging from the team of Bourguignon and Codet, continued to appear. Nevertheless, even though the publishers apparently do not stand in the way of a complete and uniform edition, one is still not available.

According to the Bourguignons (1983) Pontalis said: "It must be recognized that we have no Strachey in France" (p. 1273). I am more inclined to put the matter another way: one must recognize that France is not England, for if it were, a French equivalent to Strachey would have been found.

Such a situation does not lack for interpretations, and the Bourguignons offer a few. They cite Thivent (*Le Monde-Dimanche*, November 21, 1982), who invoked French ignorance of foreign cultural productions and also suggested that the absence of a proper translation permits those who know the original work to exercise authority over the intellectual world. This is certainly true of Lacan, who until 1953 was entrusted with the teaching of Freud's writings by the Paris Psychoanalytic Society and who used his authority for an idiosyncratic interpretation of Freud's original texts. The Bourguignons (1983) advance a related explanation: "Ever since Pichon [one of the first analysts in France, who was propelled by fervent nationalism] it has been a matter of 'rewriting Freud so that the French can understand him,' which amounted to altering, in truth, betraying, his thought" (p. 1275).

Freud was aware of the fate of his work in France and was disappointed, according to the Bourguignons, who quote Clarapède (1920, p. 849):

> Two or three years before the war, during a visit to Dr. Freud, he showed me a shelf of his library upon which his main works in the most diverse languages, English, Dutch, Russian, Polish, Hungarian, Italian . . . were lined up. "Not a single French translation," said he.
>
> And he seemed all the more surprised by this since he has never hidden the influence on the flowering of his theories of both his stay at the Salpêtrière with Charcot and the first works of Pierre Janet on psychological automatism. He thought that the Latin spirit, which is so supple, would be more apt to grasp the insight into mental life and the undercurrents of the subconscious and would accord him, if not the approbation, at least the attention that his compatriots refused him in the most discourteous way. [Bourguignons 1983, p. 1275]

Earlier, in a letter to Jung on June 14, 1907, Freud seemed quite without illusion with regard to the French: "Our difficulties with the French are probably due chiefly to the national character; it has always been hard to import things into France" (Freud and Jung 1974, p. 65). In "On the History of the Psycho-Analytic Movement" Freud wrote: "Among European countries France has hitherto shown itself the least disposed to welcome psychoanalysis. . . . In Paris itself, a conviction still seems to reign (to which Janet himself gave eloquent expression at the Congress in London in 1913) that everything good in psychoanalysis is a repetition of Janet's views with insignificant modifications, and everything else in it is bad" (1914a, p. 32). And again, in "An Autobiographical Study":

> I now watch from a distance the symptomatic reactions that are accompanying the introduction of psychoanalysis into France that

> was for so long refractory. It seems like a reproduction of something I have lived through before, and yet it has peculiarities of its own. Objections of incredible simplicity are raised, such as that French sensitiveness is offended by the pedantry and crudity of psychoanalytic terminology. . . . Another comment has a more serious ring: [that] the whole mode of thought of psychoanalysis . . . is inconsistent with the *génie latin*. Here the Anglo-Saxon allies of France, who are among its adherents, are explicitly thrown to the winds.[1] Anyone hearing the remark would suppose that psychoanalysis had been the favorite child of the *génie teutonique* and had been clasped to its heart from the moment of birth.
>
> In France the interest in psychoanalysis began among the men of letters. To understand this, it must be borne in mind that from the time of the writing of *The Interpretation of Dreams* psychoanalysis ceased to be a purely medical subject. [1925, p. 62]

The Impact of Freud's Work on the World of Literature

Freud's words usher in another part of the turbulent history of psychoanalysis in France: the surrealists and their love of the unconscious. The most enthusiastic of the literary people to whom Freud refers was André Breton. The surrealist poet greeted Freud's work with the affirmation with which it was received in other countries by at least a small group of devoted followers from the world of medicine. Other literary men, for example, Romain Rolland, Léon Daudet, and Henri Bergson, also knew and appreciated the importance of psychoanalysis. André Gide created a character in *The Counterfeiters* (1926) based upon Madame Sokolnicka, who came to France in 1921, was known in the literary circles of *La Nouvelle Revue Française*, and became Gide's analyst. But it was the surrealists who wanted to mine the unconscious for their literary creations; they were not content with expressing the irrational: they wanted art to resemble unsublimated instincts.

According to Davis (1973), Breton learned about Freud in 1916 when he served as a medical aide in a psychiatric center for mental patients evacuated from the front (he had studied neurophysiology). He initiated a correspondence with Freud in 1919 and paid him a visit two years later. Breton initially joined the dadaist group, practiced automatic writing derived from William James's and Pierre Janet's work, and later, in 1924, became the leading spirit in the creation of the surrealist movement.

The surrealists had ambitions of heroic dimensions and hailed the discovery of the unconscious in the hope of abolishing the contradictions between waking life and sleep, sanity and madness, primary process and art. This liberation was to have its repercussions upon society. According to Alexandrian (1972) "In the interview that Breton granted to the *Journal du Peuple*, April 7, 1923, he said why he prefers the human document, such as the telling of a dream, to any fabricated text: 'I have never looked for anything other than to destroy literature' " (p. 34). The unconscious was to be the vehicle for this destruction, and the surrealists wanted to be certain that they had access to it. When Breton published a collection of dreams of various artists in 1932, he asked Freud to contribute a dream, to which Freud replied:

> I regret not to be able to contribute to your collection of dreams. I must admit that I have nothing new to say about the dream. The superficial aspect of dreams, that which I call the manifest dream, has no interest for me. I have been concerned about the latent content that can be deduced from the manifest dream through psychoanalytic interpretation. A collection of dreams without associations and without knowledge of the context in which they were dreamed, does not tell me anything, and I have difficulties imagining that this could mean anything to anyone. [p. 20]

Freud's letter cautioning Breton had no effect. On the contrary, Breton was convinced that Freud did not go far enough in applying his discoveries, and he was disappointed in his meeting with the founder of psychoanalysis. As Chiland (1981) put it: "Whereas Breton anticipated finding a revolutionary in politics in someone who revolutionized psychiatry, he encountered a tranquil bourgeois" (p. 56).

Freud was evidently equally disenchanted. He wrote to Stefan Zweig on July 20, 1938, that he was "inclined to look upon surrealists, who have apparently chosen me for their patron saint, as absolute (let us say 95 percent, like alcohol) cranks" (1960, p. 441). As a matter of fact, according to Pontalis, many of the surrealists ended their days in madness or with drugs. This was confirmed by Breton who announced in 1952 that he had stopped the practice of bringing the unconscious to the surface in the interest of mental hygiene.

This chapter in the history of psychoanalysis in France is important because it contains a blend of admiration for Freud, the wish to extol the subversive role of psychoanalysis and to couple it with revolutionary politics, a concentration on the unconscious at the expense of the conscious part of the personality, and hope of finding hidden treasures in the work of the master. The French psychoanalytic literature of the past three decades is replete with interpretations and reinterpretations of Freud's work; the French keep discovering new connections between old texts, thus deepening the conclusions they draw from them. Some, like Breton, even asked Freud to reveal more intimate details than he already had. Freud for his part reacted to Breton's comments as "impertinences" (Davis 1973, p. 129). We are left to guess Freud's reaction to Lacan's setting himself up as his successor.

The Reaction of the Medical World to Psychoanalysis

The medical world learned about psychoanalysis at about the same time as their contemporaries.[2] In the beginning, those who presided over the psychiatric hospitals were medical doctors who apparently used a large auditorium at Ste. Anne's Hospital to introduce psychoanalysis to wide audiences. Interestingly enough, Henri Claude, a psychiatrist who was not himself an analyst, sponsored these lectures. According to Roudinesco (1982) they were attended by prominent figures from the world of literature and philosophy as well as those more closely involved with psychiatry.

In France, therefore, psychoanalysis reached a wide audience, but it never produced pioneers of heroic stature comparable to Ferenczi, Abraham, or Jones (Barande and Barande, 1975). Instead there were men such as Laforgue, Pichon, Allendy, Morichau-Beauchant, Claude, and Hesnard, whose names are all but forgotten. These men were prolific writers, and many of their works cornered psychoanalysis, yet their contribution to psychoanalytic theory is negligible. They were convinced of the validity of psychoanalysis, but each of them seemed to have an agenda in which other causes pressed for equal time and devotion. Eventually, an organization devoted solely to psychoanalysis had to be imported.

The first communication from France reached Freud in 1910. It was a letter from a Dr. Morichau-Beauchant, and Freud considered him the first person in France to have been won over to the cause. Morichau-Beauchant wrote a total of four articles on topics such as transference and the prepubertal sexual instinct. Freud praised his contributions in letters to Jung and Abraham. The Paris Psychoanalytic Society bestowed the title of honorary member upon him during the first year of its existence, 1926. Then he faded out of the picture. As Roudinesco observed, "it was as if Morichau-Beauchant had died in combat around 1923, whereas in reality he lived until 1951 and had ample time to watch the unfolding of the vicissitudes of a history that no longer concerned him" (1982, p. 235).

Roudinesco made inquiries and heard from Morichau-Beauchant's son that his father was perhaps more a philosopher than a physician. The son remembers hearing from his father that he saw psychoanalysis as the first attempt to approach personality and that this semiology fascinated him. He was less enthusaistic with regard to the therapy, especially since his own practice was more oriented toward general medicine. According to de Mijolla (1982), Morichau-Beauchant became a Jungian.

Another participant in the introduction of psychoanalysis was Angelo Hesnard from Bordeaux, who contacted Freud in 1912. He was one of the "twelve," that is, the twelve founders of the Paris Psychoanalytic Society. Smirnoff (1979) says merely that for many years Hesnard was the only one to defend psychoanalysis in an indifferent milieu. This abruptly ends his account of this early follower of psychoanalysis. Apparently Hesnard assigned himself the role of popularizer and did not hesitate to tamper with the product in order to merchandise it better. Nor was he disturbed by his own adherence to many views that ran counter to basic tenets of psychoanalysis. Roudinesco calls him a lightweight who refused to undergo an analysis himself.

Nevertheless, Hesnard and Régis published in 1913 an article entitled "The Doctrine of Freud and His School." It contains, according to Roudinesco, a formidable bibliographic index of Freud's works in German and French as well as Freud's translations of Bernheim and Charcot. A year later this article was enlarged and published as a book entitled *Psychoanalysis of the Neuroses and the Psychoses*. It aims at a defense of psychoanalysis but apparently is itself an example of what Roudinesco (1982) calls the "disclaimer method" (p. 274).

It is difficult to convey in English the convoluted reasoning from the Introduction to *La Psychoanalyse des Nervoses et des Psychoses* by Hesnard and Régis that Roudinesco uses to substantiate this point. Nonetheless, it is enlightening for the English-speaking reader who is unfamiliar with the climate of those fervently nationalistic years around World War I to sample their words:

> Perhaps people will be astonished to see this vulgarization of a German theory . . . undertaken by French psychiatrists who do not pass themselves off as sacrificing unduly to the current fashion of a scientific Germanism. However, there is nothing there that should surprise. It is one thing not to accept with closed eyes what comes to us from outside. It is another to ignore it or to misunderstand it. The impartial independence toward what is foreign should not be mistaken for xenophobia. [Roudinesco 1982, pp. 274–275]

According to Roudinesco the book contains two chapters that are critical of Freud for his heterogeneous vocabulary borrowed from German philosophy. Hesnard and Régis say, according to Roudinesco, that Freud's obscure syntax constitutes an obstacle to the diffusion of psychoanalysis in the Latin countries, and that it will be the task of Cartesian France to bring clarity and Mediterranean harmony to this odd collection in order to render French neuropsychiatry a service. After Régis's death, Hesnard attributed this criticism to his collaborator, but Roudinesco considers this disavowal the essence of Hesnard's willingness to compromise.

Roudinesco says that the book was criticized by those who wished to defend psychoanalysis, and that Maeder saw in it the proof that France was not ready for psychoanalysis and that nowhere was the terrain better prepared for the introduction of psychoanalysis into the French cultural sphere than in Geneva.

These were the friends of psychoanalysis. The enemies were fired by an even more fervent nationalism. According to Smirnoff, Dr. Favez (1915) called for "a French psychoanalysis, eclectic, of a logical and methodological precision that would counter the dogmatic and arbitrary psychoanalysis of Freud." Going further, the biologist Yves Delage (1915) drifted into bad taste. He judged that Freud's theory was presented "in an abstract and evolute form dear to the German genius." As to the sexual theories, they were "the obsession of a brain stricken with erotomania"[3] (1979, p. 19).

With the advent of Madame Sokolnicka psychoanalysis in

France was on firmer, although by no means reliable, ground. When she arrived in Paris in 1921, she had a cordial reception and became Gide's analyst. But the facts that she was not French and was not medically trained hampered her career. She had been analyzed by Freud in 1913. She had important contacts in the rest of Europe and had studied with Ferenczi in Budapest for two years. It was after an unsuccessful attempt to establish a psychoanalytic society in Warsaw that she came to Paris. At first she worked at Ste. Anne's Hospital, but subsequently she was rejected because she was not a medical person. The fact that her specialty was child analysis and that the hospital had an adult patient population also had made her position there difficult. At that time, she met Laforgue, who introduced her to Edouard Pichon, both of whom she analyzed, and both of whom played an important part in the subsequent history of French psychoanalysis.

Her life had a tragic end in 1934 when at age 50 she was asphyxiated in an apartment that Pichon had put at her disposal. It is not clear whether or not her death was a suicide, but Pichon, who wrote her obituary, mentioned her poverty and her rejection by the medical world.

Edouard Pichon is himself worthy of attention. He is reputed to have been a man of considerable intelligence and culture who espoused extremely right-wing views. He studied the French language and, because of this interest, is often considered the forerunner of Jacques Lacan. Pichon devoted thirty years to writing a seven-volume work on grammar with his uncle Jacques Damourette. In 1927 he married Janet's daughter and applied for membership in the extreme right-wing *Ligue d'action française*. In his letter of application he stressed his Catholicism and his sense of beauty, which was "opposed to the Jewish or Protestant spirit" (Roudinesco 1982, p. 298). He ended the letter with "one last point: I am a psychoanalyst. The results obtained by the Freudian method have honestly obliged me to accept this discipline. I have recently written an article in order to show that the adoption of psychoanalysis as a therapeutic method in no way entails the renunciation of any metaphysical, moral, or religious style" (unpublished letter to Maurras quoted by Roudinesco 1982, p. 299). Pichon's letter continues with his expression of the hope that the attacks on psychoanalysis will not preclude his admission to the *Ligue d'action française*. He was accepted.

Roudinesco describes Pichon as incapable of opportunism, fanatic, and intransigent. He invented many expressions, all of which fell into disuse except for "forclusive," which led to Lacan's "forclusion" (a more radical expulsion from consciousness than repression or denial). Inside the Paris Psychoanalytic Society, Pichon became the founder of a short-lived commission (1927–1929) for the unification of the Freudian vocabulary, and he replied to Freud's "Civilization and Its Discontents" (1927) with a series of three conferences entitled "At Ease in Civilization."

As Janet's son-in-law, he wrote to Freud and, according to Jones (1957), in order to bring about a reconciliation between the two old men, asked if Janet might call on Freud. Freud declined and explained in a letter to Marie Bonaparte that he could never forgive Janet for not correcting the rumors that Freud had stolen his ideas.

Pichon (1938) wrote about his friend René Laforgue, another founding member and the first president of the Paris Psychoanalytic Society:

> It is he, who for many psychiatrists still truly embodies psychoanalysis in France; and he could have been the uncontested head of the French psychoanalytic school . . . if he himself had known how to construct for himself a less disconcerting personality. My friend Laforgue is indeed a strange spirit: an excellent clinician, a therapist who is sometimes astonishing, he is disappointing as a theoretician. One would think that he would have great audacity but discovers in him surprising timidity. . . . Oh, René Laforgue, *mien ami*, cease to tremble before the contradictory authorities of this master here

and that doctor there. You can freely choose the road that ascends, without accounting to anyone. Our father is not of this world. [pp. 669–691]

Laforgue, the man who disappointed everyone, would himself have had ample reason to feel betrayed. He was Alsatian, therefore bilingual, and during the First World War he served in the German army. He differed from his friends precisely in his ability to span two cultures. In 1925 he applied for admission to the Viennese Psychoanalytic Society and was unanimously accepted.

His beginnings were modest. He apparently became a very gifted clinician, and the disappointments he caused others were partly due to his being more interested in his very successful private practice than in stormy ideological debates or in doing translations of Freud.

In 1923 he started a correspondence with Freud (published in the *Nouvelle Revue de Psychanalyse*, 1977) that suggests he was a well-meaning man who was struggling with his own ambivalence. He promised Freud translations he never undertook, and he attempted to convince Freud that part of the new vocabulary emanating from the pen of his friend Pichon was compatible with Freud's theories. Freud was remarkably reserved toward Laforgue and did not seem disappointed when the promised translations never materialized.

Laforgue wrote a thesis in 1922 on the affectivity of schizophrenics from the psychoanalytic point of view. In this respect, too, he presaged the French psychoanalytic movement, which focused on psychotic processes. He also collaborated with Pichon on an article entitled: "On Some Obstacles to the Diffusion of Psychoanalytic Methods in France," which blames the French resistance to psychoanalysis on the artists as well as on the vocabulary used by Freud or his Swiss or Slav translators. Laforgue and Pichon wanted to develop a psychoanalytic nomenclature better adapted to French exigencies (Roudinesco

1982, p. 292). In a letter to Laforgue dated November 1, 1923, Freud replied to this prophetically:

> I would like to caution you not to go ahead in the direction in which you are engaged in your article, you and Pichon. You obtain nothing from concessions to public opinions and reigning prejudices. This method is totally contrary to the spirit of psychoanalysis, which never uses the technique of trying to hide or to attenuate the resistances. Experience has also taught us that those who take the way of compromise, attenuations, in short, of diplomatic opportunism, find themselves ultimately separated from their own road and cannot participate in the subsequent development of psychoanalysis. [Freud and Laforgue 1977, p. 253]

Despite Laforgue's generosity in helping Jews escape persecution, he was condemned for his opportunism during World War II because he had maintained ties to the German Psychoanalytic Organization headed by Goering. He was, therefore, considered a collaborator by his colleagues after the war, gave up active participation in the Paris Psychoanalytic Society after 1945, and in 1953 followed those who split from the society. He died in 1959 on the Côte d'Azur.

"La Princesse" Marie Bonaparte

In a letter of April 9, 1925, Laforgue informed Freud that Princess Marie Bonaparte wanted to consult him. Laforgue tried to persuade Freud to accept her, even though it becomes apparent from Laforgue's later remark concerning a "displaced affect regarding the loss of the princess," that she had previously consulted Laforgue. He nevertheless pleaded her case, stating that her wishes were for a didactic analysis, perhaps to mollify Freud, but the latter answered in the negative. It is, of course, well known that Freud eventually accepted Bonaparte, probably as the result of a letter she herself wrote to him which convinced him of the seriousness of her intentions. Introducing "la princesse" to Freud was Laforgue's most important contribution to French psychoanalysis: and even though his correspondence with Freud continued until 1937 and he paid Freud various visits, his significance was eclipsed by this devoted and powerful woman.

From 1925 on, Freud's hopes for French psychoanalysis were pinned on Marie Bonaparte. She is Roudinesco's bête noire, a judgment that is as unfair as it is understandable. It is through Bonaparte's devotion and generosity with time, money, and influence that psychoanalysis in France finally became organized. The power she was able to exercise by virtue of both her link to Freud and her material resources contributed to the resentment expressed by Roudinesco.

Freud referred to the lack of gregariousness of his early supporters in France, and as usual, he was most perceptive. Into this ill-assorted group had come an emissary from Vienna, a woman who was totally devoted to Freud, well-connected and therefore powerful, seductive, nonmedical, and endowed with what to the others were her saving graces—she was rich, titled, and French.

It was a great relief to Freud that he had someone who could give his theory a toehold in France, someone who was unambivalent, who was in the midst of a strong positive transference, and who was willing to lend her social position and purse to further the cause in France. She had consulted Freud for her personal problems, foremost among which was her lifelong frigidity, but Freud was impressed with the seriousness with which she regarded psychoanalysis.

Marie Bonaparte was Napoleon's great-grandniece, and her husband was the son and brother of Greek kings and the grandson of the king of Denmark. Marie Bonaparte's father provided a stimulating intellectual environment, and in 1909 he introduced her to Le Bon, who eventually aroused her interest in Freud's work. She was apparently not snobbish, and "according to his daughter Anna, Freud later remarked that one never knew whether Marie was talking about a dog, a servant, a commoner, or a prince when it was someone she liked" (Bertin 1982, pp. 89–90).

Her dedication to the cause of psychoanalysis was matched by her devotion to her professional career. She heard about Freud through Le Bon, and as of 1923 she visited hospitals where she did extensive research based on interviews of a large number of women in order to assess the relationship between female frigidity and female anatomy. She was convinced all her life that there was a correlation between frigidity and the position of the clitoris in relation to the vagina. In this way, she undoubtedly contributed to the "biologism" that Laplanche holds against Freudian theory.

Since Bonaparte recommended and also underwent surgical interventions herself, it has to be assumed that there was a defect in her understanding of the difference between psychic and anatomical reality, a serious distortion in her interpretation of psychoanalysis. Her emphasis on anatomical manipulations attests to her need for control and runs counter to her otherwise unambivalent devotion to psychoanalysis. She never wavered in her pursuit of knowledge and used her connections in order to gather data for her research on frigidity in places as far afield as Egypt and in times as troubled as the year 1941.

Marie Bonaparte was a nonmedical analyst. Freud's attitude toward lay analysis was, of course, favorable, and he would have wished an equally favorable attitude to come from the International Psychoanalytic Association; but it did not, and ultimately Freud had to capitulate to the American Psychoanalytic Association on this matter. To some degree the French solved the matter of nonmedical analysis for themselves by creating the Evolution Psychiatrique, a totally medical organization. Thereby they assured a haven for medical analysts the year before the Paris Psychoanalytic Society, in which there was to be no discrimination between medical and nonmedical analysts, was founded.

The Founding of the Paris Psychoanalytic Society

The next "import" was the migrant Polish Jew from Berlin, Rudolph Loewenstein, who settled in Paris with Bonaparte's help at the end of 1925. He was not French, but he was a medical doctor. All accounts attest to his having received a cordial reception just as another foreigner, Madame Sokolnicka, had before him. Laforgue and Claude helped him establish himself, and he eventually became the analyst of many of the leading figures in the French psychoanalytic world. It is interesting that a group that guarded its national character so carefully seems to have been quite wholehearted in accepting these foreigners sent by Freud. Those, like Roudinesco, who regard submission to any external authority as a cardinal sin, interpret this imposition of Freud's authority in a dark light; but at the time of Loewenstein's arrival, there was no discrimination against him, and Nacht, Lagache, and Lacan, three of the main actors in the split of 1953, were his analysands.

But then, the leading analysts had expressed their ambivalence toward Freud and Vienna by founding the Evolution Psychiatrique in 1925, one year before the Paris Psychoanalytic Society saw the light of day, and even before the arrival in Paris of Bonaparte and Loewenstein. This organization issued a publication by the same name, and both are still in existence. The ostensible purpose was for psychoanalytic psychiatrists to make inroads into the world of psychiatry, but this apparently was not the only goal. Eitingon was amused to find in the preface to the first issue of this publication the statement, "Leaving the too deliberately dogmatic and doctrinaire terrain onto which German psychoanalysis has slipped. . . ." (Roudinesco 1982, p.

413, quoting a letter from Eitingon to Laforgue). Seven of the founders of the Paris Psychoanalytic Society were part of the Evolution Psychiatrique, and according to Smirnoff (1979, p. 35), who quotes Lamoulen, Laforgue wrote in his diary in 1954, "I was struck from the beginning by the fact that something did not 'work' in the mentality of psychoanalysts around Freud. . . . The movement of the Evolution Psychiatrique permitted a little escape from psychoanalytic dogmatism, the causes of which I did not yet understand."

When the Paris Psychoanalytic Society finally came into being in November 1926, it did so in large measure because of Bonaparte's initiative. Apparently with Evolution Psychiatrique as insurance against the loss of their identity as medical persons, the founders finally decided to come together in a psychoanalytic organization. The twelve founding members were Marie Bonaparte, René Allendy, Eugenie Sokolnicka, Adrien Borel, Henri Codet, Angelo Hesnard, René Laforgue, Rudolph Loewenstein, Charles Odier, Georges Parcheminey, Edouard Pichon, and Raymond de Saussure. De Saussure and Odier were Swiss citizens who spent long periods of time in Paris. Such nonmembers as Spitz, Rank, Hartmann, and Eitingon passed through Paris partly as a way station on the road to emigration. While they were in Paris, however, they participated in the activities of the society. Loewenstein, who was himself analyzed by Hans Sachs, conducted most of the didactic analyses. Bonaparte supported the acquisition of an office for the newly founded society and remained in many other ways a powerful, if not decisive, voice in Paris psychoanalysis. Unlike the psychoanalytic societies of other countries, however, this group was essentially composed of individuals with strong patriotic leanings and an attachment to the national cultural values. In other countries the introduction of psychoanalysis was almost entirely dependent on individuals who were accustomed to a less parochial outlook.

It should not be surprising that the new organization

headed straight into controversy. What would be its position with regard to Freud? Laforgue wrote to Freud to keep him abreast of developments:

> We have, as you have learned from the princess, been able to take a decisive step forward. We have from now on a well-organized group and the possibility of publishing a review. . . . My proposition to publish the review under your patronage has not been accepted because of the counterproposal that we should also ask Claude for his patronage in order not to seriously offend him. [Freud and Laforgue 1977, letter dated November 7, 1926]

Psychoanalysis had reason to be grateful to Claude since he had allowed psychoanalysis to be taught at Ste. Anne, had hired Laforgue, and subsequently made room for Loewenstein. Claude, however, was not himself an analyst.

Freud replied by return mail to Laforgue's letter: "It would have been a genuine pleasure if you had put my name on the title page, and the idea that Claude could take offense would never have occurred to me spontaneously, since certainly he could hardly have illusions about his slender participation in psychoanalysis" (Freud and Laforgue 1977, letter dated November 11, 1926).

Bourguignon (1977) thinks that for Freud the essential thing was that the review not remain under Claude's influence and that it establish the affiliation with the International Psychoanalytic Association in order to counter any suspicion of opportunism or eclecticism in matters of analysis. The first issue of the *Revue Française de Psychanalyse* appeared on June 25, 1927. The title page bears Freud's name as the patron, but affiliation with the International is not mentioned. Bourguignon thinks that this was a compromise between the chauvinistic minority and the majority directed by Laforgue: the minority yielded on the question of the unique patronage of Freud, but obtained a concession on affiliation with the International Psychoanalytic

Association. Laforgue prevailed with the second issue, and the words "Section française de l'Association Psychoanalytique Internationale" appear.

Compared to the turbulence that preceded them and the tempest that was to follow, the 1930s seem to have been fairly calm within the organization. The social contacts among the members were cordial. Roudinesco describes dinner parties at which Pichon entertained with old French songs while Loewenstein unpacked his Jewish stories.

The Institute of the Paris Psychoanalytic Society was founded in 1934. Bonaparte located the premises and contributed financially to their upkeep. But despite the relative calm, there were political alliances and tensions among the Parisian analysts almost from the start. Bertin, M. Bonaparte's biographer, mentions one source of controversy within the Paris Psychoanalytic Society even in the 1930s. Lacan had to wait from 1934, the year of his election to associate membership, until 1938 to attain full membership, whereas Daniel Lagache went that same road in one year between 1936 and 1937.

As Bertin (1982) relates the story, when Laforgue was voted out of the presidency, a rift developed. Laforgue's faction, which included his and Pichon's analysands, opposed Bonaparte, Loewenstein, and their followers. Heinz Hartmann, already famous for his book *The Ego and the Problem of Adaptation*, was proposed for the presidency. However, Pichon opposed Hartmann because he was a foreigner. In order to help secure the election of Hartmann, Lacan was admitted to full membership in the society, although he had not finished his training analysis with Loewenstein. Through his wife's family's connections, Lacan was well launched in Parisian avant-garde literary and artistic circles, and soon he was a force within the society. But by 1939, Pichon, the linguist, had changed his mind, and he wrote that language for Lacan was "an armor made out of the jargon of a sect and personal preciosity," and that Lacan's style was "hermetically sealed and inexact" (pp. 206–207).

With the outbreak of World War II the society came to a standstill. The institute closed down, the publication of the *Revue Française de Psychanalyse* ceased, and the curtain fell on the opening acts of the history of psychoanalysis in France. There were a few individual practitioners who continued their professional activities during the German occupation, but the majority did not.

Notes

[1] I retranslated this sentence from the original German.

[2] I use the word *medical* to encompass the world of the psychiatric hospitals. The issue of medical versus nonmedical analysis has been officially resolved, but I think that it plays a greater part in the history of psychoanalysis in France than is generally acknowledged. At the appropriate times, I attempt to clarify its role in the evolution of psychoanalysis.

[3] Smirnoff attributes the Favez quotation to *La Psychanalyse Française*, Paris, 1915, and the Delage to La théorie du rêve de Freud, *Bull. Inst. Gen. Psych.* 1915.

3

History after World War II

Rebuilding the Society after World War II

In 1939 there were twenty-four members of the Paris Psychoanalytic Society. In 1945, along with the rest of Europe, the society faced a sad accounting: only four of the twelve founding members remained in France. Pichon and Allendy had died at the beginning of the war, Borel had resigned, and de Saussure and Loewenstein were settled in New York. Laforgue had come under a cloud because of the accusation that he had collaborated with the occupying forces and therefore was a member in name only. The same was true of Hesnard, who had never undergone an analysis himself and who had settled in Toulon. There were therefore eleven survivors, including the second generation—that is, those who had started their training before the war and had joined the membership—but not even all of them were active. Marie Bonaparte resumed her former level of leadership within the organization; Nacht was elected to the presidency in 1947 and remained in office until 1953. Lebovici, Bouvet, Lacan, and Lagache are names that appear on the roster as of 1948, and they must be counted among those who rebuilt the society after the war.

After the war the tendencies embodied by Pichon, chauvinism mixed with royalist and Catholic sentiments, were a thing of the past. It would be unfair to say that the *Ligue d'action française*, to which Pichon belonged, was fascistic, but until the actual invasion by the Germans, the ideologies of the *ligue* and of the fascists did not differ greatly. Both were elitist, nationalist, and anti-Semitic, but the *ligue* allied itself with Catholicism and was committed to a more honorable and less destructive elitism.

When the impetus to create a typical French version of psychoanalysis resurfaced after the war, Lacan was the dominant figure. He was able to make common cause with those imbued with left-wing ideology fostered by the suffering of the war. And his contacts with the surrealists, to whom he was related by marriage (his brother-in-law was André Masson, the painter), enabled him to feel kinship with the most important intellectual currents in postwar Paris. Within psychoanalytic circles, his need to find a new terminology made Lacan into Pichon's heir.

Although he was a physician by training, Lacan was less so than Nacht by inclination and not at all academic like Lagache; he was given to philosophical speculations (de Mijolla 1982), and despite his kinship with the various currents, including structuralism at a later date, he went his own way. He became active in the politics of the Paris Psychoanalytic Society, especially right after the war. He was a member of the training commission as of 1948 and was elected to the presidency in 1953.

This happened despite the fact that by the end of 1951 Lacan's technique had come under fire, and he eventually promised that he would not apply his new custom of shorter or variable sessions to the didactic analyses he was conducting.

This promise was not kept. His supporters asserted on June 16, 1953, in *Ornicar?*[1] that "Dr. Nacht authorized Lacan to expose his ideas on the possible shortening of the analytic sessions to the society, in December 1951," and they interpreted this as a permission to continue this practice (Miller 1976, p. 87).

The relationship between Nacht and Lacan was close, and they were political allies. There seems to be little question therefore, that the former tolerated Lacan's innovations until 1953, with the proviso that he not practice them as part of didactic analyses.

Bonaparte opposed Lacan from early on, perhaps not only because of his innovations but also because she considered herself the true interpreter of Freud's thinking, a position to which Lacan aspired. As the history unfolds it can be seen that the manifest reason for the attack on Lacan, that is, his irregular practice of analysis, was determined by a multitude of motives that have not all been fully revealed.

The fat was in the fire when the Paris Psychoanalytic Society was assured of financial support by the Rockefeller Foundation for the reopening of the Institute of Psychoanalysis. This generosity was based on the international connections established by Bonaparte and by the ties between those analysts who emigrated and those who stayed. The conditions attached to this offer were that the members themselves also contribute, which they apparently did generously, and that appropriate premises be found.

Ironically, Lacan was placed in charge of drawing up the statutes, doctrines, and rules of the training commission for the new institute. Smirnoff (1979) questions whether the published report had been revised because it contains some non-Lacanian statements, such as that the duration of the analytic hour should be at least three quarters of an hour and that trainees not call themselves analysts until they had been approved officially. It is equally possible that the rules were drawn up during the time when Lacan was still eager to be conciliatory, or as de Mijolla

(1982) states, that Nacht was the author and classed psychoanalysis with neurobiology, as a "branch of scientific activity . . . useful and necessary in psychopathology," and in medicine, especially psychosomatic medicine (p. 56).

According to Smirnoff (1979) the intent of the document is quite liberal, declaring that a medical education may be recommended for analytic training, but it is not required, nor does it preclude the admission of an "autodidact."

The Years of Discord: 1951 to 1953

In November 1950, Lagache, the academician, found premises in which the institute could be housed, but his choice was turned down for reasons that he attributed to excessive medicalization by Nacht and his followers. On June 17, 1952, Nacht proposed himself as the director of the institute for five years, and during the summer months he found and rented its premises. This meant that he would be both president of the society and director of the institute. Lagache was outraged and contacted Lacan in order to set up an extraordinary meeting for December 2, 1952, at which the majority challenged Nacht on issues of authoritarianism. The latter resigned but was then reinstated. The dissatisfaction, judging from a later document (June 16, 1953, position paper by Lagache, Dolto, and Favez-Boutonnier, *Ornicar?* 1976, p. 87), was based on Nacht's autocratic and secretive demeanor and the sentiment that members no longer knew what was going on in their society. At the end of December Nacht resigned once more, and this time Lacan briefly assumed the direction of the institute, until his election to the presidency of the society in January 1953.

In this election, Bonaparte had proposed Michel Cénac as an alternate candidate for the presidency, thus opposing Lacan. She also reproached Nacht for his wish for a rapprochement between psychoanalysis and medicine.

According to Bertin, Bonaparte's belief that Nacht was

antagonistic to nonmedical analysts had been reinforced by the position he took in a lawsuit in June 1950. Margaret Williams, an American child analyst practicing in Paris, was sued by the medical association for practicing medicine illegally. Marie Bonaparte was struck by the importance of this lawsuit and when, according to Bertin, Nacht joined those who opposed Williams, her animosity toward him increased. She supported Cénac, who is quoted as having said: "If the French physicians, after having scorned and vilified it, now claim analysis for their own, it is because they have realized how profitable it is" (Bertin 1982, p. 234). This determined her position in the election, along with the fact that she held against Nacht his political alliance with "this madman" as she called Lacan in a letter to Loewenstein (quoted by Bertin 1982, p. 236).

Marie Bonaparte's position was difficult. Her antagonism to Lacan was not yet shared by Nacht, who otherwise could be considered the upholder of traditional analysis. Yet the possibility of her forming an alliance with Lagache, who wanted to forge a closer relationship between psychoanalysis and the academic world, had no other basis than their joint opposition to the medicalization of psychoanalysis. Lagache was, after all, a candidate for the vice presidency of the Paris Psychoanalytic Society under Lacan.

The Lacanians like to think that A. Freud brought about the reconciliation between her close friend, Bonaparte, and Nacht. This may indeed be true because Nacht and Bonaparte together could maintain a close tie to the International Psychoanalytic Association, a contact favored by Freud, which might have been endangered by Lacan or a nonmedical person.

After a confrontation between Nacht and Bonaparte in which she accused him of being engaged in a vendetta against psychologists, and he said he thought she held him in contempt (Bertin 1982), a reconciliation took place. Marie Bonaparte renewed her attacks on Lacan in the hope that those whom he had trained by his brief method would not gain admission to membership and thereby threaten the majority. Loewenstein wrote to Bonaparte on February 22, 1953:

> What you tell me about Lacan [his former analysand] is distressing. He has always represented a source of conflict for me; on one hand there is his intellectual worth which I value highly, though I disagree violently with him. Nevertheless the misfortune is that much as we agreed that he would continue his analysis after his election [to membership in the Society], he did not do so. One does not cheat on such an important point with impunity (this between us). I certainly hope that his hastily analyzed (that is to say incompletely analyzed) trainees will not be admitted. [Bertin 1982, p. 245]

The Split of 1953

On May 15, 1953, Jenny Roudinesco, mother of the author of *Histoire de la Psychanalyse en France*, addressed a letter in the name of the candidates to Nacht and to Lacan objecting to the rules drawn up for the new institute (*Ornicar?* 1976) and stating concern about the validity of former commitments made to them and by them. It is evident that Lacan's trainees had the most to fear, and he was accused of instigating the students. In *Ornicar?* there is a draft of a reply to the students that can only be described as very similar to Marc Antony's funeral oration at Caesar's grave. This reply was apparently never sent, and Lacan remained officially passive, but unofficially he met with the candidates, something for which he was later reproached since many of them were his analysands.

On June 2, 1953, the confrontation between Nacht and Lacan finally took place. Bonaparte was not present at the meeting at which the discussion was held calling for a vote of confidence in Lacan. She was in London attending the coronation of Elizabeth II. According to Bertin (1982) she was certain that Lacan had chosen this date knowing she would have to be absent. She wrote to Loewenstein that "Lacan had promised, in March 1951, to cease his practice of short analyses, but he has not kept his promise. Nacht confronted him at a meeting with the students (in June 1953). Lacan said that since he had explained his technique some months ago before the society, he had been released from his promise, and that moreover he had said that he might change his technique but not that he would do so. Each called the other a liar" (Bertin 1982, pp. 245–246, letter of June 17, 1953).

In de Mijolla's (1982) account of the administrative meeting of June 2, 1953, Cénac reproached Lacan for his presence among the students, considering that he was president of the organization and a training analyst. There was a motion of no confidence. Nacht introduced the issues of the shortening of sessions, to which Lacan replied that he had conducted all didactic analyses in regular-length sessions since January, however he did not commit himself as to frequency. The minutes show that Lacan recognized that he had been imprudent, that he had taken dangerous liberties. He appealed for understanding, stressing how much he had given of himself to the organization. His only hopes were to continue working in friendship for his colleagues, that the institute would live, and that he would be able to work there. He wanted a vote of confidence and promised to do what he could. This vote was tabled until the meeting of June 16, at which these minutes were accepted after a discussion.

The issues appear in all their complexity when one realizes that the tabling of the vote of confidence was opposed by three members, according to de Mijolla. Those were Daniel Lagache, Francoise Dolto, and Juliette Favez-Boutonnier, and their attitude was not prompted by their sympathies for Lacan but by their opposition to Nacht and the institute. In preparation for the next meeting, they continued to work on their project for a new and freer society.

The meeting of June 16, 1953, Lacan received a vote of no

confidence and was asked to resign the presidency. He was no longer in the meeting room when Lagache, who was supposed to succeed him, announced his resignation from the Paris Psychoanalytic Society. The two women, Dolto and Favez-Boutonnier, resigned also. Later that same night, Lacan decided to announce his resignation from the Paris Psychoanalytic Society.

I think that it is important to stress that Lacan did not initiate the split; on the contrary, he appealed for understanding and expressed his wish for the institute to thrive. Previously a potential split was feared from Nacht, and when it happened differently it seemed as if, had Lacan been tolerated, he would not have chosen to become the antagonist. Lagache initiated the split and wrote, along with Dolto and Favez-Boutonnier, a strong indictment against the secrecy and autocracy of Nacht's administration. Lagache's attitude was consistent. He was acting in the interest of greater freedom and independence for psychoanalysis. In the process, he made common cause with Lacan.

At first, Lacan's passivity may seem mysterious, but the mystery is soon cleared up when his actions are understood as those of a man who hoped to remain within the organization, defend it weakly (even to the students), and attain a majority within the foreseeable future. To attribute greater ideological motives to his stance seems unwarranted, and the only sense that emerges is that all explanations, including Lacan's subsequent pose as the defender of this or that cause, were afterthoughts and rationalizations. Lacan's aim throughout his career was power.

It is tempting to think that Lacan was either the original thinker who would put French psychoanalysis on the map, or the usurper who went too far. Yes, he started a tradition of Wednesday seminars reminiscent of Freud's Wednesday meetings. But his actions were not those of a man who was defending a cause. The sequence of events instead suggests that Lacan made himself into a cause. Why else was Nacht, the man most at ease with the Americans, Lacan's best friend and ally, when Lacan himself struck a pose of such virulent anti-Americanism after the split?

The impression of a man who consciously constructed his own public image is confirmed by one of Lacan's American supporters, Stuart Schneiderman. He thinks that Lacan was complicitous in his own sequestering because he withdrew from the worldwide analytic community. In addition to Lacan's idiosyncratic use of language, Schneiderman (1983) notes the importance of Lacan's "presence, his attitude, his bearing, his dress, even the tone of his voice," as vehicles for communicating his thoughts. It is, Schneiderman says, "next to impossible for readers to pick up a text and to evaluate it on its intellectual merits alone, to formulate a judgment outside of an established system of belief" (p. 92). Lacan himself said that "everything that is published . . . coming from my pen, horrifies me" (letter of October 11, 1976, quoted in *Ornicar?*).

Chasseguet-Smirgel, who is by no stretch of the imagination a supporter of the faction that left the society, declared in an unpublished manuscript (1984a), "What I know through colleagues whom I consider trustworthy and sufficiently neutral, is that one cannot render judgment on the split without taking into account that before the creation of the institute by Sacha Nacht, Lagache, professor of psychology at the Sorbonne, found premises for an institute which he hoped to tie in one way or another to the university and that, in a manifest manner, the affaire Lacan derived from this first and fundamental quarrel. It is a choice derivative since the Lacanian practice, that of short sessions of variable length, five minutes sometimes, with an analyst who is almost totally silent, is indefensible."

Furthermore, she points out that the three protagonists, Lacan, Lagache, and Nacht, were analyzed by Loewenstein and also suggests that the issue of an *analyse à la française* underlies the quarrel in a subterranean and unconscious way.

Smirnoff (1979), a former Lacanian, asks:

> Is it really necessary to accumulate so many documents, anecdotes, details, and files? There is no doubt that the behavior of the ones and the others were not always courteous. That each one wanted to justify himself and to make others shoulder the responsibility for the split, that's good warfare. That is not what is important, because, even if one considers that the split of 1953 was above all a political affair, a fight for power, it remains true that it had its basis in an ideological disagreement. [p. 49]

Smirnoff thinks that France was left without a tradition. The English-speaking psychoanalytic groups attained a legitimacy that only Bonaparte had in France. "She was respected, certainly, but, despite her publications, she could not be considered the holder of a doctrine. She had a certain power because of her relations, the influence and the esteem in which she was held. That was not enough to embody the French psychoanalytic school: she would have had to have a wider scope than that of faithfulness and devotion" (p. 50).

According to Smirnoff there were those who were influenced by the American current, and he names Bouvet, Lagache, Lebovici, and Nacht as examples, which again suggests to him that the originality had to come from elsewhere. Others, he feels, were engaged in a Freudian tradition that was becoming defunct. In this way of thinking, Lacan opened the way for an original approach to psychoanalytic theory in France, something that seemed essential from Smirnoff's point of view, which is that of an ex-Lacanian.

One of Lacan's former disciples, Pontalis (1979), suggests that the issues around Lacan ultimately were centered not on substance but on transference. He said that when the "veterans," i.e., former Lacanians, got together, "we all said: at this date no one could not be Lacanian; at this other, one could no longer be Lacanian. But the dates were not at all the same depending on the persons concerned" (p. 9). He draws an analogy between their situation and that of the disillusioned Stalinists, Arthur Koestler, Ignazio Silone, Stephen Spender, and others who contributed to the anticommunist manifesto of 1950, *The God that Failed*, the case of former communists.

The American sociologist, Sherry Turkle (1978), whose work on Lacan is most enlightening although her comments on the rest of the French psychoanalysts are extremely biased and dismissive, thinks that the essential unorthodoxy of Lacan's approach is rooted in the fact that French psychoanalysis itself had its start with poets and philosophers rather than with physicians. Lacan would thus be following the path of those who used psychoanalysis to revolt against established authority rather than to adapt to it.

I consider it impossible to dismiss as unfounded the accusations by Nacht's opponents that were leveled at the medical establishment and at the relationship between Bonaparte and A. Freud. Indeed, if the documents published by Jacques-Alain Miller are to be trusted, it is evident from the record of the discussion at the Seventeenth International Congress in London in 1953 that A. Freud's position was one of easy acceptance of the split, which she likened to a divorce during which the children inevitably must suffer (*Ornicar?* 1976, p. 139). She did not seem to share the regrets and the reluctance of some of the other participants in the discussion, notably Loewenstein. The split was especially traumatic for the analysands of those who left the institute because they were forced to choose between their analysts and the institute.

In order to comprehend Lacan's impact fully, the situation in France in the 1930s and 1950s can be compared to the early years of psychoanalysis. Freud, too, worked with analysts who "warmed their soup at his fire," and Lacan can be compared to Jung. Abraham cautioned Freud about the danger to his theories years before he himself saw it. Once he was aware of the basic incompatibility between his theory and the innovations theorists like Jung, Adler, and Rank wanted to introduce, he devoted himself to the explication of the differences between them. In the same way, Lacan's basic incompatibility was not recognized by many, especially not by those whose unfamiliarity with German precluded their ability to discern that Lacan's reading of Freud was based on misinterpretations, nor by those who were pleased with his departure from the link to biology underlying Freud's earliest formulations and Marie Bonaparte's excesses.

The French Psychoanalytic Society: 1953 to 1964

The organization founded by those who left the Paris Psychoanalytic Society was named the French Psychoanalytic Society. It applied for membership in the International Psychoanalytic Association immediately after being established but was refused on the recommendation of the investigating committee in 1954. In 1959, the French Psychoanalytic Society renewed its application, and the new investigating committee accorded it study-group status in 1961 upon the condition that Lacan and Dolto not assume the functions of training analysts.

It had been the intention of the new group to affiliate as soon as possible with the International Psychoanalytic Association, especially, as de Mijolla (1982) puts it, because Lacan threatened immediately to become a state within a state. Affiliation with the international psychoanalytic community would have acted as a counterweight to Lacan's power. Having got out from under what they considered Nacht's tyranny, they did not want to have to submit to a new prince.

As Chiland explains (1981),

> The members of the S.F.P. [French Psychoanalytic Society] were confronted with a dilemma: either to remain loyal to colleagues or to recognize the validity of the criticisms formulated by the I.P.A.

> [International Psychoanalytic Association] committee . . . . The names of Lacan and Dolto were ultimately withdrawn from the list of training analysts in 1963. Lacan and Dolto refused to accept the majority decision. This resulted, finally, in the dissolution of the S.F.P., the majority forming a subgroup recognized by the I.P.A. and the minority establishing an independent splinter group. Neither group retained the title of the S.F.P. The society eventually established by Lacan was initially called the *École Française de Psychanalyse* (French School of Psychoanalysis) and subsequently, the *École Freudienne de Paris* (Freudian School of Paris). [p.58]

Lacan Opens His Own School

According to de Mijolla (1982), Lacan declared on June 21, 1964, "I am founding—as alone as I have always been in my relation to the psychoanalytic cause—the French School of Psychoanalysis, of which I shall personally take on the direction for the next four years, with nothing at present to prevent me from making this commitment (p. 101).

The majority group after the breakup became the Psychoanalytic Association of France and was admitted to the International Psychoanalytic Association in 1965 as a fully accredited member (Chiland 1981). Since then the relationship between two officially recognized groups, the old Paris Psychoanalytic Society and the newer Psychoanalytic Association of France, has been friendly, although de Mijolla (1982) rightly points out that the correspondences between the two have also been exaggerated and that indeed each clan ignores what the other produces, "inaugurating a kind of ostracism in bibliographic references that only hardens with time" (p. 80).

The École Freudienne grew rapidly because of the lack of formal requirements. Lacan took upon himself privileges that he did not accord to others, such as signing his name to the articles he wrote whereas other members did not have this privilege. Moreover the practices used to designate "*Analystes de l'École*" were confusing and led to an exodus from Lacan's École Freudienne and the establishment of the French-language Psychoanalytic Organization, also known as the Fourth Group, which has not attained nor, as far as I know, sought affiliation with the International Psychoanalytic Association. The best-known member of this group is Piera Castoriadis-Aulagnier, whose work is included in the last section of this book.

In 1980, Lacan himself dissolved his own group, an action that was illegal and was challenged by some of the members. He founded the Freudian Cause and, according to Chiland, reserved for himself the right to decide on the admission of members. Those who had wanted the École Freudienne to continue were unable to unite and function as an organized group. Instead, thirteen splinter organizations emerged from the crisis of 1980 to 1981 (Roudinesco 1986). Lacan died in 1981 and with him a unity of purpose.

After the second split, Lacan's antagonism, which departed very rapidly from any question of substance, took shape. Once the International Psychoanalytic Association refused the newly founded French Psychoanalytic Society recognition in the form of affiliation, and the refusal was based on a rejection of the practices of Lacan and Dolto, the attacks of the Lacanians on the International assumed the form of accusations of McCarthyism. It was forgotten that the first gesture of the new organization had been to seek affiliation with this group that they subsequently maligned.

The noise, the numbers, and the idea of a French psychoanalysis were attached to the École Freudienne. This was the seat of the ferment until Lacan's death. Psychoanalysis was the topic of intellectuals, housewives, and newspaper and magazine articles; psychoanalysis became fashionable. Meanwhile, relatively little took place in the original Paris Psychoanalytic Society because it continued on the course on which it had embarked. The institute was established under Nacht's direction, and the Paris Psychoanalytic Society has remained immune to further splits, although at times there have been strong protests against certain policies that were considered authoritarian. Many of the present-day French distrust any power, including that involved in imposing and upholding requirements for training. They agitate to dismantle as much of it as possible, as if the imposition of standards were abusive in and of itself. A group of eight dissatisfied members even instituted a lawsuit against the organization, but it remained without serious consequences.

The Two Orthodox Groups: 1964 to Present

With the reforms that were adopted (for example, the institute was merged with the society in 1986), the Paris Psychoanalytic Society may have one of the most open training programs within the International Psychoanalytic Association. It is much larger than its sister organization, the Psychoanalytic Association of France. Roudinesco claims that the organization that was conceived as a brotherhood became in effect a group of aging chieftains threatened with extinction. Some of its best-known members are Laplanche, Pontalis, and Anzieu.

French psychoanalysts have become increasingly visible on the international scene: Lebovici was president of the International Psychoanalytic Association recently, the *Language of Psychoanalysis* has had wide circulation, and an increasing number of books by Chasseguet-Smirgel, McDougall, Green, and Grunberger have been translated into English, so that the psychoanalytic community at large has become familiar with their names if not their work.

In France, psychoanalysts are active in areas elsewhere reserved for specialists in other disciplines. They teach at many universities and medical schools, and they have an impact on the study of psychosis, psychodrama, group analysis, and the treatment of psychosomatic illness. A free psychoanalytic treatment center has been opened at the Institute of the Paris Psychoanalytic Society. Their journals and books, issued by many publishers, are too numerous to mention; psychoanalytic debates often reach the popular press. But at least part of this popularization is caused by the enlargement of psychoanalysis itself: the proliferation of methods used by Lacanians has caused the term "analysis" to be used indiscriminately.

Psychoanalysis and Communism

In France, psychoanalysis was a vehicle for political causes. The relationship between the individual analyst and psychoanalysis as an institution was much more debated in France than elsewhere because "in the French analytic milieu, the 'splits' maintain a climate of constant acrimony: one cannot be an analyst in France and maintain the studious neutrality of a research worker" (Smirnoff 1979, p. 57).

Yet, the issue of world politics, which concerned the French analysts so greatly from after the war until the 1970s, has abated. It arose because of the tendency of French intellectuals to be politically involved, the great suffering the war had inflicted, the bonds of friendship it had forged with Russia and communism, and the fervent wish that such a tragedy could be avoided by means of a new world order. The other reason why socialism and communism were such burning questions to many of those studying psychoanalysis was that in France the issue between the two important deterministic theories of the twentieth century was not settled, as it was in the rest of the world where, with few exceptions, dyed-in-the-wool communists turned away from psychoanalysis. In France, the confrontation between the two has resurged periodically, as it did in 1949 when the Communist Party required that the analysts in their midst sign a self-critical text which was subsequently published (Roudinesco 1986). Lacan emerges as the one who seemed least deterred by the inherent contradictions between left-wing causes and his esoteric approach to Freud. Others reconciled themselves to the necessity of a choice.

According to Barande and Barande (1975), the official left

periodically attempts a rapprochement with psychoanalysis. "All along the episodic ups and downs of this impossible and tumultuous philosophical flirtation between Freudism and Marxism, in the forms of different argumentations according to the cyclical variations (from Politzer to Althusser, Deleuze, Guattari, and Castel), the same utopia can be met regularly, reopening each time the same false case: a condemnation of psychoanalysis for not being the ideological system one would have wished it to be, and in the name of which one rejects it" (p. 18). In recent years most analysts have accepted the idea that a choice between the two systems of thought is necessary.

If a marriage between psychoanalysis and Marxism proved to be impossible, flirtations and even liaisons have occurred between psychoanalysis on the one side and existentialism and structuralism on the other. Thus Lacan developed an intellectualized version of psychoanalysis based on structuralist assumptions which became the guiding light to the student revolt of 1968. His version of psychoanalysis provided the background for slogans such as "Consider your wishes as reality," or "Be realistic, demand the impossible." This could be called "psychoanalysis in the service of subversion."

Psychoanalysis and Psychology

At this point, a few words are in order about the relationship between psychoanalysis and psychology in France. It has been stated repeatedly that the Paris Psychoanalytic Society does not discriminate against psychologists as the affiliates of the American Psychoanalytic Association do, but it is equally true that in France, academic psychology has a friendlier relationship to psychoanalysis.

Anzieu (1979), on whose article the following material is based, says that psychoanalysis actually helped psychology in France to define itself. Until the end of the war, psychology in the universities was splintered among the disciplines of philosophy, biology, and medicine. On the other hand, psychoanalysis was received so ambivalently that psychology could be helpful in its propagation.

Daniel Lagache, a psychoanalyst, was chosen in 1947 for the psychology chair at the Sorbonne. And with the institution of a diploma in psychology, departments were created that graduated teachers, clinicians, and researchers. Some of those trained by Lagache and Favez-Boutonnier later decided to study medicine, others decided to remain pure psychologists. Anzieu quotes a remark by Lagache: "Now that the license in psychology exists, take it and give yourself psychoanalytic training: medical studies will not be necessary anymore; psychology is in the process of acquiring its specificity; it will be sufficient for you and you will promote it" (p. 62–63).

Anzieu claims that two thirds of those who teach clinical or pathological psychology have had firsthand experience with psychoanalysis. (This is of course not the case with research psychology.) French universities have truly been friendly to psychoanalysis, which provided psychology with a needed network of theories that constitutes a discipline in its own right and removed it from both philosophy and the natural sciences. Lagache wanted it to be "humanist" and "clinical" as against naturalist and experimentalist. Its methodology was clinical and projective rather than relying on tests and measurements. Furthermore, according to Anzieu, Lagache was instrumental in initiating the *Language of Psychoanalysis*, which Laplanche and Pontalis not only completed but also purged of some terms that they considered overly psychological.

Anzieu thinks that the psychologists were more resistant to Lacan than their medical colleagues were. He thinks that Lacan's structuralist approach derives from French rationalism, whereas the French psychologists are closer to empiricism and therefore to the Anglo-Saxon tradition.

According to Anzieu, nonmedical analysts did have a problem of gaining acceptance in the Paris Psychoanalytic Society, and many applicants went to the French Psychoanalytic

Society for training between 1953 and 1964. Since the time, however, the two societies have had equal proportions (approximately 20 to 25 percent) of nonmedical members, but there is no quota that maintains this proportion. "The basic reason [for this lack of medicalization] is that the French medical milieu was then very hostile to psychoanalysis, that it had refused to consider psychoanalysis as a speciality and even as a medical matter and that it was paradoxical to accuse someone of illegal practice of medicine which, in another context, was not admitted as being medical" (p. 71).

Psychologists were particularly welcome in psychopedagogical centers and child therapy, which, according to Anzieu, is the poor relation of adult analysis.

Basically, however, a conflict cannot be totally avoided. Psychoanalytic training itself cannot be obtained within the confines of the university so that in the end, it might still seem that psychoanalysis is not a psychology.

Anzieu (1979) is aware that the relationship between psychoanalysis and any of the established professions is problematic, and he sums up the problem in the following way:

> A concrete outcome of this impasse that can be established is that psychologists tend to become, for better or for worse, "psychoanalysts" in quotation marks and that these quotation marks are reassuring. Their depsychologization makes them attractive in the eyes of the young Lacanian generation. . . . Simultaneously, it renders them increasingly suspect in the eyes of the defenders of the so-called "scientific" psychology as well as those of the defenders of medical privilege and it exposes clinical psychology to many disappointments and dangers as much in the administrative realm as in the realm of a devaluation of psychology and of the psychologist in the public opinion.
>
> In this way history—at least history of mentalities—pursues, here as elsewhere, its pendular movement. After the risk of a "psychologization" of psychoanalysis, there is now the risk of a "general psychoanalyzation." [p. 75]

Typically, Anzieu cautions against yet another source of excesses in a milieu that might just be too receptive to psychoanalysis.

The Current Status of Psychoanalysis

The French have become wary of excesses. Psychoanalysis occupies a unique place there: not identified with any of the established disciplines; enjoying a rare popularity, sometimes for the wrong reasons; maintaining independence with regard to the major foreign theoretical systems; and functioning in a wide arena outside the analytic situation. Some of the French have established friendly relations with their colleagues abroad, and Braunschweig and Fain (1975a), assess how the French analysts function internally:

> It seems to us that the Psychoanalytic Society of Paris and the institute which depends on it have always benefited from what we could call a true ecological equilibrium. If this equilibrium sometimes resembles a tempest of discord, its objective product is a sum which surpasses every systematized point of view. The majority of the members of the society value this equilibrium which resembles from the outside a sum of scattered tendencies, each in business for itself, thus evoking the organization of the unconscious. Despite certain attempts, no leader has succeeded in ruling this society, and this eventuality is hardly to be anticipated in the future. [p. 199]

It is difficult to imagine anyone other than a Frenchman suggesting as a model for the structure of a social group the organization of the unconscious!

Notes

[1] *Ornicar?* is the name of the review of the Lacanians. The name seems to have no other significance than its connection with *fornicare*.

4

Training and Transmission

Recently, Chasseguet-Smirgel (1984a) and Smirnoff (1979) each suggested that the recurrent problem of psychoanalysis in France starting with Pichon has been the attempt to create a *psychanalyse à la française*. The history of psychoanalysis in France lends ample support to the validity of this point of view. There was however, a time, roughly between 1967 and 1981, when the problems of French psychoanalysis were studied as part of the general problems of psychoanalysis. During that time, the French examined their dilemmas around the transmission of psychoanalysis as if they were not limited and unique to their culture so that what they wrote is relevant to non-French analysts. This literature includes both the training process, which they came to call transmission, and the dissemination through writing. Both elicited many comments that call into question practices common beyond the borders of France.

Training

The controversies around the training of candidates generated many interesting ideas about Freud's "impossible" legacy. Girard (1984), who gave a long report on the issue of the transmission of psychoanalysis in 1983, calls it a crisis "which has become a chronic process, the way of life of our institution, with its symptoms, its compulsions, its resistances, its dramatizations, its acting out, its perversions: family life" (p. 148).

The challenges to the structure of training launched by Nacht's opponents prompted many debates centered on accountability, the exercise of authority, and, implicitly, the issue of submission versus insubordination—sometimes termed personal autonomy as against dependence on an authoritarian structure. The discussions, however, covered a broader field and led to questions concerning the nature of psychoanalysis and its reproductive system.

What name to give the teaching process? Girard describes with considerable irony the questions that were raised. The term *transmission* was bounced around, he reports. "It was newer and more pleasing than *course* or *didactic*, less forbidding and constraining than *formation*, less technical than *teaching* and less normative and lighter than *education*. *Transmission* turned away from healing and seemed to ennoble the goals of analysis; it was associated with the mysteries of the spirit and touched ever so lightly on initiation because its object remained quite elusive." In fact, Girard says, "this term attracted thunderbolts." He reports that R. Barande claimed not to know what transmission meant. Girard argues he knew only too well, and he took exception to the analytic process it hints at: "an objectifying of the analytic process through a transmitted object, knowledge, theory, doctrine, profession, which orients the process between two poles signifying the activity of the analyst toward a passive analysand, a reductionist and mechanistic view of transmission." Barande proposed the notion of "sensitizing to the process" to put the accent on the prospective notion of discovery, "of revelation of an aptitude which the subject carries within himself since forever except when counterindicated." Girard responds, "This reduces training and institutional functioning to psychoanalysis" (Girard 1984, p. 151).

With the accent on self-discovery, transgression against established rules, and the influence of Lacan's self-authorization, it is indeed often difficult to fathom how some of the most extreme challenges to the training process intend to differentiate between the personal analysis of the analyst and his training within an institution. Girard makes a historical comparison: Eitingon favored the institutionalization of training and the integration of technique with a method that could lead to the "obsessionalization of the spirit of psychoanalytic training" . . . . Ferenczi counters this method with the liberty gained from a long analysis and with putting these gains to technical use without fear of the "affective trance."

> Both have a grandiose vision of the transmission of psychoanalysis and of its mission, anchored in the pursuit of their primordial request of Freud: Eitingon to be taught, Ferenczi to be cured, two permanent modes of entry into the analytic training process. 'Two complementary modes also of the organization of training since the Ferenczian perspective still largely dominates the curriculum, with regard to form, to the length, to the ideal, and somewhere perhaps also, let us hope, with regard to the results.' [p. 120]

These contrasting views of the psychoanalytic training process can typify the contrast between the French and American approaches to the problem. Americans are temperamentally more at home with the structured approach, and many of these controversies are not aired in the United States with the same vehemence and depth. The American analysts tend toward pragmatism: they find a solution, make the necessary changes, create a spirit of consensus, and work. The French approach highlights the latent controversies that in America are kept at bay, perhaps too forcefully, in the interest of consensus.

It is difficult to ascertain the practical ramifications of these debates. There were reforms as a result of the unrest of 1968, which had an impact on the psychoanalytic societies as well as the rest of the nation; but with the French, what they do is never as interesting as what they say.

In 1982 Sandler compiled statistics that reveal some interesting differences in the various institutes affiliated with the International Psychoanalytic Association. She shows that at the time her study was conducted the Paris Psychoanalytic Society had 288 members and 353 candidates, whereas the Psychoanalytic Association of France had forty members and eighty candidates. The latter designates 78 percent of the total membership as training analysts, whereas in the former, 19 percent of the members analyze candidates.

Sandler differentiates between the so-called open and closed institutes on the basis of whether or not the curriculum was fixed. In this respect, both French institutes are open. This leads to a larger student body because it takes the candidates longer to complete their training than if they were ushered through a set program or eliminated in a more active way.

It is evident that despite the accusations of conservatism leveled at the training institute of the Paris Psychoanalytic Society, its curriculum is structured quite loosely by our standards. It is interesting to note that in a culture that prizes intellectuality so highly, a candidate's analysis starts before the course work. Some think that this accentuates a masochistic submission, but most defend this practice, reiterating the precedence of personal analysis over intellectual mastery.

According to Girard (1984) a frequency of three sessions per week is considered acceptable, group supervision for at least one case is obligatory, there is freedom in the choice of analyst and supervisors, and there is flexibility in the length and the structure of the program. At the present time, training analyses are conducted only by senior analysts *(membres titulaires)* who are ipso facto training analysts. Preselection interviews, for example, at the beginning of the training analysis, were made optional in 1967. Thus one of the major hurdles in the life of a candidate is the application for supervision. It is the granting or withholding of the right to conduct analyses under supervision that gives the Institute its major screening power. The approval seems to be based exclusively on the progress of the candidate's analysis.

There is no curriculum committee that rules on either the suitability or the level of any given course, and any member can propose to give a seminar. The obligatory education, programmed as to the number of years, was abolished in 1961 and was replaced by seminars to which free access was given. The responsibility for a balanced exposure to psychoanalysis is left entirely in the hands of the candidate, with the result that a one-sided learning process is a real possibility. The validation of a candidate's curriculum aims at eliminating this pitfall, but in practice the effectiveness of the method depends on the composition of the examining committee. Everything points to a comparative distrust of knowledge because of its phallocentric implications, as against a process in which receptivity and femininity is given a major role. With minor modifications, the training requirements of the Psychoanalytic Association of France are similar. As for the Lacanian groups, they have no official requirements. However, *la passe*, the process by which one could become *Analyste Membre de l'École*, eventually introduced an important and traumatizing step into the communality of the followers of the master, Lacan.

Chiland (1981) describes this Lacanian invention in the following way: "To become an 'Analyst of the School' (a term corresponding to full member or training analyst in the other societies), a confirmed analyst, with many years of experience, must discuss his own analysis ('theorize on it') with two candidates (or *passeurs*) still in analysis and selected by their analyst. A jury, presided over by Lacan, makes the decision on the candidates' status, after listening to the candidates' observations" (p. 58).

I have considered Chiland to be an impartial and reliable source of information, and I was quite unprepared to find another version of *la passe.* According to Schneiderman (1983), a candidate selects two *passeurs* to represent him or her to a committee that judges the merits of the candidacy. Schneiderman explains that the basis of this practice rests on the dismantling of the self and the accentuation of the other. In the examination, the candidate is literally the other, or the Other, and this is somehow connected with a fundamental Lacanian belief in the place of the subject and the relationship to death.

A former *passeur*, Jeanne Favret-Saada (1977) adds to this account that *passeurs* were candidates in the last stages of their analysis, selected by their analysts, themselves *Analystes de l'École.* The candidates for *la passe* drew at random the names of two *passeurs* with whom they spent a year or two theorizing about their analysis. The *passeurs* presented the candidate's case before a jury headed by Lacan and judgment was passed. Favret-Saada is not stingy with words expressing outrage at having analysts confer the designation of *passeur* on an analysand during an ongoing analysis. In addition to the peculiarity of not having a candidate present at the time he or she is being judged, it perverts the analysis of the *passeurs* because of the narcissistic gain inherent in being chosen by one's analyst.

The Lacanian practice of *la passe* demonstrates the extremes he was willing to go through to implement his vision of the uniqueness of psychoanalytic training. He disguised his own autocratic practices and suggested that the members hold a franchise. Be that as it may in Lacan's camp, the struggle to maintain the uniqueness of psychoanalytic training by devising equally unique methods of differentiating the qualified from the unqualified practitioners preoccupied many, especially the younger analysts of the established organizations. They started with the important premise that psychoanalysis is not a natural science, that it must not become alienated from its own true nature, nor must it be left to the happy few since it should not attain the status of a secret society, open only to the initiated or to the true believers. However, Gressot (1975) suggests that the problem of the transmission of psychoanalysis is not unique to it, and to prove his point he shows that one of the chief detractors of psychoanalysis, Eysenck, continuously predicts its demise, thereby setting himself up as a oracle, contrary to the spirit of the scientific method he seeks to extol.

The discussions around the existence of two types of analysis became the vehicle for many comments that apply to training and beyond that to the authority of the analyst.

Cournut (1979) raised the possibility that the practice of training analyses could be corrupting. He enumerates the pitfalls in the tacit agreement underlying the notion of training analyses, especially when they are conducted by analysts who have to earn the privilege of being called training analysts. "The institutionalization of the didactic analysis . . . has brought about a paradoxical situation, that is, that those who should as a matter of principle be best analyzed (in order to defend the 'cause' and to train 'good analysts' themselves) are those whose analysis has been mortgaged from the start by means of a reaction which is poorly founded in theory" (p. 244). He mentions that what Freud did in relation to Adler, Jung, and Ferenczi is now being done in relation to other analysts. The fear of heresy brings with it distrust and a reinforcement of the institution using the didactic analysis as a key instrument. It could lead to two types of analysis, one for training and one for therapeutic purposes, and the further separation of analysts into those "for the lead of a psychotherapy with analytic leaning on the one hand, and on the other, the training analysts for the gold of a pure psychoanalysis, assuring its transmission" (p. 245).

Cournut also points out that didactic analyses have not prevented deviations and dissidences, and that the differentiation between didactic and therapeutic analyses falls prey to the error of taking the manifest content of the wish to become an analyst as grounds for the choice of this or that analyst recognized by the institutes as a training analyst. Instead, he says candidates should be urged to undertake a personal analysis in which their desire to become an analyst is taken as content for analysis along with their other wishes. "There is no 'future analyst.' There are only patients undergoing analysis, some of whom may eventually approach a committee for permission to undertake supervised analyses; this should take place after their wish to do so has been analyzed within the treatment and their wish further been subjected to the scrutiny of the examining group" (p. 241). According to Cournut, the present practice of consulting someone from a list of qualified analysts only suggests an endorsement of the stated wish, which is then acted upon before it can be properly analyzed.

Braunschweig and Fain (1975a) state that he who teaches is not an analyst. They say that an analysis that becomes the key to analytic practice is in danger of not being a true analysis. They defend the need for an analysis into which no extraneous elements intrude for fear of a return to what they call messianism—a situation in which an analyst becomes the defender of a point of view, as may happen, for instance, when the analyst teaches. This leads them into an investigation of the messianism of Lacan, the return of the foreskin in Christianity, and no particular statement about the didactic analysis, to be or not to be.

Le Guen and Roustang studied the process of transmission as it concerned Freud personally. Roustang (1976) says that the International Psychoanalytic Association is organized like a church, and Le Guen (1972b) suggests convincingly that by having chosen the youngest among his "sons," that is, Jung, as the head of this church, Freud recreated the situation described in *Totem and Taboo*: the murder of the father by the youngest brother. Both works merit closer attention and will be discussed in the section devoted to the French literature on Freud. They illustrate the fairly widespread French distrust of the International Psychoanalytic Association because of its function as an enforcer of standards and rules.

In this vein, Robert Barande (1979) questions the notion of transmission as reifying analysis. He insists that the essence of analysis is a process, and as such it cannot be transmitted. Translating transmission into German, he finds kinship between that word and transference (Uebertragung) and suggests that transmission-transference could act as an agent of identification with the analyst. "The analyst 'midwife' does not create nor does he transmit: he helps to facilitate the rediscovery, the free restitution of the conditions of the possibility of instinctual life to each individual and not the analyst's" (p. 219). According to Barande, this does not mean that all institutions have to be abolished, but he urges that the certainty inherent in the term *transmission* be revealed in its fundamental contradiction of the uncertainty of the theory and practice of analysis. Furthermore, he points out that the term is antithetical to the upkeep of psychic functions that undergo indefinite elaborations. Barande has renamed his own practice of control analyses to eliminate the connotation of institutional surveillance. He calls his activity "*écoute assistée* (assisted listening), which is more adequate to account for the function of this practice aiming at external sensitizing, complementing the internal sensitizing assured by the personal analysis" (Barande and Barande 1975, p. 54).

Laplanche (1981b) adds that analysis should never lead to a certificate implying privileges, and if it does, it no longer is analysis. He defends teaching psychoanalysis at the university because it is founded on the communication that each listener has with his or her own unconscious. Laplanche does not fear institutionalization: the personal analysis is outside the reach of both the university and the psychoanalytic training organizations.

In this respect, his point of view differs from that expressed by Pasche and Renard (1984) when they point out that a training analysis differs in an important point from an ordinary analysis: it gratifies. Laplanche's admonition that it should not lead to a diploma glosses over the fact that in a sense it does, and I think that Pasche and Renard accurately point out that treatment concerns *being* whereas admission to training concerns *having*. Since the effectiveness of their analyses is one of the most important criteria by which the candidates are judged for the beginning of their analytic work with patients, the training analysis gratifies one of the major wishes of future analysts. They obtain a privilege as a result of their work. This, it seems to me, is indeed a factor that is best acknowledged as being inevitable and therefore subject to analysis rather than to attempts to avoid facing it.

Cosnier (1979) stresses the creative aspects of analysis leaning somewhat toward the idea of a transitional phenomenon described by Winnicott. According to Cosnier, analysis is both found and created, like the transitional object, and therefore the candidate can only learn to hear creatively. She asks: "Is not an open system the transcription of a fantasy of penetration susceptible to being resexualized . . . does not a closed system represent an attempt for a definite protection against castration threat?" (p. 229). She would opt for an alternation between the two attitudes that also characterized Freud's work: consolidation, openings, introduction of new concepts, and so forth, for each analyst. This could never be the equivalent of an identification with one's analyst. On the contrary, she advocates that one of the goals of treatment is the analysis of the marks of identification.

There seemed to be a general affirmation that analysis can and must be perpetuated within an institution, preferably one that keeps itself apart from other affiliations. "We must not resign. Transmission can take place through treatment, through single papers, but also through the institution and meetings; the problem remains the same for all these forms of transmission. Only the suffer-learn, *patheinmathein*, the learning by trial, the suffering in order to understand cannot be transmitted, being the eternal part of being human" (Gillibert 1979, p. 259).

Guillaumin (1979) thinks that it is inevitable that a part of the idealizing process enter into the positions taken by all psychoanalytic groups and that there is no alternative but to interrogate oneself about one's own unconscious motives rather than to interrogate the ill will of others.

These writings reflect some of the vigor and rigorous questioning which I consider stimulating and challenging. It is not at all clear to what length those who highlight the flaws in the present institutions are willing to go to erode the authority of those in power to grant or withhold the right to recognition. There are few references to pragmatic issues that would give a clue as to the author's stand on the types of remedies that he or she would favor, but there seems to be a general understanding that they would be reluctant to emulate the situation that exists in the Lacanian institutes.

Barande (1984), one of the most vociferous and adamant critics, challenges the necessity of an either-or choice between conservator, member of a society on the one hand and anarchist, destroyer of the institution on the other. "Rather [to be] not only Moses conservator of the tables of the law since they are necessary, but also, without God or master and revolutionary, available to break the tables of every transmitted law, if only to better rediscover it" (p. 329). This seems to him the best way to transmit Freud's message, which is never finished, in order to leave it open for new discoveries.

Those who defend the existing structure accuse those who challenge it of bringing about chaos. The critics are undeterred and show an enormous willingness to take an issue to its ultimate implications which suggests that there is an implicit faith that the structure that they are examining, attacking, and analyzing will not be destroyed in the process. This may actually have been truer in the 1970s than it has been lately, when these debates have abated.

Didactic Analysis

At that time, too, the members who wrote critically of didactic analysis seem to have been in the majority. However, this may have been an artifact, since the defenders of the status quo may not have felt the need to be so vociferous.

In Grunberger's 1980 defense of didactic analysis, he contrasts the oedipal attitude to the narcissistic one and points out that the latter entails a seduction away from the reality principle. According to him, this seduction manifests itself in psychoanalytic organizations as a negative attitude toward training. He suggests that the Oedipus principle as well as the father principle aim at of truth, conforming as they do to reality; the individuals resist thereby the seductions of the mother, who embodies the pleasure principle and the principle of self-deception. Grunberger, contrasting a narcissistic solution of the conflict with a truly oedipal one, points out that the father of the fundamentally narcissistic Oedipus is not a person. In fact, the literal Oedipus rivalry is not involved here, but rather the Oedipus principle structuring the world in conformity with its derivatives; it is the parental function in the widest sense of the term. On one side stands the subject in his wounded narcissistic omnipotence, and on the other, the paternal function, the ambient world, reality—all of which the narcissist considers his antagonist. Reality reminds him of his failure to master the complex and achieve postoedipal drive organization. Applying this view to his defense of didactic analysis Grunberger argues that the narcissistic analyst cannot endure the notion of training, since being trained means organization, hierarchy, "establishment," and the notions of difference and maturation, without mentioning manipulation by instructors (p. 620).

This leads Grunberger to analyze the obsession with language of the "narcissistic analyst" who comes into the world as a fully formed analyst. It is, according to Grunberger, one more manifestation of the tendency to return to the archaic mother and the games they played forming sounds and words. Furthermore, he draws attention to the pendular movement of history favoring the matrilineal tendency with narcissistic regression supported by the primal mother imago. He is concerned with the reorientation of psychoanalysis, with the inversion of the oedipal tendency and the principles derived from it, and the negation of clinical reality as such. "Instead, the cathexis of the narcissistic intellectual activity of the analyst displaces the focus to the regressive superficial expression of the psyche in a position that is a defense against the principle of oedipal maturation" (p. 624).

Grunberger defends a point of view that is greatly in need of defense in France. He sees no necessity to avoid a training process based on the prototype of a parent–child relationship undergoing a subsequent process of maturation. Whereas this may not be an issue in parts of the world where these facts are readily accepted, these debates can also enlighten those who may indeed err on the side of excessive submissiveness to a proclaimed and idealized father (or mother).

Insufficient working through of the conflict peculiar to didactic analysis in which the analyst is both the transferential rival (father substitute) and the rival in real life with regard to professional practice may lead, according to Grunberger, to conferring greater status to those who have written than to those who have devoted their time exclusively to clinical practice.

Transmission through Writing

Colette Chiland (1981), herself a French analyst, suggests that the tendency to use a literary style in scientific writings can become excessive. "The taste of the French for brilliant discourse and philosophical speculation leads them to scorn the more 'down-to-earth' spirit of inquiry of the Anglo-Saxons. For the French, obscurity harbors profundity. Intellectual terror, thus, reigns: there is a tendency to be elliptical, obscure, to forgo explanation; those seeking clarity are called imbeciles" (p. 64). "A fruitful obscurity is worth more than a premature clarification" states Green (1977, p. 140), who is not immune to elegantly convoluted phrasing. And none other than the current president of the Paris Psychoanalytic Society, Michel Fain, has deplored precision of language as fetishistic because it does not reflect the workings of the unconscious.

The French not only do not object to ambiguity, they welcome it. Consider, for instance, how Laplanche and Pontalis (1973, pp. 131–132) treat Hartmann's efforts to distinguish between *ego* and *self*, in the face of Freud's use of *Ich* interchangeably for both: ". . . Freud *exploits* traditional usages: he opposes organism to environment, subject to object, internal to external, and so on, while continuing to employ *Ich* at these different levels. . . . He plays on the ambiguities thus created. . . . It is this complexity that is shunned by those who want a different word for every shade of meaning."

Pontalis (1979) makes an apt comparison between the French preoccupation with the written word and the relatively untortured, unself-conscious use of a format by Anglo-Saxon writers. It portrays the differences in methods of approach beautifully, and the quotation itself demonstrates the author's own brilliance of observation and analysis.

> Let us give some examples of those questions which have gripped the French psychoanalysts. For most of them, the question of the transmission of the experience of analysis by means of writing, the question of the possibility itself of this transmission, is strongly present, no matter what its adopted route: whether it intends to lead toward 'science' or 'literature', whether it depends on demon-

> strative logic or free association. It does not matter that this preoccupation is judged excessive by some, nor whether or not some complacency enters into it: the fact exists, to the point that we were able to consecrate a whole issue of this review *[Nouvelle Revue de Psychanalyse]* to the difficulty inherent in the project 'writing psychoanalysis' and that Bernard Pingaud can even pin down, without fear of contradiction, a new genre called 'psycholiterature'. This would be disconcerting outside our [national] borders, judging by the current production one can find, for instance, in the *International Journal of Psycho-Analysis* which is supposed to represent the whole of the analytic community. Our colleagues hardly seem to be prey to the torments of a writing style which was not too inadequate to what it is supposed to recount. The majority of articles follow a standardized scheme: hypothesis, recension of the studies on the questions (with numerous quotations, of oneself and other Anglo-Saxon authors almost exclusively); collection of 'clinical data,' in the form of case histories or 'vignettes' (sic) illustrating explicitly the initial hypothesis; conclusion; summary. Therefore, surely, no risk of 'contraband.' [p. 6]

This facetious remark about there being no risk of contraband suggests the sobriety of Anglo-Saxon texts. They define the terms used, present the reader with an operational definition, and thereby assure that no parameter permeates the surface. The contraband Pontalis refers to are those very parameters that seep through a text when it is less precise, more evocative, and poetic. Americans, because of their greater concern for respectability as embodied by the natural sciences, especially avoid the evocative mode of expression in their psychoanalytic writings. The French clearly do not because they want their verbal expression to reflect the ambiguity and the density of human exchange. This is why the unwary often feel as if they were walking into the middle of a conversation that had preceded their arrival. Americans, on the other hand, define their terms at the beginning so that there can be no doubt about other levels of meaning lurking beneath the surface. Nothing is hidden. In comparison to the French, the Anglo-Saxon approach sometimes seems oversimplified, whereas at other times it constitutes a refreshing reprieve from the French tendency to preciousness.

As a result of the comments made by the various observers of the way the French use language and the dangers inherent in the love of beautiful diction and phrasing, I was led to reflect on the differences between their approach and ours, which also has its pitfalls. In their mode of expression, the French want to cut through layers, and this sometimes leads to a tortuous approach compared to which Anglo-Saxon analysts seem to be naive and unconcerned like a traveler on a good road with a good roadmap. Since every one knows that the map is not the equivalent of the terrain, there is no danger ever that a driver will mistake the map for the road. The map gives the driver a sense of security, a sense that he knows where he has been and where he is going. But when, as so often happens everywhere, psychoanalytic terminology is used as if it were the scenery instead of a map, it can confuse thinking instead of clarifying it.

Pontalis, who is practiced at spotting derailments, hints that the unself-conscious way in which psychoanalytic literature in English glides into a pseudoscientific jargon is a problem also worthy of attention. He and others like Fain and Braunschweig fear that psychoanalytic concepts can become reified or act as fetishes. They think that the scientific approach is too clean, too clear, and too secure for the subject matter. They are afraid that the substance might get lost or falsified. Braunschweig and Fain (1975b) dramatically claim that "Representations through words don't deal with lack (*le manque*) and therefore have a fetishistic reassuring quality. The search for precision through language is in the service of the denial of what is missing" (p. 198).

They emphasize the need to remember that the word is a stand-in for a thing–representation in the unconscious, and what Braunschweig and Fain call the fetishistic aspect of words, is the potential of words to convey something that does not have a representation in the unconscious—the capacity of words to support the illusion of restitution by means of language and thereby avoiding the impact of loss and mourning.

In this country, Jacobson (1971) made a similar observation in her study of denial. Unlike her French colleagues, her remarks were made in the course of her clinical assessment in which she described denial as presupposing "an infantile concretization of psychic reality, which permits persons who employ this defense to treat their psychic strivings as if they were concrete objects perceived" (p. 125). She never addressed this observation to the general use of language, but she did point to the possible pathological implications in the concretization of psychic phenomena inherent in the use of terms such as aggression, sex, or love. I consider this caution against the reification by means of terminology very important.

The solution to the problem of reification attempted by some French analysts, that is, to create a style of writing that, through its imprecision, imitates the workings of the primary process, has questionable results. The liberties they have taken with a process that should be purely secondary have led Anzieu (1977) to the following remarks:

> We are dealing, at least in France, with increasingly proliferating psychoanalytic writings in which the beauty of the style serves as ornament and as narcissistic screen for the banality of the thought, where the subtleties of discourse only serve to give evidence of the singularity of an individual's journey into territory which is supposed to be deciphered and superdeciphered, and where the seductive spirals, typical for alexandrian decadence, flourish on the body of psychoanalytic knowledge declared closed and cadaverous. [p. 128]

The solution adopted by many American analysts, which stems partly from the fascination with what is new, has led to a continuous need for more precise terminology. One has to question whether we are really discovering ever new psychic phenomena and if so, whether they are precise enough to warrant increasing subdivisions of terms or whether we are exhibiting our own infatuation with novelty and natural science.

We can turn to the French and their acute ear for the uses and the abuses of language to remind us of what we are suffering from. Green (1975a) is critical of the genetic approach since he considers it used by those "who took away from the total edifice of psychoanalysis and caused the concept of 'deferred action' (*Nachtraeglichkeit, après coup*) to be eclipsed and who replaced the temporal dialectic with a linear view of development" (p. 114). He and Le Guen have often publicly deplored the case histories that are made up of events that are stacked and sealed off from each other. Both advocate the approach, tacitly used by many of their French colleagues, derived from Ferenczi (1923) who stressed that events occurring earlier in psychic development are imbued with the meaning of later experiences or, more generally, who advocated viewing psychosexual phases as interpenetrable. This approach condenses aims and zones from different phases in a way that is not current here. Psychosexual phases are telescoped into one another so that references to an anal penis or a devouring vagina are not rare at all; some writers do not distinguish passivity from femininity, all of which can appear arbitrary compared to the precision Americans like to achieve. The advantage of this point of view lies in its capacity to remain with drive theory. Ultimately, it is a kind of shorthand that becomes a matter of personal preference and training and is not immune to abuses.

It will become evident from the later chapters that the few case studies that are available make ample reference to body parts and body processes. It gives them a certain Kleinian flavor, but the interpretations are based on psychosexual processes other than the oral that so dominates Kleinian thinking. The French have given the body the central position in their psychoanalytic thinking, and in this way, they believe themselves to be in direct line with Freud's original intent. They do not require a new "action language" because drive theory provides them with that. Actually, what one sees very little of is the action of the environment on the patient. Sometimes I have missed the references to real events and have wondered whether the difference of approach reflects a difference in the culture of the patients. I have speculated that French analysands might be more at home with the reflective verbal approach and are better able to distinguish thoughts from reality than our more action-oriented, less reflective patients. Therefore I have questioned whether their approach would create too unreal an analysis for American patients.

Thus, it appears that their practice and their excesses are of a different order, perhaps even opposite, but the questions they have raised are not. The missionary zeal with which the French struggle for the uniqueness of psychoanalysis is relevant everywhere. Many of those whose work was discussed expressed their concern for maintaining and propagating ideas in a way that does not resemble traditional education either in form or in affiliation. Their outlook in this respect is reminiscent of that of their predecessors who were so reluctant to recognize Vienna as the capital of psychoanalysis. Their continuous striving for purity is as admirable as it can be self-defeating, and it is difficult to know whether to cheer them on or to chide them for expecting the superhuman in a profession that must resign itself to or pride itself on being only human.

5

Freud As Son, Jew, and Father

Many French scholars have studied the relationship between psychoanalysis and the culture into which it was born in order to identify those elements of psychoanalysis that were predicated on Freud's time, location, religious heritage, and personality. Some conducted these studies so as to deepen our understanding of the influence on psychoanalytic theory of Freud's personal choices. Others, in a less positive vein, engaged in what has been a constant effort among the French: to return to a true psychoanalysis, one that is not dependent on the practitioner's being Freud's disciple or follower. Some of these studies implicitly question the need to adhere to Freud's formulations, with the unstated assumption that if indeed it could be demonstrated that psychoanalytic theory is based on certain contingencies related to its founder, then. . . . Well, then it must be remembered that the consequences are never spelled out concretely and that we are meeting again examples of the French tendency to pose challenging questions without serious concern as to the outcome. It is a luxury of which pragmatic Americans do not avail themselves. In fact, they are likely to counter with a request for instructions in applying this wisdom, but this request would be in vain. One has to be willing to be stimulated and charmed by the questions, admire the cleverness of the French, and put aside thoughts of application for the moment.

Freud's Jewishness As an Influence on Psychoanalysis

Of those who were most positive, Pasche (1969) studied the relationship betwen Judaism and psychoanalysis and drew a distinction between the Judeo-Christian tradition and gnosticism. He suggested that Jung veered into the gnostic tradition whereas Freud remained grounded in the idea that man is not good, that he is limited by nature, and that those limits cannot be analyzed away because they reside as much in his flesh as in the rules that surround him. "Judeo-Christian asceticism is a sublimiation of desires, not their eradication, a metamorphosis of flesh, not its annihilation" (p. 131). Furthermore he states that in this view of the world, man is not a microcosm in relationship to a macrocosm that is greater than he: Judeo-Christians are not idealists. On the contrary, the macrocosm is less than a man. This tradition endows life with the significance of an end in itself rather than the means to a higher goal. Pasche believes that "Merger experience and oceanic feelings inspire the greatest mistrust in theologians. We could say that the relation to God must be established beyond the preverbal stages—from relations with a distinct father" (p. 133).[1]

As to the superego, "The Freudian analyst does not consider himself to be a superego any more than a Judeo-Christian believes himself to be God. He must know that he is under the jurisdiction of his own superego and must be careful not to give the contrary impression" (p. 151). Pasche concludes that psychoanalysis is an atheistic version of Judeo-Christian anthropology.

Compared to Pasche's serious study, Besançon's 1974 article is an example of lightweight musing. Besançon suggests that the choice of the Oedipus myth as the key to psychoanalytic thinking was not inevitable. Forgetting that Freud needed his hero to be a son and that a theory that presupposes submission to a real and powerful God would make psychoanalysis into a branch of religion, Besançon raised the question as to whether psychoanalysis is imbued with elements that are rather arbitrary and much more predicated on Freud, the person, than on objective factors. The inquiry centers on Freud's choice of Oedipus over Abraham as the central figure in psychoanalytic theory.

Besançon, a historian, challenges the necessity for the tragic hero as against Abraham, the biblical patriarch, and Moses, the lawgiver. Why did Freud refuse to choose another hero? Freud mentions Abraham only twice as an alternate choice for the protagonist in the central drama in human development, once with regard to filicide and once to attribute by mistake to Moses the notion of alliance through circumcision. Besançon thinks that Freud deprived Abraham of his status as Father as well as robbing him of his alliance with God. Moses, who is not a father through the flesh but only through the book, is made into a stranger, an Egyptian. Thus the law comes from an external superego.

According to Besançon, this enables Freud to assume (one is even inclined to think of the word *usurp* when reading this) the position of the father and the lawgiver, a place that is threatened only by the disciples. Because of his feelings of apprehension, Freud invented the story of the father who is endangered by menacing sons. The murder of the father by the sons is created as a new mythology in *Totem and Taboo*, the work that ignores the Jewish heritage. This is the myth of the father according to Freud, a myth that runs counter to the story of Oedipus.

Besançon stresses that compared to the story of Abraham, who can keep his son since he promises to obey his God and who is the patriarch of many subsequent generations, the story of

Oedipus is tragic. In Freud's choice there are no offspring, and "The paradigm of the father is Laius, the father who abandons and tries to kill his child" (p. 33). The fate is inescapable and resides in every one of us. Jocasta aligns herself against the father, whereas in the Bible there is no such conflict between Abraham and Sarah. Abraham can become Father on the condition that he accepts being the son of the father whose gift he wants. In this way the chain of generations is fixed through obedience, which does not amount to a negative Oedipus complex. There is no transgression that is fatal.

Besançon thinks that this outlook is personal to Freud who speaks about an inexorable fatality. It should not be binding on psychoanalysis as a movement, which should not encompass a *Weltanschauung*, that is, a metaphysical view of the world. Besançon suggests that there are literary styles other than tragedy and that, by implication, Freud's tragic view should not be imposed on future generations of analysts. Indeed, it has not always been. Implicitly, many new theories agree with Besançon's wish for a more optimistic outlook: the current psychoanalytic literature frequently departs from the idea of unavoidable conflict, such as the theories that stress developmental arrest in which there is no conflict or in some object relations theories in which blame converts the process of understanding into one of finding the culprit, mostly the unempathic mother who has been elevated to the level of original sinner. Besançon may believe that Freud had no right to pass down a philosophy as well as a psychology. However, I think that the theory of inevitable conflict depicts life as it is, and if this passes over into the realm of philosophy, so be it. At least it avoids the danger of psychoanalysis becoming a theology, as Besançon's choice does not.

Marthe Robert (1974) also examined Freud's relationship to the biblical hero Moses, but not with an eye to making psychoanalytic theory into a comedy. She studied the choices made by Freud in order to situate them with reference to his Jewish background and his attitude toward it. Schur made a similar attempt in *Freud: Living and Dying* (1972). It differs from Robert's in that he believed that Freud's attitude toward his Jewishness was unambivalent, therefore not problematic; Robert finds significance in Freud's basing his theory to a great extent on non-Jewish myths and depriving one of his heroes, Moses, of his Jewishness. Robert thinks that Freud's fear that psychoanalysis might remain a Jewish affair was an important influence on his work and an impetus to his need to tie his work to Western culture as a whole.

She brings to her study her vast knowledge of both psychoanalysis and the historical situation of the Jews before and during Freud's time. She undertook this study because she felt that the close bond between psychoanalysis and the Jews, which has been taken for granted especially by Freud himself, had remained unexamined. She thinks there is a paradox in Freud's belief that Jews were at an advantage, being unencumbered by a mystic tradition and being outside of society, and his belief that his theories can attain a universality beyond their Jewish origin. Also, according to Robert, psychoanalysis, which supposedly is conceived by a Jew because only a Jew is capable of this kind of universal thinking, borrows from Greek mythology its most important explanatory concept.

Robert, a "Germanist" and the French authority on Franz Kafka, concludes that the fathers of both Kafka and Freud transmitted a more ambiguous heritage than is generally thought. She points out that Freud, like Kafka, who considered himself part of a generation that was in transition, experienced the Jewish heritage only vaguely. For this, she faults "all the Hermann Kafkas" who brought a bit of authentic Judaism from their rural ghettos and demanded from their children a vague faithfulness to tradition, at the same time tacitly consenting to their children's wish for a break. Thus, the son is an unhappy animal no matter what he may do, "fated to live between two worlds and to deceive himself about his own duplicity." She cites this situation as the origin of the revolt against the father—himself the victim of circumstance and sinning only because of banal opportunism and lack of enthusiasm (pp. 22–23).

This father is at the origin of the conflict that psychoanalysis first explained to a spiritually and socially uprooted Jewish generation. As Robert points out, the actual father is Jacob Freud, the cause of the conflict that led to his son's well-known discoveries. He is a Gallician Jew, not a Greek king. Therefore Jacob is kept in the background, and his disappearance at the end of Freud's life has been displaced onto Moses. Robert calls it a return to him whose power Freud had to overcome.

In an interesting study, *Les Visiteurs du Moi* (1981), de Mijolla suggests that Freud may have identified mainly with his paternal grandfather, Schlomo, after whom he was named, inasmuch as his own father could not well serve as a model for sage or patriarch. Instead he had to be castrated and artificially transformed into an old man in order to appear in his son's writings. According to de Mijolla, the model of the wise man comes first and foremost from this grandfather, who died shortly before Freud was born. De Mijolla's thesis, which seems plausible and well documented to me, draws on the assumption that identifications are often based on the model of the parents' oedipal object rather than on the model of the parents themselves.

Robert's interpretation of Freud's relationship to Rome and Athens is that they epitomized for him "the other side," both antiquity and Catholicism, a world that was unknown to his father and in which the older man probably showed no more interest than he did in the books for which Freud spent so much of his hard-earned money. Marthe Robert suggests that Freud was both as comfortable with his Jewish heritage as he seems to have been when he uses the anecdotes that had come to him from his forefathers and as bedeviled by the wish to be integrated into the larger society and to enjoy the privileges bestowed on those who are born into it as he seems to have been.

Freud's access to this world was through the road of intellectual pursuit. Jacob, who had loosened the bond to his ancestors and who did not urge his son to maintain a closer tie to his religion, left his son in an ambiguous position. Robert observes that whereas all of Freud's daughters are named after Jewish women he revered, his sons received the names of his heroes from "the other side": Cromwell, Charcot, and Bruecke. "Freud is therefore revolutionary as a Jew from time immemorial, and conservative as a Jew of today who is half brought to the level of the middle class, timid or even fearful where he has appropriated for himself the ethical and intellectual norms of a borrowed culture but insubordinate and capable of all the temerity where he continues the dream of an intractable people, fiercely attached to its ways and to what it believes to be the truth" (p. 90).

He appropriates the learning of the others, possesses it better than they, and thereby also seemingly converts his science into something that could be called Jewish in the way of the Jewish intellectual who has access to the knowledge of all times and all cultures. Nevertheless, Freud's attachment to the secular culture surrounding him has the quality of a restricted classicism since he rejected the other innovations of his time introduced by artists who were as revolutionary in their fields as he is in his.

Robert points out that the tie between classic humanism and ideology is equally apparent in the timidity of Marxism. For Freud, she thinks, it is a case of a real religious cult of antiquity that demands of him the sacrifices of money for the purchase of relics and pilgrimages that equally tax his means from another point of view; yet the torment with which Heine is afflicted as he struggles with what he considers a necessary choice between the two worlds does not appear to afflict Freud. The struggle exists, but less obviously. Robert thinks that Freud was prevented from "completing the long secret road toward the Rome of his dreams and entering the real Rome which he had forbidden himself until then" (p. 131) by his own inhibition against undertaking the necessary steps toward the attainment of an academic post, rather than by anti-Semitism. Where he is at home, as in the Jewish tales, he is not the scholar; and where he patiently applies his gift for research, he is not immediately, nor even for much of his career, completely at home. Eventually, this paradox enables him to understand the "family romance of the neurotic," that is, the wish to give himself a different origin (though not in reality, since Freud never seriously turned his back on his Jewishness).

According to Robert, Freud's identification with Moses leaves him nothing in common with the Jew and renegade son that he fears becoming when he reaches the root of his ambition; he is "the inspired leader, the political and spiritual guide, the unique legislator of the Jewish people, and as such he is above suspicion" (p. 180). But, to follow Robert a bit further, if Freud has not avenged his father as did Hannibal, neither has Rome succeeded in winning him over. "He undoes the city in his own way, by destroying the tight web of fallacious ancient images that changed it into an inviolable place, sacred in the dual sense of the word: saint, impure for the profane and protected by a moral taboo" (p. 217). Ultimately, he does not bend his knees.

Robert points out that Freud's lifelong struggle was not resolved until close to the end, in 1937, when he killed Moses. At this point he had already succeeded in imposing upon "the other side" his way of thinking and unmasking for them their baser natures, and he had moved from speaking of the wish to kill the father to the actual killing of the hero of Judaism. It almost seems as if the guilt had to be erased through the disappearance of the angry Moses whom he feared. "He breaks the chain of generations and frees himself forever of all fathers, parents, ancestors, who take him back to the scandalous limitations of being" (p. 275). Freud is no one's son and everyone's father. "So that at the moment of leaving the stage where he has so valiantly played his part, he can say that he is no longer Jew, or German, or whatever it may be that carries a name; he only wants to be no one's son from nowhere, the son of his work, which like that of the assassinated prophet, leaves the centuries perplexed as to the mystery of his identity" (p. 278).

Thus Freud can commit the oedipal murder without guilt and impose himself as the new leader of mankind by removing Moses from the line of Jewish ancestry. He can be an unfathered father, better than Narcissus, who loses his way toward his fellow man.

Marthe Robert's impressive study reveals an important conflict that existed for Freud. Whereas far too much has been made of Freud's comfortable relationship to Judaism, not enough stress has been placed on the fact that Jacob Freud was actually a poor model for the castrating father. Time and again, it is forgotten that Freud's theories concern not real people but imagos leading to the prototypical fantasies into which real life events are molded and that therefore his thinking remains relevant, especially since the stability of his own environment has been exaggerated by those who want to detract from the applicability of his findings.

By creating this difficult bridge between two civilizations, Freud kept hidden the nature of his own particular struggle, and thereby he also provided another alibi for those who wished to reject what he had found. One reads so often that the Oedipus complex belongs to a phase in history when the father was unequivocally dominant. This is clearly contrary to fact. As Robert's study shows so cogently, the choice of Oedipus as the central character in psychoanalytic history is the result of a dramatic resolution of conflict. It is not a self-evident choice stemming from Freud's peculiar family situation. On the contrary, it is predicated on Freud's ability to transcend his own specific drama and to find in his own fantasies that which has univerality. Robert's understanding of his motivations and conflicts, while of necessity speculative, seem entirely convincing.

Robert's study addresses Freud's conflicts, especially since they are reflected in the dreams he divulges. Her emphasis on his conflicted relationship to Judaism leads to additional insights about him. None seems to me as important as the assertion that the murderous wishes directed against the parent by the oedipal child are always accompanied by an awareness of some cooperation from the parent, who is never, except in fantasy, a powerful king at all times.

Freud As the Son of His Father and the Father of Psychoanalysis

In Freud's case, the best-known illustration for the disillusionment with his father is the story of the cap that the father was forced to pick up from the ground, a story which diminished the father greatly in the son's eyes. It is undoubtedly a screen behind which are hidden many other stories and events. Jacob Freud was simply not an imposing figure, not the kind of father Freud imagined in his theory of the Oedipus complex. The problem of a beloved man who does not play the part of a hero repeats itself with Karl Abraham, his most trusted colleague and disciple. From the correspondence between the two men it becomes clear that Abraham had Freud's affection, but Jung was his ideal. The conflict played itself out throughout Freud's life, and according to Robert, culminated in Freud's diminishing Moses by theorizing that he might have been a non-Jew, an Egyptian.

Probably every father has had to take his hat out of the gutter at least once in a child's awareness, and this brings about the gray area, in which fantasy and reality intermingle. Fathers are humiliated; fathers die; children have hostile wishes toward fathers, and the failures of the fathers lend tacit support to the fantasy that these harmful wishes can come true. Freud himself is the best example that one does not have to be the son of a king in order to fantasize about a strong, invulnerable father. I think that Freud may have used the image of his grandfather Schlomo as the raw material for his Oedipus complex, but this is speculation. Robert's study emphasizes that complexes are not based on one's real parents. Freud's oedipal struggle, as it is described in her study, is one with which we can identify even more fully than we can with the one Freud postulated in his writings.

The failure to differentiate between the role of the father in reality and in fantasy is illustrated by the interpretation given to a woman patient who had a psychotic father. Her former analyst had assured her that her father meant nothing to her. This was based on the father's withdrawal and eventual psychosis, but it overlooked the patient's regular visits to her father when she was a child. If he did not talk to her, she stayed with him nevertheless. She took her friends to play at her father's house. Even though her family remembered him only as an object of ridicule or pity, he liked to read, and occasionally she could talk to him about books. He did not represent for the patient a genuine oepidal object, but those visits gave the patient an object for identification in relation to the negative Oedipus complex, for the idealization of his independence and aloofness, and thus the underpinnings for a triangle. Most importantly, the father's presence limited the impact of her mother's stance of omnipotence.

The problem of the seemingly voluntary abdication of authority by many fathers, including Freud's, complicates the oedipal problem. The demarcation between the wish and the deed shows itself to be less secure than we would like to think, and every oedipal victory in fantasy may also be accompanied by that piece of reality that makes the victory all the more frightening and inhibiting. The awareness of the parent's weakness converts the child's struggle into something that just might be possible in reality and is therefore more terrifying. As Robert's study demonstrates, this was the case with Freud.

Freud's relationship to Moses was studied in a different way by Claude Le Guen (1972b) in "When the Father Is Afraid or How Freud, Resisting His Fantasy, Has Instituted Psychoanalytic Societies." Le Guen thinks that the essence of *Moses and Monotheism* is that in this work Freud asserts that he has found historic evidence for his discoveries. Here he treats the murder of the father as a historic event and not a fantasy stemming from the mental life of the individual or possibly from a shared mythology. Therefore, Le Guen thinks that Freud gives us in *Moses and Monotheism* his ultimate assertion of reality many years after the seduction theory had been abandoned. What was stated as a hypothesis in *Totem and Taboo* in 1913 and was alluded to in subsequent articles, finally emerges as a fact of history at the end of Freud's life.

Le Guen suggests that Freud never recognized this idea as his own unanalyzed fantasy. Instead, he acted upon this fantasy, that is, the fantasy of his own death as well as the annihilation of his leadership of psychoanalysis, in relation to his own disciples. Freud's preoccupation with his own death has been amply documented. However, Le Guen is the first to point to the parallel between Freud's idea of the murder of the father by the youngest son and Freud's elevation of Jung, his youngest disciple, to preeminence, thereby passing over other collaborators from Vienna as well as his most loyal friend, Karl Abraham. Le Guen claims that the organization Freud helped found was not set up as a group of learned men but rather seemed to be modeled after those schemes Freud did not like: the church, the army, the state. He was suspicious of dissidence, and after his disappointment in Jung he probably gave up the thought of an unthreatened future. Le Guen cites the letter to Jung in which Freud says, "If I am Moses, then you are Joshua and will take possession of the promised land of psychiatry, which I shall only be able to glimpse from afar" (pp. 196–197). In the disappointment he suffered because of Jung, Freud identified with the father of *Totem and Taboo*, and later his choice of a leader fell upon a woman, his daughter Anna. Le Guen suggests that psychoanalytic organizations have been marked by the imprint of Freud's actions and that all subsequent splits bear the stamp of the issue around the father of psychoanalysis. (Le Guen himself proposed a different theory concerning the fantasy of the murder of the father, one lodged in the history of each individual, which will be discussed in Chapter 10.)

Whereas Le Guen drew a convincing analogy between the themes of *Totem and Taboo* and Moses on the one hand and Freud's actions toward Jung on the other, Roustang (1976) examined Freud's relationship to his disciples with the aim of showing that there is an inherent contradiction between discipleship and personal integrity. He, too, took as his point of departure Freud's relationship to his younger colleagues, but he did not single out Jung from among them. Roustang set out to show that Freud was keen on attaching his followers to his own person which, Roustang believes, can only happen in an unresolved transference relationship. He thinks that the same state of affairs prevailed between Lacan and his followers. They, too, had to break away in order to attain their independence.

In one of those games with paradox that the French seem to love, Roustang reaches the conclusion that only the psychotic fantasizes for himself. This is why he cannot form a transference relationship. "From there it derives that there is a proximity between delusion, theorizing and liquidation of the transference relationship" (p. 80). Therefore, says Roustang, adherence to a theory without analyzing the transference to the theorist becomes a symptom or a defensive system. In analysis the patient must learn that he is the one who has the knowledge and not look upon others as its source. "Analysis is therefore at the heart of science since it abolishes belief. But if you take analysis as a science you act as if transference did not exist" (p. 88). Therefore, both the status as a science and the irrationality of transference are at the heart of psychoanalysis, which Roustang interprets to mean that psychoanalysis is not a science but a process of scientificity or scientification. The analyst must avoid becoming like the psychotic, who does not exist except through received ideas.

Roustang points out that Freud was not totally immune to the notion of thought transmission himself and was therefore tainted in the sense of showing some psychotic mechanisms. This may be why he was not so repelled by the idea that his followers should be the recipients of his thoughts. Roustang thinks that Jones, of all Freud's followers, was the most immune to received ideas because for Jones and rationalists like him, Freud's discourse came from the side of science. Paradoxically, they could believe in it without being aware that as disciples they reproduced a fundamental trait of psychosis: they were programmed like computers by means of the discourse of another to which they did not have access. "By making disciples for himself, Freud protected himself. His theoretical discourse, at the outskirt of delusion, was no longer delusional for him to the degree that it was accepted by men of science" (p. 133). But Tausk did not want to wait for the word of the master. He wanted to be involved in the process of creation. The difference between two men, according to Roustang, was that Tausk could experience ambivalence toward his mother, whereas Freud could not. He wanted that part of his psyche as well as his work to be left undisturbed.

Turning to the last would-be disciple discussed by Roustang, there was Groddek, a man who was conscious of his homosexual attachment to Freud but who wanted to work independently. This relationship, too, came to grief.

The point of the study, which resembles nothing as much as erudite gossip aiming to shock, is its emphasis on the contradictory aims of discipleship and the psychoanalytic process. Roustang links psychosis with "being-disciple," which, according to him, is related to psychoanalytic societies. Whereas Roustang considers the ultimate disciple to be the one who only receives ideas and has no desires of his own, he does not think that the counterpart, the disciple who theorizes for himself, has the solution for what constitutes good analytic practice. Roustang tells us that psychoanalysis is often transmitted by means of a transferential attachment to a master. This type of attachment is to be distrusted, and Roustang blames Freud for preferring that his disciples be attached to his person, which is contrary to what Freud actually wrote in a letter to Abraham: "I do not require . . . that you should make considerable sacrifices for my own person, but for the cause" (Freud and Abraham, 1965, letter of October 11, 1908, p. 64). Roustang may have evidence to the contrary, but ultimately to credit or to blame Freud for this state of affairs detracts from the issue and obscures the frequency with which psychoanalysis becomes a personality cult.

But Roustang also points to the defensive aspects of theorizing, that subtle form of negativism and intellectualization, the opposite of discipleship, that occurs frequently in the analyses of persons familiar with popular or professional psychoanalytic literature. The analysand observes himself and tries to continue to form a theory about his observations and thereby controls his thinking. While this looks like self-observation, it amounts to control, competition with the analyst, or self-punishment and is the opposite of the freedom required by the analytic process. The same phenomenon can be observed in the beginning practitioner who theorizes about a patient whereas a more experienced analyst would suspend judgment about the global meaning and concentrate on the more immediate events within an analytic hour. By calling attention to the pitfalls of discipleship and independent theorizing, Roustang challenges us to independence without the excesses inherent in narcissistic defenses.

Anzieu Introduces "The Maternal Dimension" in Freud

Another study of the influence of Freud's personality on psychoanalytic theory was undertaken by Didier Anzieu (1975) in collaboration with a group that discussed his findings with him.[2] He studied Freud's self-analysis and verified some of his thoughts with colleagues and also reexamined Freud's dreams in terms of their relevance to the discovery of psychoanalysis. Anzieu approached this work, which was started in 1959, with the idea that there was an aspect of personality development that had to be added by later theorists, especially Klein, because Freud's view was necessarily limited by his own personality, which Anzieu calls hysterophobic. He found that the maternal dimension is missing in Freud's analysis of himself and others.

By demonstrating the determinants within Freud's personality in the theory he has enunciated, Anzieu takes inventory of those characteristics belonging to the schizoparanoid type of personality that Freud did not formulate.

Anzieu finds parallels between the problems within Freud's personal development and those within the psychic apparatus he is in the process of depicting and then applies these to the dreams that, seen in this light, constitute an identifiable, orderly series bearing a relationship to the discovery of psychoanalysis.[3]

Anzieu (1975) meticulously traces the sequence of Freud's discoveries through a chronological examination of the vicissitudes of his insights. He suggests that there is an analogy between the diversity of Freud's early environment and his subsequent attempt to unify the psychic apparatus according to principles of psychic health as opposed to the alienation of neurosis. In other words, Freud sought to "find a system of transcription between the various languages spoken by each of the subsystems of this apparatus in order to be forearmed against the exodus of one of them and against the 'Babelization' of the whole" (p. 39).

Anzieu suggests a link between the diversity of generations, languages, and cultures surrounding Freud in his earliest years and the diversity of layers composing the psychic apparatus. Freud's self-analysis is, and is only, the mental formulation of depressive anxiety. (Persecutory anxiety would call for a biochemical solution.) This is why, for instance, Freud postulates that there is no representation of death in the unconscious, something that Anzieu and others, who believe in the death instinct, question.

Anzieu points out that Freud was able to mourn his own

future death rather than feel persecuted by it. This corresponds to the notion that depressive anxiety accepts the cause as coming from inside whereas persecutory anxiety would be the result of a projection.

Viewing Freud's dreams from the same perspective convinces Anzieu that the Irma dream aimed at reparation; it refers to the incident concerning Emma in order to close and to bar the road to doubt that had insinuated itself about Fliess's moral honesty and value as a professional (p. 202). In fact, according to Anzieu, the Irma dream constitutes the expression of Freud's wish to analyze himself. As such, it is a program dream for the future discoveries that would become the basis of psychoanalysis. Freud "enunciates the identity of the body of the dream and the dream of the body. The unconscious of which Freud undertakes to establish the corpus is experienced as a corpus delicti from which he wants to exonerate himself, since it represents symbolically and contains metonymically the body of the mother, which must not be grasped" (pp. 216–217). However, that which must be renounced as a possession on the carnal level can be grasped again symbolically.

In this sense then, the interpretation of the dreams becomes the accomplishment of fantasized incest. Anzieu (1975) points out that through the discovery of the Oedipus myth, Freud fully accomplishes this triple movement, objective, subjective, and autofigurative: the discovery of a universal truth, discovery of himself, discovery of itself. We mean by this last expression, the discovery of the process itself through which the principal discovery takes place. "By inventing the Oedipus complex, Freud realizes symbolically his own Oedipus complex. The dream . . . is for him, for all analysts, perhaps for everyone, the body of the mother, a place for the original fulfillment of the wish of the child. To understand dreams, one's own dreams, that was repossessing this lost body" (p. 328).

The transference relationship to Fliess, which at first leads to the acceptance of the theory of periods enunciated by the latter, eradicates the difference between the sexes but not in the usual phallic direction. Men are assigned the same signs of castration women are supposed to have suffered. In the same vein, Anzieu points out that Fliess's theory of bisexuality was at first an ideology that could serve as a defense against castration anxiety, since what he speculated might be a biological fact returns to Freud somewhat later as a psychic process. The difference between the two theories of bisexuality explains why Freud knew about bisexuality through Fliess long before he could truly integrate it into his own theory. Then, as Anzieu documents amply, it came to him almost as if it were his own creation, which in a way it was, since it had changed its psychic location. In addition, says Anzieu castration anxiety furnishes Freud with the means to think about death anxiety, which he feels without understanding or identifying it. "Freud has the premonition that he is on the verge of recognizing the Law of the Father, fundamental for psychic organization, but he is afraid of paying with his life for the price of the triumph" (p. 255). Here, as in other areas, such as when Anzieu refers to transcription that takes place between the topographic levels, a certain Lacanian influence can be sensed. This is equally true of the sensitivity to analogies between writing and movement of ideas within the mental topography.

But the dominant influence on Anzieu's work lies in the Kleinian theories, and it is because of them that Anzieu is convinced that certain psychic mechanisms could not be discovered by Freud and must therefore be added by later generations of analysts. Anzieu states that death, in the fantasy of the child, means losing the mother, and losing her by the child's own fault. This concept of death is typical of depressive anxiety, which for Freud is the motor for his self-analytic work. It is only with great difficulty that Freud conceived of the fantasy of the mother as destructive, fundamentally nasty, even lethal; he had conceived of the child's fantasy of violent death only at the hand of a cruel father. The need to protect an idealized maternal image is for Freud a dominant trait and undoubtedly facilitated by the presence in his infancy of two maternal persons, Amalia and Nannie, whom he split respectively into good and bad. Ultimately, he discovered the image of the phallic mother, which he describes in his studies on Leonardo and on the Medusa's head. But he is able to formulate neither the imago of the bad mother nor the concurrent notion of persecutory anxiety.

Thus, according to Anzieu, Freud's unconscious activity fulfills the fantasy of controlling the bad objects by naming them, without ever becoming conscious of what he is doing. This is also what limits psychoanalysis for those who would want to remain where Freud stopped. Time and again Anzieu suggests that those who present different personality structures have to be treated differently and that the method discovered by Freud is particularly counterindicated in such cases. He is led to speculate about what would have happened if it had not been Freud who discovered psychoanalysis, and his answer is that whoever would have invented it would have brought to bear upon it the particularities of his own personality. A hysteric like Fliess would have been too taken with the physical experience of the fantasy; an obsessional like Breuer or Charcot would have been too systematic and too biased in conceptualizing; a prepsychotic like Tausk or Reich sometimes too subjective and sometimes too abstract. "Thus as Freudian psychoanalysis is the fruit of a formation of the depressive position, Kleinian psychoanalysis is the fruit of the formulation of the schizoparanoid position" (p. 742).

It is, of course, due to the strength of Freud's personality structure, permitting firm boundaries as well as their permeability, that he could attain the insight he did. According to Anzieu, today's personalities tend to have an impoverished preconscious compared to Freud's. Thus, the counterphobic and antidepressive concept of psychoanalysis is not only inoperative but counterindicated today, in the face of the anxiety of depersonalization and persecution. To be faithful to the spirit and to the genius of Freud is to be aware of the historic contingencies that handicapped his concepts of treatment, the limitations that treatment presently has, and the power that remains if only analysts can meet patients without too many affective prejudices and exercise their intelligence without too many theoretical prejudices.

Comparing recent generations with the older ones, Anzieu sees the newer generation as one for whom everything is allowed and less and less is possible; they are often treated by their parents, who have spoiled them, as the repository for everything that is bad. Narcissism has overshadowed oedipal problems, and the subdivisions of the personality are generally not as firmly in place as they once were. Still, it is Anzieu's conviction that it is possible to attain insight into this new structure just as Freud once did into the old, as long as someone meets the problems with genius, determination, and courage.

Pontalis (1977) seems to disagree with Anzieu. He asks whether it is the patients or the analysts who have changed. The latter have become increasingly attentive to the latent—which would largely explain the length of treatment. They interest themselves more in the "container" than in the "content." He speculates that the content has become less structured as a result of a sociocultural evolution that has rendered the referents for identification unstable and vague, "as if the identity crisis were no longer linked exclusively to the adolescent phase of life but constituted a permanent state" (p. 208).

Pontalis cautions against that point of view, since it results in an analysis of society. The danger in this resides in the fact that without knowing it, one exchanges one's analytic chair for that of the "commissar who claims also to act only in the name of the law" (p. 208), in other words, there is a temptation to make normative statements.

And so the French go on: from the studies that concern Freud's person as it influenced the course of psychoanalytic theory, there have been in this chapter excursions into neighboring territory related to questions of the nature of psychoanalytic theory. Some of these observations strike me as accurate and perceptive, and the warnings seem to have their place. However, to think that psychoanalysis can ever become abstracted from the persons who practice it is probably fallacious and undesirable. If we analysts are not influenced by elements that were present in Freud's life, we can be quite certain that there will be other factors influencing our approach and that the French will be studying the relationship between our work, our unconscious conflicts, and some as yet unexplored hero or heroine of Greek or biblical mythology.

Notes

[1] Interestingly, he classifies the autonomous ego among the disembodied entities, because it is taken out of its flesh and conflict.

[2] Anzieu has used his understanding of group dynamics for many purposes; the discussion and deepening of the study of Freud's dreams is only one of the many applications he mentions in his most recent book (Anzieu 1986). It is not within the scope of this present work to expose in greater detail the work of Anzieu's group.

[3] Le Guen (1981) takes Anzieu to task for going so far with the interpretation of dreams. Le Guen thinks that there is nothing to prove or disprove Anzieu's analysis because Freud's associations are missing beyond what he gives in *The Interpretation of Dreams*. In other words, he is opposed to analyzing written documents. Le Guen thinks that this is equally true when psychic content is converted into a topography or when a history is stratified according to a genetic sequence. In each case, according to the author, it is a matter of putting psychic events in a place rather than considering them as organic and fluctuating.

Le Guen thinks that post-Freudian developments encourage the type of thinking that leads to a notion of inscription. This, according to him, is what gives the Kleinian interpretation its degree of sureness, leads Lacanism in the same direction, and despite the few formal appearances to the contrary, places the genetic schools, such as Mahler's, in the same tradition.

Whether or not Le Guen's criticism invalidates Anzieu's study must be left to the opinion of each individual. The variety of sources upon which Anzieu drew is such that his work seems more than a textual analysis. Wherever he could, Anzieu examined the events in Freud's life at the time of the dream and at the time of the memory to which he was associating.

6

Psychoanalysis beyond the Couch

In the French psychoanalytic literature, interest in the way the Judeo-Christian tradition manifests itself in psychoanalysis also led to a study of the religions' underlying philosophies. Instead of focusing on Freud, one controversial book attempted to analyze the student revolt of 1968 and the dynamics prompting it by finding an analogy between the modern events in France and the thinking of the early Christians.

One cannot but agree with Pontalis's claim that analytic neutrality not be guaranteed when analysts apply their knowledge outside the consulting room. Such studies remind me of what I heard early in my career: that any interpretation that does not respond to a request is a sign of hostility. I believe this to be true, but it does not exactly invalidate the interpretation, any more than we can deny the accuracy of some comments made by psychotic patients, whose defenses prompt them to read the unconscious processes of others. Accuracy of observation is not predicated on neutrality.

Analysts Examine Current Events

Such lack of neutrality was the case in this passionate book published in 1969, a year after the student revolt. It was so controversial that the writers used the pseudonym André Stéphane in order to protect their own patients from the controversy. It is called *L'Univers Contestationnaire* and its authors are now known to have been Grunberger and Chasseguet-Smirgel. They made a comparison between the protest movement and other manifestations of mysticism throughout history.

The authors document their contentions with quotations that support their conviction that the protestors of 1968 aimed at nothing so much as the dissolution of structure and materialism. The book demonstrates convincingly the regressive phenomenon inherent in the revolutionary literature of that period in which matter is confused with fecal matter and therefore rejected in favor of a spirituality that is not rooted in material reality.

This study is relevant to many situations in which mysticism and idealism become factors in protests against the bourgeoisie and organized society. These are usually less well rationalized than they are in France, but the authors' analysis seems equally valid and applicable to situations elsewhere, for example, the flower children, the hippies, the religious movements, and so forth.

In essence, the authors distinguish between revolution and contestation in order to differentiate the genuine wish for social change from the phenomenon of which they are so critical. They do not present themselves as defenders of the status quo for its own sake.

They have read widely, including a statement in which Lenin himself mentioned that he considers leftism to be a disease. They have attended the meetings of the protesters and are at home in the Old as well as the New Testament. This book has a definite point of view, which the authors do not deny; but it is also rich in documentation that gives substance to assertions that might otherwise seem to be only politically motivated. When they say that they consider the protest movement a phase of Christianity, they show through quotations placed side by side the similarity between the thoughts expressed in the New Testament and those voiced by the leaders of 1968. If, in addition, it is remembered that the decline of the popularity of protest movements has been followed by an upsurge of interest in religions, especially those rooted in mysticism, the thoughts expressed in this book gain in validity, since subsequent events have confirmed the direction of their analogy.

In contrast to Pasche's (1969) work, which opposed Judeo-Christian thinking on the one side to Gnosticism on the other, this study differentiates between Judaism and Christianity and attributes a strong idealistic current to Christianity. In the authors' opinion, the "Christian religion, especially Catholicism, constitutes the attempt to solve the Oedipus complex which for 2,000 years has castrated man. The guilt with which matter is sullied and concomitantly the flesh and earthly goods, still weighs on humanity" (p. 11). They contrast the commandment "You will love your father and mother so that your days on Earth will be long," with the later Christian "My kingdom is not of this world," which constitutes a movement of rejection of the worldly order. In terms of psychic economy, this attitude is impossible to maintain and therefore has most frequently led to projections of the instincts that are denied or repressed. In the protest movement this projection is aimed at the middle class or consumerism and has led to an intolerance of the other, who is the representative of those denied parts of themselves. The authors contrast this attitude with other contemporary revolutionary movements that were not particularly Christian and point out that the French workers in 1968 resisted making common cause with the student movement precisely because of the element of mysticism. The workers' aim had always been to improve their own condition by attaining a little more of the worldly goods the students so despised.

In the Grunberger and Chasseguet-Smirgel study, the authors consider Christianity the prototype of all later dissidence, such as leftism with regard to socialism, Jungism and Lacanism with regard to Freudism. In this sense Protestantism was a return to material reality, away from the mysticism of the hereafter, since it gave rise to modern capitalism, as Max Weber pointed out. The authors are well aware that generalizations are inherently dangerous and that Christianity and Catholicism are open to various interpretations. They recognize that the notorious wealth and corruption of the church was as much responsible for the Reformation as anything else. They also know that the early history of the rule of Christianity involved a struggle between the Church of Rome and the Gnostics around the issue of the humanity of Christ in which Rome, defending the manhood of Jesus, prevailed.

Nonetheless the book offers a convincing analogy between the religion of the son and the participants in modern protest movements, who benefited from the high regard in which youth is held in the cultures in which those protests took place. The writers stress that asceticism is frequently a part of adolescence, and that this also corresponds to a Christian ideal. The early phase of adolescence is dominated by the wish to escape from the fundamental facts of biology: the instinctual urges. Both in Christianity and in many social movements this wish becomes incorporated into the group and leads to ideology that unites the members in the manner described by Freud (1921).

This ideology replaces the Oedipus complex, in a manner discussed in great detail in this book. "To attack the father, to destroy him, can mean a total refusal to identify with him, that is, it can be linked to the suppression of the parental function pure and simple and an attempt to eradicate the unconscious wish to become 'father' and 'mother' oneself and not wish to take his place" (Stéphane 1969, p. 24). Instead, there is a desire to erase the distinction between parents and children by magical means. The ideologues want to place themselves outside the succession of generations. And, according to the authors, a similar effort can be recognized in those who would want to understand their own characteristics by consulting the astrological signs under which they were born rather than to compare themselves to their own biological parents. The same impulses led to the destruction of the Jewish cemeteries in Nazi Germany.

On the other hand, a total inability to identify with the aggressor leads to the search for a victim with whom to make common cause. Thus Israel became devalued as soon as it had military victories against the Arabs, toward whom sympathies shifted rapidly as of 1967. Subtle anti-Semitism, disguised as anti-Zionism, is directed at the Jew as victor, that is, one who has gained through aggression, and not at the Jew as a victim of persecution, which is, after all, also part of his identity. But as the authors point out, the aim is to project the aggression and then condemn the objects on whom it has been projected.

This process of idealization leads to the suppression of a part of the object's humanity, and this defense runs counter to identity formation in the subject since an important part of his own instinctual life has been split off. They point out that Jesus had to establish himself both as the emissary of God and as loving him so as to remove any suggestion that aggression might have been involved in his attaining the exalted position that he occupied with regard to the father. They further comment that Judaism and Christianity, with their parallel opposition between the religion of the father and the religion of the son, differ sharply in their views on education. Jehovah, the strict father, gives his people strict regulations extending over all acts of life and chastises them every time they turn away from the straight road. The history of the Jewish people can be seen as alternations of happy phases of obedience on the one hand, and of deviations punished by God on the other. He who loves well, punishes well. As to Christianity, we see that it has liberated the believer from the yoke of the law and it demands no other religious activity than faith. The Christians' sins are forgiven in advance. At most they are asked to recapitulate them in front of an innocent mediator who is there to make them innocent at the price of certain rather scant formalities" (p. 50). Baptism makes them children of God, who sacrificed himself for them, and God showers them with honors upon their entry into life. These honors last until their entry into paradise. Are they not the spoiled children of God?

At another point the authors contrast circumcision, which is a pact with God inscribed in the flesh, with baptism, which washes off all traces of the origins of carnal birth and conception through the father. "In this sense, baptism expresses and confirms the contestation of the father, whereas circumcision attests to the *tie* to the father. Baptism, by contrast, expresses rejection" (p. 65). Thus Judaism is seen as the religion of the father, not only the divine one, since honoring mother and father is part of the proscription of the commandments, and the reward of a long life on this earth is seen as desirable. This attitude contrasts with the emphasis in Christianity on the hereafter and the otherworldliness of the kingdom of God.

Furthermore, submission to the father, as required in Judaism, implies renunciation of the mother and a resolution of the oedipal triangle. By contrast, the son takes on a larger role than the father in Christianity, and the role of the mother eclipses that of the father. This structure of the religion does not, of course, spell out how it fits into the life of the individual. As the authors point out, the number of neurotic Jews proves this. Actually, the genuine resolution of the oedipal conflict would preclude the practice of any religion.

In a study of faith and miracles, the authors point to their link to narcissism, which has an affinity for events that take place magically, without human manipulations. The object is to lift man out of the realm of material reality: the spirit against matter. But through their contempt for matter, the protesters have shown that they equate all matter with fecal matter, thereby demonstrating their failure to resolve the anal phase. The young protesters enacted the regression that is artificially induced through the analytic process, as the authors amply demonstrate through quotations from their writings. They gratified their wish for mirror relationships that permit quasi-absolute fusions. "Whoever is not I is an agent of the repression which is exercised upon me" (p. 109). In order to escape from this repression, there is a wish to abolish most criteria for examinations of competence, replaced by autoevaluations. Again, this is due to the projection of anality and aggression onto the outside, which renders the outside untrustworthy.

The authors refer to certain pseudo-epistemophilia. The investment of intelligence permits the young people to skip the maturational process. It avoids the oedipal confrontation with the father. In the same way, knowledge pertaining to certain aspects of reality, such as the difference between generations, is repressed. Culture frequently supports this process.

> Christianity presents an attempt of man to remain son, and nevertheless to become God, recovering his narcissistic omnipotence through a pseudo-identification with the divine father, short-circuiting thereby the relation with the historical father, whose function is annulled through baptism, that is, second birth.
>
> In Genesis, on the contrary, the myth shows us human beings in paradise, that is, in a state of narcissistic regression—elated, unconscious happiness. Sexuality and drives in general seem to be symbolized by the serpent (the tempter), whereas transgression against the divine (paternal) taboo becomes one with knowledge (to eat the fruit of the tree of knowledge is to know, to have carnal knowledge in Hebrew). Knowledge implies facing the difficulties of existence; pain; the need to find subsistence; and above all, giving up paradise, that is, narcissistic regression. In short, knowledge is *the commitment to the long and painful road of maturation.* [Pasche 1969, p. 118]

This view encourages the individual toward reason and reality as against a romantic, anti-intellectual stance in which faith and poetry are considered superior to fulfillment in the material world. Grunberger and Chasseguet-Smirgel do not imply that both attitudes are necessarily mutually exclusive, but rather that it is already a mark of regression when the two are juxtaposed. For instance, they quote Picasso to the effect, "This is very nice, but one must also reflect" (p. 121), thereby demonstrating that artists recognize the need to impose control over their thinking. They add, "Verbal and conceptual motor functions are not used as a narcissistic compensation for the avoidance of the Oedipus" (p. 122). Rather, where this is the case, "it is the matter of a poetic work permitting the maintenance of a certain relative equilibrium with regard to complexes in which the catharctic effect plays an important role" (p. 123). The narcissistic world of "being" refuses to recognize the world of process, the only one in which real change can occur, the world that the authors call the anal universe, the one that allows for modifications and transformations.

Furthermore, they demonstrate that a certain self-hatred is generated when the anality has not been completely projected but cannot be integrated and narcissistically cathected. This is the case for all those who have been touched by the ideology and have made it part of their ego ideal without, however, having been able to control their impulses in accordance with superego demands. They note that "things become serious when intellectuals, who supposedly are tired of using reason, adhere without reservation and without criticism to myths and slogans and attribute to themselves the mission of imposing on others an archaic view of the world that, in reality, they impose on themselves by their internal conflicts" (p. 167). From this comes an irrational intolerance of machines, even those machines that have made life easier and better. Since they are viewed as projections of our biological reality, they tend to be rejected by those who favor a more romantic and idyllic vision of the good life. In the process of analyzing this kind of *Weltanschauung*, the authors take on Marcuse, who they say favors a kind of pregenital sexualization, in that he pits himself against a procreative sexuality and postulates an external and repressive superego. "Daily clinical practice and the entire work of Freud indicate that the demands of society cannot be equated with those of the superego, nor of the Oedipus complex, that is to say, the result of the internalization of the incest barrier in order to escape castration anxiety" (p. 187). Thus, contrary to Marcuse's view, the Freudian superego could induce regression rather than prohibit it.

The authors demonstrate that this kind of regressive phenomenon is present throughout history in one form or another. The reason for the greater temptation of regressive solutions to conflict today is the affluence in Western society, which confronts people in a direct way with their sense of being mutilated and fated to dissatisfactions.

A return to some form of religion has been the heritage of the protests of the 1960s, especially in America, because progress and abundance have been disappointing in terms of solving man's problems. Therefore, people experience themselves again and again as fallen gods who have lost the hope of reintegrating the heavens from which they have fallen. And with the advent of an attempt to return to God and old-fashioned religion (at least in the United States), the projection and persecution is directed at the criminal on the street, who has in actuality transgressed. Fortunately it has not taken the form of the racism known from previous periods. The Moral Majority attacks immorality, but has not as yet attacked any one racial or societal group as being the bearer of evil.

The authors point out that those who protested are those who did not have to struggle for a livelihood; they are the spoiled children of parents who may have suffered greatly either because of the war or material deprivation. The combination of indulgence and weakness coupled with a misplaced permissiveness, further heightens the tendency to eclipse parental functions and disparage the need for the satisfaction of material needs. The children, in order to circumvent the inevitable confrontation between their need for material goods and their need to disparage the products they use, attempt to take the latter for granted so as to ignore their origin. The dream of automatic gratification is continued by the child as well as the parents, who ask their children to be happy, as if this were part of man's condition instead of their own dream of paradise. The sexual freedom of the children serves as proof of transgressions that count more heavily than actions. The children form couples from chance meetings that come closer to autoerotism than to love. This mode of relationship resembles mirroring, rather than a relationship between a subject and an object.

Parents project guilt about their own affluence onto the Third World, which they want to save in order to save themselves from imagined persecution. Those members of the Third World who refuse to grant affluent Westerners this role of savior plunge them back into guilt and a renewed attempt to identify with those who are in need of salvation. (I think that it might be interesting to analyze fashions in this light as well. Current trends capitalize on the wish to appear poor by wearing loose, torn, and rather ill-fitting clothes. The popularity of camouflage-like prints and of khaki reflects another attempt to imitate the drabness of poverty and the trenches. It is doubtful whether those who have experienced war firsthand are attracted by these fashions.)

The authors think that the tendency to politicize these conflicts constitutes a provisional channel for tensions and avoids depression. They call it a cosmic anality.

> A narcissistic position based on the realization of a 'cosmic anality' is not at all equivalent to a mastery of the object . . . nor to an anal-sadistic relationship, since it does not have the qualities of precision and limitation. If the immature person flees from the

> Oedipus, he remains equally incapable if he fecalizes the other, that is, if psychologically the other stops existing, so that he finds himself alone (with others like him) in his narcissistic universe. [p. 259]
>
> If anality proper constitutes above all mastery and object relations, fecalization annuls the object in a way, after having transformed it into garbage, and results in an objectless, *narcissistic state*. [p. 261]

Here then, the authors differentiate relating in an anal-sadistic way from fecalization, which is more primitive and is reminiscent of the anality described by Abraham before the stage of retention and conserving the object. It is related to contempt, which is not what typifies the more object-directed anal-sadism. Anal-sadism is, after all, a precursor of love; it is a wish to control, which must be distinguished from contempt and fecalization.

The authors equate the level of regression with the relationship to the sadistic, overfeeding mother; the accusation against the society of overconsumption is an accusation leveled at her. Thus, the writers postulate that social hierarchy promotes the Oedipus complex. Even socialist states return to forms of privilege and private property; otherwise they would constitute maternal systems.

"True revolution must of necessity be oedipal" (p. 287), the authors declare. "Contestation is an affective movement with a secondary content, whereas revolution pursues above all a goal in which the affective elements mobilized through it are subordinated to it" (p. 293). And finally, "The true revolutionary . . . incorporates the past that is the parental universe and surpasses it. The contestant cuts himself off from his roots and can only, if he is artist or writer, create inauthentic works. The new is only really new when it contains the old and transcends it" (p. 299).

L'Univers Contestationnaire has a systematic point of view that applies the understanding of defensive mechanisms to social phenomena, in keeping with Grunberger's and Chasseguet-Smirgel's clinical theories which will be discussed in subsequent chapters. The authors defend their method of approach on the basis that Freud set the precedent by also regarding social phenomena as open to psychoanalytic interpretations. We are dealing here with a controversy that permeates the field of psychoanalysis and does not seem to find a resolution.

In a recent publication, Anzieu (1986) recounts his experiences during the events of 1968. At the time of the student uprising, he was a professor of psychology in one of the newer and most liberal universities. He points out that revolts always start with a small group. In this case, he thinks that the young people were plunged into an overabundance of knowledge and a void in terms of cultural models. He too thinks that this leads to utopian thinking, but not of the kind that germinates in the mind of one individual. Rather it was a utopia that was improvised collectively from day to day. The protesters refused to plan ahead because to anticipate would mean to impose and therefore to arrogate to oneself a new power.[1]

Very recently, Chasseguet-Smirgel added yet another chapter in the application of psychoanalytic knowledge to social phenomena. She examined the unconscious guilt of the German nation concerning the fate they imposed on the Jews during World War II and found evidence of repressed national guilt in the political phenomenon of the Green Party.

She examines documents published by the Greens to demonstrate that "the very acute guilt of an Ego faced with a gigantic task, a measureless work of reparation, is experienced as an assault on the Ego by a demanding and pitiless agency" (1986a, p. 109). In the case of the Greens and their fears about pollution of the environment, the agency is projected and returns to consciousness as a fear of being poisoned and exterminated in the same way as the Jews were. It is as if the guilt of the fathers were going to fall on the children, and the children's fears are embodied in ideas that incorporate the deeds of the fathers.

Chasseguet-Smirgel justifies this interpretation of the Green phenomenon because it has become so pronounced in Germany, whereas in other countries it has not attained such importance (unless we include the United States, where possibly it could relate to guilt concerning the first use of the atom bomb). She contrasts the pacifist movement in Germany with that in France and argues that since the dangers of another war are the same for both—the Russians could reach France as well as Germany with their missiles—the strength of the movement must be related to psychic factors. "In cases where a belief is shared by a group, individual reality testing is swept away in favor of the group reality, that is, its belief. This makes it possible to believe one really is the victim of car-exhaust gas in exactly the same was as the Jews were, without bursting into laughter at the scandalous nature of such a statement, or breaking into tears rather, because one can never overestimate the immense grief that the Green illusion must turn into persecution at all costs" (p. 127).

The evidence and the rationale they supply for their interpretations seem to me to support adequately their beliefs. As with all beliefs, it is undoubtedly true that we are convinced when we want to be, and it is possible that another person does not find the facts as they are presented compelling. To my knowledge, no one has reinterpreted those same facts to draw a different conclusion. The criticism, when it came, was aimed at the conclusions, which are political in nature, not at the possibility of faulty reasoning.

Notes

[1] When the universities resumed their activities, Anzieu was asked by Faure to enter his Cabinet.

7

Psychoanalysis off and on the Track: Dissidence and Dissidents

In the Preface, I referred to the French attitude of stewardship in intellectual matters including psychoanalysis. This attitude, interestingly enough, led French psychoanalysis into two totally divergent directions for the same stated reason: faithfulness to Freud's heritage. Those who took the direction of classical analysis call those who took another direction *dissidents*.

The dissidents found in Lacan the embodiment of the dream that has accompanied French psychoanalysis from its inception: to have a French analyst sit in the chair vacated by the master. Lacan arrogated to himself the right to dictate which way psychoanalysis had to go in order to be true to itself, and he seduced many into following him in this endeavor. Those who never were seduced and those who later became disenchanted were equally motivated to analyze what had happened to psychoanalysis so as to guard it against further derailments. Lacan's opponents demonstrated how he deviated and attempted to define the temptation to alter the basic nature of psychoanalysis;

undoubtedly they also tried to master, at least intellectually, their own disappointment with the fact that professionals are not immune to seductions and illusions and that training does not ameliorate the animosities within analytic groups.

Chasseguet-Smirgel, Grunberger, Pontalis, Laplanche, and others think that Lacan embodied the image of the analyst chafing under the constraints imposed by psychoanalysis, and they found parallels in Ferenczi's work of psychoanalysis gone astray. They believe that the source of the fascination both men exerted lay in part in their basic insubordination or negative transference to Freud, which neither acknowledged to exist. But since Lacan and Ferenczi used totally different vehicles to attain their independence from Freud, the similarity between them consists only of their motives and of their roles as brilliant rebels. Their methods were diametrically opposed: Ferenczi mothered his patients, whereas Lacan remained silent and shortened his contact with patients.

Lacan's Return to Freud

Lacan called his endeavor a return to Freud, but he hardly assumed the role of Freud's disciple. He reinterpreted certain texts of the master, ignored others, and imposed himself as the new authority. According to Roudinesco (1986), he "translates Freudian discourse into a language familiar to the Catholic culture" (p. 274). Perhaps this is true, especially in view of the fact that after he lost his connections with the world of medicine and the International Psychoanalytic Association, he requested an audience with the Pope.

According to Schneiderman (1983), an American Lacanian, Lacan believed that "Freud did not expect his followers to advance the theory of psychoanalysis; he wanted it guarded until someone else came along to pick up the flame" and that he, Lacan, was the one to do it (p. 31). Lacan (1966) said:

> If the place of the master is left empty, it is due less to his death than to the growing obliteration of the meaning of his work. [p. 244]

> Every return to Freud leading to a lesson worthy of this name, will only come about through the way [*voie*, meaning both way and roadway] from where the most hidden truth becomes manifest in the revolutions of the culture. This way *[voie]* is the only training which we can pretend to transmit to those who follow. It is called: a style. [p. 458]

A style is not the same as substance. Lacan "wants to be and calls himself the messenger *[le porte-parole]* of the unconscious by using its language" (Bär 1974, p. 481). This results in Lacan's letting himself be the patient who suffers the irruptions of the unconscious.

With his style, Lacan attempts to evade the logic of secondary process thinking. By becoming himself the embodiment of the unconscious, he disbands the cohesiveness of the ego. This notion of tampering with the commonly accepted structure was in the air in Paris. It was evident in the efforts of the surrealists, specifically Breton who wanted to undermine literature, and in the influence of structuralism. Equally in the air was the problem of texts that were impossible to read. Bär states that by all accounts, Lacan is unreadable.

> Lacan ironically takes with one hand what is given with the other, and his reader finds himself in a game, with the marbles of truth hidden in one of Lacan's fists which, upon opening, frequently turns out to be empty. . . . Lacan seems to be eaten up by his own style, much to the discomfort of some of his readers. As the messenger of the mythmaking unconscious, he is as difficult to understand as what he speaks of, that is, dreams, hysterical behavior, hallucinations. And that need not be. However, it is very much in accord with his theory of communication, which beautifully and consistently shows why form is everything and content negligible:

The content, if any, is provided by the reader or listener himself. [p. 483]

This description is in keeping with all other comments concerning Lacan's writings. Bär (1974), whose study is the most complete, scholarly, readable, and respectful I have read, repeatedly refers to the fact that Lacan is confusing and that his terminology is ambiguous. He clarifies the multiple meanings of the terms used by Lacan. But the ambiguity and confusion confront the reader with two choices: a posture of modesty in the face of a complexity that exceeds one's own intelligence, philosophical knowledge, and erudition; or a rejection of Lacan's complexity because it hides confused thinking and fundamental errors. I have opted for the second attitude, and I hope to be able to demonstrate enough of Lacan's errors and deviations to substantiate this point of view. Anyone interested in a detailed and scholarly analysis of Lacan is well advised to consult Bär.

Lacan (1966), like the surrealists before him, was interested only in the unconscious, not in its biological underpinnings. He stated that it was structured like a language or that the individual is taken into the web of language. "The unconscious is the discourse of the Other" (p. 814.). The notion of an unconscious that is supposed to irrupt and find conscious expression prompted the surrealist enterprise. Breton, as was mentioned earlier, aimed at a breakthrough into art of unsynthesized unconscious material. He opposed the notion of sublimation in artistic creativity; instead he wanted art to be the work of the instincts (Roudinesco 1986). Freud's reaction to the surrealists is cited in Chapter 3, and there is no reason to believe that his reaction would have been any more favorable had he lived to witness Lacan's idea of the relationship of the unconscious to the rest of the personality.

Lacan's method of interpretation relies on irruptions by the unconscious, such as words that act as nodes, parapraxes, and dreams, but not on the other Freudian notions of day's residue, dream work, nonverbal cues, and so forth. He thereby gave short shrift to affects and syntheses such as those inherent in the defenses, compromise formations, and derivatives. Laplanche (1981b) asserts that Lacan's theory typifies the concretization of language. He suggests that in Lacanism the dissociation between representation and affect leads to an absolute priority accorded to the representation, the primacy of the signifier. It has led to a rejection and a contempt for the affective. Emphasizing the rules of linguistics,[1] Lacan relies especially on metonymy, metaphor, and word games. This is a method Freud also used in the *Interpretation of Dreams* (1900), but with Lacan it eclipsed all others.

Lacan (1966) justifies his radical departure from Freud's idea of the unconscious, its structure, its function, and its relation to other parts of the individual by claiming to know Freud's intent. For example, he declares that Freud's "*Wo Es war, soll Ich werden*" (1932, p. 86) should not be interpreted as it is in the Strachey translation—"Where id was, there ego shall be" (1933, p. 80). According to Lacan, if Freud had meant to say this, he would have used the article *das*—"*das Es*" and "*das Ich*"—to indicate that he wanted to designate the mental structure. This is unquestionably a misinterpretation of the German. The capitals alone indicate that Freud intended the words to be nouns. The lack of an article preceding them is immaterial. Used as nouns, *Es* and *Ich* refer to the psychic structures, the id and the ego. Lacan, however, ignores this, and in his discussion of his interpretation of the quotation he omits the capital letter when writing *es* and translates *Ich* (capital remains) as *je*. Thus he treats both words as pronouns, which suits him better, despite the fact that in German pronouns are not capitalized.

Lacan (1966) then arrives at the following mistranslation: "*Là où c'était, peut-on-dire, là où s'était, voudrions-nous faire qu'on entendit, c'est mon devoir que je vienne à être*" (pp. 417–418). Or, as translated by Bär, "Where it was itself, it is my duty that I come to be" (1978, p. 529). There can be no mistake, despite Freud's omission of the article, that he intended these words to be nouns, otherwise the capitals would be an error in spelling. Lacan is either deliberately misrepresenting Freud, or his knowledge of German was not adequate to the task.

But Lacan could not accept the idea that Freud gave a central place to the ego instead of the more amorphous *I*, which was the term used by Lacan and his followers. With this distortion, and an apparent unfamiliarity with German among the French analysts, Lacan could successfully claim that he understood Freud's meaning better than those who said Freud gave the synthetic function of the ego an important place in his theory. It is difficult for me to believe that no one did this simple grammatical research before me, but I have not seen any evidence of it.

Central to Lacan's theory is the notion of the divided subject. The division is caused by repression; this idea is different from the more widely accepted view only because there is no access to the *other* except through the rules of linguistics, so that the division postulated within man resembles more a split than the compromise formations inherent in neurotic symptoms and neurotic character which provide access to the unconscious as it is traditionally conceived. Lacan speaks of an alienation of one part from the other. In the Lacanian universe desire is for something else, or *otherness* (as Bär translates Lacan's *autre chose*), not an object that is an other and loved as such. Lacan's *desire* cannot be satisfied and remains elusive and allusive because it is always the desire of the other. Says Lacan (1966) "*Et les enigmes que propose le désir à toute philosophie naturelle, sa frénésie mimant le gouffre de l'infini, la collusion intime où il enveloppe le plaisir de savoir de celui de dominer avec la jouissance, ne tiennent à nul autre dérèglement de l'instinct qu'à sa prise dans les rails, -éternellement tendus vers le désir d'autre chose-, de la métonymy*" (p. 518). Or, as translated by Bär (1974, p. 509): "The puzzles which desire imposes on any natural philosophy, its frenzy which infinitely pursues the void, its intimate collusion of knowledge, power and pleasure, are due to no other malfunctioning of the instinct but its being caught—eternally longing for the desire of otherness—in the rails of metonymy." Instead of wishes that become altered partly because of maturational factors, Lacan postulates an absolute desire that can never be attained and has to be guessed at in analysis because it has been transformed according to the linguistic laws of metonymy and metaphor.

Lacan (1966) believed that the fundamental division of the subject takes place through the mirror stage during which he receives an inverted image with which he identifies as he does with others in his environment in a dual or specular relationship. He speaks of the mirror image symbolizing "the mental permanence of the I at the same time as it foretells its alienating destination" (p. 95). Since it comes from the outside and is inverted, it is the first instance of an alienation that is central to Lacanian thinking.[2] A further alienating factor stems from Lacan's notion "that man's desire is defined by the desire of the other, not because the other holds the key to the object of desire but because his first objective is to be recognized by the other" (p. 343). In Lacan's theory, desire, unlike the Freudian drive, does not have an object. Instead it addresses a person who recognizes the desire of the subject. The notion of satisfaction appears to be absent, and its substitute is confirmation. This strikes me as a purely narcissistic striving. Here is "where it can literally be verified that man's desire alienates itself in the desire of the other, structures the drives discovered in analysis" (p. 343).

The following quotation actually constitutes an important change in the meaning of what Lacan calls the desire of the Other. "If the desire of the mother is the phallus, the child wants to be the phallus to satisfy it" (p. 693). This leads to a complex interplay between what the father is, what he has, what he forbids, and what is left for the child, that is, not being the phallus that satisfies the mother, assuming his castration, and incompleteness. Partly this is due to the *Nom-du-père*, a play on the word *nom,* the sound of which is identical whether it means *no* or *name,* which inscribes itself upon consciousness and enters into the child's constitution. The desire always being the desire of the other somehow becomes the desire for something else and cannot be realized.

It is evident that Lacan's references to desire and anatomy are strictly metaphorical and concern neither instincts nor erogenous zones.

> Final satisfaction of one's desires is impossible for two reasons. First, the figure of the father forbids it; that is, the father, cultural symbol of the law, prohibits the infant from being everything (symbolized by the phallus) for his mother. Second, it is impossible because it has as its origin the irreparable failure of being incomplete, symbolized by the postnatal separation which traumatically (Rank 1924) lays the basis for the castration complex. Here the phallus is the cultural symbol of totality and instantiates the absolute nature of the system Unconscious. [Bär 1974, p. 495][3]

Thus the Lacanian literature mentions desire that lacks the specificity of aim, source, or object associated with drives. It is a paradox, like so many in Lacan's thinking, that the mirror image and beyond it the notion of the father enter into the formation of the *I* while leaving Lacanian psychoanalysis totally non-environmentalist. There are references to others, as we have seen, but the aim is to arouse their desire. The subject cannot satisfy itself with an object because its search always concerns its own identity: solipsism and narcissism appear to be the norm for human existence and communication is doubtful: "The function of language is not to inform, but to evoke," says Lacan (p. 299). "Human language constitutes a communication where the sender receives from the receiver his own message in inverted form" (p. 898).

Lacan appealed to those who were critical of the so-called biologism and medicalization of psychoanalysis. He satisfied the

French inclination to study the unconscious, but his theory provides shaky ground for that which is real, even though he postulates a tripartite division between the symbolic, the imaginary, and the real. Since the real can only be described within the symbolic, there does not seem to be a postulate of anything existing beyond it. Thus the idea that attains the greatest reality is the Name of the Father, or the Law of the Father, leaving matter, reality, and the nature of objects outside Lacan's psychoanalytic sphere. Perhaps this attitude is fruitful in the analysis of psychosis, but Lacan's appeal was less selective.

Pragmatically, as perhaps only an American can be, Schneiderman (1983) asserts that one could probably argue that interest in Lacanian psychoanalysis in France was furthered by socialized medicine with the government control of fees, by the high unemployment of philosophy students, and by the fact that "psychoanalysis in France was traditionally a cash business' (p. 52).

Anzieu (1986) recounts his experiences as Lacan's analysand poignantly and concretely:

> At the beginning of my analysis, he gave me sessions of normal length, forty to forty-five minutes, and he saw me at the prearranged times. After two years of work with him, the analytic framework developed a snag. The length of the sessions was reduced to thirty then to twenty minutes. The waiting room became filled with persons anxious to know if they would be received—Lacan opened the door, designated the chosen one, who would retrace his steps ten or fifteen minutes later in order to leave. I read. Lacan tapped me on the shoulder: it was my turn to pass in front of everyone or to find myself sent away to come back another day. . . . The master, heaving a deep sigh, confided in me, as in a friend, that he was overloaded, that he had to make an unforeseen appointment, face a difficult case, giving me to understand that I was not one, that I could therefore come back, and that he was sure that I understood him. This reinforced my narcissism, which did not need this, and made it difficult for me to express my astonishment,

> my criticism, my disagreement, that is, a negative transference without which a psychoanalysis is not complete.
>
> During the sessions, Lacan was intermittently attentive. Sometimes, instead of sitting in his analyst chair, he paced back and forth in the room in order to stretch his legs, to take a book; he sat at his work table and read, leafing pages covered with Chinese letters, which, apparently, he was learning. . . . Sometimes, his maid knocked on the door, to bring tea, sandwiches, the mail, or to alert him that he was wanted on the telephone. Lacan gave instructions for the answers or even went to answer himself. "Don't let this prevent you from continuing your session during my absence" he told me once as he disappeared from the office. [p. 34]

Anzieu includes many more details than can be repeated here, but one last example, touching on the subject of fees, is particularly revealing. Anzieu relates that when he decided to terminate, Lacan immediately reduced the number of his sessions from three to two to one. "But he made me 'pay' for this concession: 'So that the effort on your part remains the same, you will continue to give me every week the same sum of money as you did when you had three sessions' " (p. 36).

According to Schneiderman, Lacan based some of the changes in his practice on the fact that Freud failed to symbolize death and that he, Lacan, taught "how to negotiate and to enter into commerce with the dead" rather than teaching people how to get along with other people, interpersonally, and that the analyst's silence represents death within the analytic hour (p. 63). Therefore his role is never as the one who has the answers. Schneiderman suggests that at best, Lacan was a questioner who even behaved like a Zen master at times. He himself remained an enigma; he was even reluctant for his work to be published. His theory held that this place was "that of the Other, the capital Other or the grand Other" (Schneiderman 1983, p. 81).

According to Bär, Lacanian analysis aims at letting oneself

(analyst and patient) be dominated by a word to which one must correspond and listen. It speaks in him. Nevertheless, analysis must remain interminable and the subject divided because the alienated part helps it survive. With his usual playfulness, Lacan alludes to splitting by suggesting that Freud's article on the subject was left unfinished: *"Ici s'incrit cette Spaltung dernière par où le sujet s'articule au Logos, et sur quoi Freud commençant d'écrire Die Ichspaltung im Abwehrvorgang (1938), nous donnait à la pointe ultime d'une oeuvre aux dimensions de l'être, la solution de l'analyse 'infinie,' quand sa mort y mit le mot Rien."* My translation: "In this context is inscribed this last *Spaltung* (split) through which the subject links itself to Logos and about which Freud, beginning to write, gave us at the last point of a work as large as being, the solution of the 'infinite' analysis, when his death placed there the word Nothing" (1966, p. 642). With the absolute subjectivity of language, little brings the analysand out of his own world if the analyst only attempts to decode the meaning of words in order to help the patient introject the Other, living within himself. The analyst is "death," "nothing," and the "void" (Bär 1974, p. 531). Says Lacan: *"C'est à cet Autre au delà de l'autre que l'analyste laisse la place par la neutralité dont il se fait n'être ne-uter, ni l'un ni l'autre des deux qui sont là, et s'il se tait, c'est pour lui laisser la parole"* (1966, p. 439). My translation: "It is to the Other beyond the other that the analyst yields his place through the neutrality by which he is not, *ne-uter*, neither one nor the other of the two who are present, and if he is silent, it is to let it (the Other) speak." Because the Other has an unpredictable timetable, the analyst does not have to be bound to the patient by a mutually agreed upon schedule. The timing of the session is dictated by the Other, supposedly.

Bär concludes by suggesting that Lacan has to be appreciated for his literary and esthetic side: "And as no criteria are given here, the question 'Why then believe in it?' is answered simply by 'Because someone (Freud, Lacan) could intelligently think of it' (p. 536). Lacanian analysis remains guesswork and a great art, and the divided subject, as one also finds in Winnicott, provides a romantic image of man that is hard to resist.

Roustang, a former Lacanian, gave his 1986 study the title *Lacan de l'Equivoque a l'Impasse (Lacan from Ambiguity to Impasse).* He stresses that despite Lacan's strong connections to the arts and philosophy, he wanted psychoanalysis to be treated as a science. He lectured in the setting of a public forum in order to educate other analysts. In this way, these lectures became spectacles in which curing illness had no part in the project. He liked to draw diagrams using letters, as is done in algebra. Psychoanalysis was to be the science of the sciences and the holder of truth.

Roustang (1986) stresses how Lacan considered symbols to be more real than what they symbolize. Paraphrasing Lacan, he says that it is the world of words that creates the world of things, and that man becomes man through language. Roustang also notes that it is a disincarnated subject that is being treated. Thus Lacan's notion of a divided subject is emptied of flesh, humanity, affect, and so forth, in order to be made into a mathematical object that has either one dimension or none at all. As such it cannot be divided.

Roustang points out the language that is used in psychoanalysis to reach the unconscious is the instrument, which Lacan confuses with the object of psychoanalysis, that is the unconscious. Because of this emphasis on language, everything becomes the domain of psychoanalysis because everything is communicated through language. Its underlying substance is denied.

The real is the impossible, that is, impossible to symbolize, which comes from Lacan's understanding of the meaning of the pronouncement that that which cannot be symbolized comes back as real, or as hallucination in psychosis. This logic is an example of how Lacan plays with texts that describe a truth belonging to one realm and attempts to generalize it to a broader field, made possible by his emphasis on symbolization beyond which nothing exists.

The futility of Lacan's enterprise becomes evident when he claims that the psychotic is rigorous and in this sense he is rigorous. What is not expressed in language does not exist, is lost, empty, dead; and what is left is a language that can be manipulated in the most rigorous fashion by logicians and psychoanalysts and can therefore be scientific. It just happens not to be alive, but then Lacan claims not to know about experience, *le vécu*.

Because of this level of abstraction and divorce from sensory experiences, nothing is relative. According to Roustang, if something is not all, it is lack or absence. As an example, since only phallic enjoyment can be spoken, the sexual pleasure of women cannot be verbalized and as such does not exist. She enjoys something that she cannot describe, of which she knows nothing except that she feels it. Therefore Lacan (1966) disclaims the existence of any pleasure other than phallic.

Roustang calls it the triumph of failure. The logic depends on an unfolding of thinking that is based on fundamental misconceptions. It is antirationalistic and celebrates the irrational while submitting it supposedly to the rules of science, albeit by denying matter the status of reality.

A sense of disintegration underlies much of what is described in "*La Pensée 68 Essai sur l'Anti-humanism Contemporain*" ("The Thinking of 1968, Essay on Contemporary Antihumanism") by Ferry and Renaut, two philosophers. They claim that although the student revolt seemed to be about the refusal to be integrated into anything that would deny the young person's individuality, and therefore seemed to be putting value on the person, the motto for the revolt derived from the undoing of the subject, taken in the sense of the one who is being subjected.[4] In reality, the revolt of 1968 had more in common with today's individualism than with a humanistic tradition, but philosophically the students were guided by Lacan's 1955 pronouncement that "the true center of the human being is, since Freud's discovery, no longer in the same place assigned to it by humanistic tradition" (1966, p. 401). Man as an end in himself was no longer the cry of the day; on the contrary, the evils of the day were ascribed to humanism.

According to Ferry and Renaut, the thinking of those days placed the emphasis on the structures that are lived out through the subjects. Anyone insisting on a discussion based on principles of identity, or noncontradiction, was considered naive; conscious discourse was treated as if it were a symptom; statements of fact were superseded by interpretations; and the revolutionaries practiced suspicion. They did not appeal to the ego to integrate itself into a project; instead it was supposed to burst apart. There is no room for will in this pulverization of subjectivity. It is actually inserted by force into a logic that is not inherent in it. The subject is deprived of the mastery of what it says leading to the perverse effect of an interpretative delirium (1985).

Ferry and Renaut also say that the death of man is linked to the discovery of the break in the subject: the demonstration of his opacity to himself. The other avenue to the death of man comes from becoming the object of science, no longer subject, but object. Freud's goal, according to this perspective, leads to the *ex-centricity* of the subject in relation to the ego. According to the authors (1985) Lacan uses the Heidegger concept of truth being unveiling, "the unveiling of being as such is at the same time and in itself the dissimulation of being in its totality"—every manifestation is effected only on a background of absence and invisibility, not through derivatives (p. 237). Therefore Lacan's notion implies a person who is possessed by the unconscious, an idea that is foreign to Freud.

The authors specify how Lacan believed that the child receives a unified picture of himself during the mirror stage, how this image is linked to the desire of the mother, that is, the phallus, and leads to an identification with the object of mother's desire. But it is not the real father, it is a metaphor that goes from the wish to be to the wish to have. With the idea of identification with a metaphor we see a subject who is not the cause of language but its effect. "If true speech is that which knows that it does not know what it says; if true discourse, on the contrary, fools itself by believing that it knows what it says; is it not coherent to be incoherent?" (p. 254). "It speaks in me," I do not speak.

Lacan's misplacing the role of language in psychic topography led to the question as to whether some of Freud's oldest psychoanalytic formulations were rendered obsolete. Lacan robbed the concepts of the preconscious and conscious of Freud's theory of one of their main functions, that is, attaching words to images. In her analysis of the problem, Chasseguet-Smirgel (1975a) refers back to Freud's well-known differentiation made in 1900 between the thing (in the unconscious) and its representation (in the preconscious), a differentiation, as she says, that is dependent on the maintenance of the organization of the psychic apparatus that Freud envisaged when he conceptualized the unconscious and the process of becoming conscious. "The discovery of the thing behind the word, the attachment of the symbolized behind the symbol, necessitates . . . retracing the passage along associative links that end with the body of the mother and the breast" (p. 599). She says that avoidance, like phobia, cuts this chain of associations short and stops with the symbol, which is conceived as preexisting.

In her judgment, the system Lacan built in which he says that the unconscious is structured like language, is clearly unthinkable without altering fundamentally Freud's idea of the unconscious as the repository of imagery. She suggests that the investment of the word at the expense of the thing comes from a phobia of the primary object or its persecutory character, and that the prevalence of words tends to liberate man from the limits of his physical existence. According to Chasseguet-

Smirgel, this type of thinking illustrates the realm of regression where fantasies of narcissistic omnipotence dominate. Symbols can be formed only when there is a differentiation between self and nonself. When this is not the case, the word is treated as if it were the thing, and language has lost its symbolic and substitutive character.

The Relation between Linguistics and Psychoanalysis

In the face of so much mischief concerning the relationship between psychoanalytic theory and linguistics, Balkanyi (1976) concentrates on the latter and says that linguists do not like to collaborate with psychoanalysts because they know unconsciously that language is a phenomenon of restitution. "They prefer to remain in the domain which touches abstract and verbal relations and fear the rapprochement with psychoanalysis which touches upon human relations in their living, sexual, and affective aspects" (p. 723). In her opinion psychoanalysts are not very interested in language, and this gap between the two disciplines is furthered by the technical jargon in each. "The definition of 'jargon' implies that those who use it aim unconsciously not to be understood by the noninitiated" (p. 726).

Balkanyi points to Freud's and Abraham's interest in language and to the sparsity of attention given to language and verbalization by analysts outside France, with the notable exception of Ella Freeman Sharpe. She thinks that even today when there is a much more widespread interest in language, there is still a lack of clinical material and a preponderance of theoretical speculation. If the renewed interest in language serves only to reinforce the split between the two disciplines, of course, nothing is gained, and the study of linguistics helps only "to flee from the difficulties, the anxieties that come up in the consulting room, in favor of a speculative domain where only the symbols of reality are observed. Such a regression would be a danger for psychoanalysis and would bring nothing to linguistics" (p. 728). Balkanyi disagrees with Chomsky's theory that syntactic structures are inborn and thinks we have not sufficiently explored the process of introjective identification in this connection. Furthermore, she implicates the oedipal situation in the difficulties of language development and the evolution of mutual understanding.

Balkanyi offers the following interpretation:

> You want to penetrate the heavens with your penis and you want to create like God and cause things to exist by naming them—let your organ be forever limited in its power of communication. The restriction in linguistic communication is added to the oedipal chastisement of castration. To understand and to speak only the language of the immediate family, to erect partitions, linguistic barriers which will last forever—all this implies a definitive fixation. . . . . Such could be the meaning of the myth of the tower of Babel. [p. 731]

As a result of the Lacan phenomenon, the tower of Babel was built right into the French psychoanalytic world, and it is a rare analyst who knows both the Lacanian and the non-Lacanian literature. Schneiderman (1983) says that "the lack of dialogue with people who were not believers, who did not share the passionate commitment to Lacan, created an intellectual hothouse in Paris in which everything was related to the Master, whose words were quickly elevated into sacred dicta" (p. 87).

Linguistics threatened the "extraterritoriality" of psychoanalysis in France, as sociology, biology, or excessive emphasis on the scientific model has done elsewhere. And around the world, analysts convey their thoughts in such a diversity of technical vocabularies that communication between them is often all but impossible.

As mentioned at the beginning of the chapter, the French became interested in dissidence in a more general way, not only as it is manifested through the misuse or misplacing of language.

They admired and studied Ferenczi to a much greater extent than is the custom here. To them he is an often-quoted authority, and therefore his deviation aroused greater interest in France than here, where his work has suffered neglect.

Ferenczi's Contribution to Psychoanalytic Technique

Two issues of the *Revue Française de Psychanalyse* were devoted to Ferenczi's contribution to theory and technique. The first issue delineated the nature of Ferenczi's deviation and the causes for it; the second (1983) tried to show the positive aspects of his contributions to psychoanalysis.

Cahn (1983) suggests that Ferenczi returned to the seduction theory long since abandoned by Freud. But because of this, Ferenczi also drew attention to the traumatizing potential of the analytic framework. According to Cahn, it is Ferenczi who discovered the advisability of including interpretations based on the impact of the analytic reality (behavior, lapses, and other frustrations inherent in the analytic relationship) in the analytic work.

Cahn (1983) thinks that "the actualization by means of a fault within the framework, which might actually be related to an induced countertransference, reiterates in reality the real failure of the object at a stage prior to all symbolization" (p. 1111). Or, to put it more clearly, the analyst may be countertransferentially induced to frustrate the patient in the same way as the early object did, so that some of the early deprivations and failures can be understood by means of the disappointments the patient experiences with the analyst. Cahn thinks that Ferenczi deserves our recognition for this type of analysis, which has made an important contribution toward the understanding of the more difficult patients that are now part of the practice of many analysts. However, he stresses that the attention to the presence of the analyst should not constitute a gratification aimed at restitution in the way Ferenczi intended it late in his career. Rather it represents "the recognition of the nucleus that constitutes the subject like the mythical moment when he existed already, without however being differentiated from the other and of the damage that he might have suffered at that time" (p. 1123). In other words, for better and for worse, Ferenczi introduced the early mother into psychoanalysis.

Donnet (1983) assigns an important place to Ferenczi with regard to the role of repetition within the treatment. And Donnet draws an interesting conclusion: he suggests that Freud never completely overcame his unease with regard to his discovery that treatment often repeats the past rather than leading to immediate recall by means of the recovery of forgotten memories. He points out that after the initial shock of recognition of the role of transference, it seemed that Freud had made peace with the resistance through repetition, often in the transference, of that which seems to have been otherwise forgotten. But if it were true that Freud was reconciled to the need to repeat, why do we find the repetition compulsion on the side of the death instinct in *Beyond the Pleasure Principle*? Donnet thinks that this theoretical leap expresses Freud's ambivalence toward acting, and I am inclined to agree with him. For Freud's reason for assigning a special status to repetition is far from cogent. Repetition could just as easily be said to be in the service of pleasure, and Freud himself seems to contradict his reasons for assigning a special status to the need to repeat in the course of the very work that did the assigning.

In order to develop his point further, Donnet distinguishes between construction and interpretation in analysis. He thinks that construction draws upon preestablished knowledge, whereas interpretation emerges from the session. He points out that interpretation emanates from the transference. By interpreting, the analyst resumes his function as the guardian of analytic playing. The correctness of the interpretation is not based on a fact outside the analytic setting; it obtains its meaning from the analytic situation and is therefore perfectly unique.

Defined in this way, interpretation is imbued with contingency and therefore with nonscientific elements that may well displease those who wish to assign a different status to the work of analysis. Donnet thinks that Freud was among this latter group, since he favored construction over interpretation toward the end of his life. Construction has greater recourse to previously acquired knowledge and may have suited Freud's temperament better. Donnet thinks that this preference was further enhanced by Freud's negative reaction to Ferenczi's excesses in the use and abuse of the experiences during the analytic hour.

The immediate experience of the patient within the analytic hour has been stressed by many French analysts, who emphasize the introjective and projective processes that take place during a session and use those concepts as the basis for interpretation. In this respect, their interpretations are aimed at impulses and their derivatives outlined by Ferenczi to a far greater degree than is common in America.

Grunberger (1974) links that particular conduct of analysis with Ferenczi when he asserts that Ferenczi has extended the notion of symptom formation to the global behavior of the analysand and that in this respect "we are all his students." As an example of this approach, Grunberger (1954) said to a patient who missed half a session and entered complaining about gastric upsets, "You eat half of the session, my session, and thus you render it unusable" (p. 446). This type of interpretation is fairly common in French circles and shows to what degree the French are indebted to Ferenczi's attention to introjective processes taking place within an analysis. Needless to say, they divorce themselves emphatically from Ferenczi's attempts at restitution, as did Klein, who pursued this relatively id-centered approach without supplying the patient with extra-analytic gratifications.

It also differs from Gill, who concentrates on the here and now of the analytic hour without, however, giving it symbolic interpretations.

Grunberger (1974) quotes Marthe Robert who suggests that all heresies seem to have only one aim, that is, to reestablish the previous state of psychology, in other words, to "render null and void . . . the scandal of Freudian thought" (p. 523). Grunberger, despite his high regard for Ferenczi, whom he calls the second-greatest analyst, demonstrates how Frenczi negated an aspect of infantile sexuality by attributing conflicts to external forces. Grunberger suggests that all dissidences are maternal systems, that they are regressive and that this explains their charm. He is applying the same criteria as he did in his article, "The Oedipus of the Analyst" (1980), to which I referred earlier in relation to training and transmission. Grunberger thinks that Ferenczi's identification with the analysand further illustrates the regressive tendency in his method. Ferenczi helped to create a sadomasochistic process within his active technique without submitting that process to a transference analysis. Grunberger thinks that Ferenczi placed all the impulses pertaining to the child's life on the side of the adults, that is, an external source of the seduction of the child; nevertheless the anxious guilt is somehow transmitted by the adult.

"We have to ask ourselves if in this case the analyst can have another role in the analysis than that of the *exorcist*" (p. 544), Grunberger points out. He says that Ferenczi inverts the order of the generations, therefore reality; avoids the Oedipus complex; suppresses the psychosexual stages, the conflicted dialectic, and the notion of maturation; and jumps over the anal-sadistic phase, as do the theoreticians of dissidence and as does, in the realm of neurosis, the hysteric.

Taking the same point of departure, that is, Ferenczi's active technique, Chasseguet-Smirgel (1971) examines the use of mechanisms that are sublimated in the functioning of the analyst and which had derailed to some degree in Ferenczi's case. She thinks that the conduct of a classical analytic treatment often rests on the result of masking and utilizing that which represented a difficulty originally, be it in the patient or the analyst. As with transference, which was first experienced as an obstacle and was then made into a tool, so it is with many aspects of analysis conforming to the manic mechanism akin to the sense given to it by Klein. The manic mechanism is motivated by the need to control the bad object and to vitiate its destructive character toward the ego and the good object. Chasseguet-Smirgel maintains that this mechanism, when it is not entirely imbued with negation and remains therefore under the dominance of the reality principle, should not be confused with the psychotic mechanism bearing the same name. Thus, overcoming an obstacle in the way of any creative pursuit is satisfying, but it is doubly gratifying to use it as a positive element and to make it serve the achievement of a final goal.

She thinks that Ferenczi's active technique does not sufficiently take into account the influence on the transference of the analyst's need to do better in terms of dominating the bad objects. The motives underlying excessive rigidity of structure, which Chasseguet-Smirgel attributes to the fear of the destroying object, stem from a depressive core. Yet too great a sense of freedom vis-à-vis the basic rules stems from the negation that anything could happen to the object or to the ego, and from the maintenance of a feeling of omnipotence. The author points out that it is easy to reject in the name of analytic purity everything that Ferenczi has left us in his writings on the active technique. This would avoid, at the same time, the narcissistically injurious reality of the difficulties therapists encounter. It is sometimes easier to hang on to rules than to depart from them; hanging on does not require imagination, "the mind of a researcher, nor creative capacities, all qualities that can be used gladly by one who lacks them against the one who possesses them" (p. 175).

One Man's Psychoanalysis Is Another Man's Dissidence

The question of dissidence and its nature was also the focus of a meeting on *The Ways of the Anti-Oedipus* that took place in 1973 and resulted in a small book by the same title.[5] Once more, the germ of its own corruption inherent in Freud's work was examined. Thus Chiland (1974) states that "the theory of infantile sexuality that is central to psychoanalysis is not finished in 1897, nor in 1900, nor in 1905, nor, let me add, at Freud's death, nor even today" (p. 41). It therefore requires further elaboration, and in the process there is always the danger of doing violence to one or another aspect of the psychoanalytic approach.

Anzieu (1974), in an article entitled "The Imprint of Its Origins on Psychoanalysis," mentions that Freud undertook his self-analysis because of his depressive tendencies. Anzieu thinks that psychoanalytic theory bears the imprint of Freud's neurosis, and that his form of thinking repressed or even denied the other forms of psychopathology. He states: "The book on the Anti-Oedipus is scandalous in certain aspects and unfair; but the scandal, the injustice, aren't they the necessary bias through which the repressed, the denied content, comes back and imposes itself on consciousness?" (p. 159). In Anzieu's opinion Freud's theory and technique have supported the establishment of obsessional defenses against depressive anxiety. Those who lean more toward the realm of schizoparanoid defenses are poorly accepted, and he postulates that the excessive concern with structuralism based on language has unnecessarily delayed in France forays into the realm beyond neurosis taking place elsewhere. (He is referring to the English-speaking countries, with whose literature he is very familiar.)

Chasseguet-Smirgel contrasts the search for truth as epitomized by Oedipus with the love for pleasure embodied in Jocasta, who wishes to impede this quest. She quotes Ferenczi, who said, "The Oedipus complex is not only the nuclear complex of the neurosis . . . [but] the kind of attitude adopted toward it also determines the most important character traits of the normal man, and in part also the greater or lesser objectivity of the scientist" (Ferenczi 1912, 1956 ed., p. 218). She stresses that Freud himself realized that what was won through analysis could be lost almost as easily as insight is within the analytic setting. Here she reminds the reader of the Freudian postulate that intolerable impulses are projected so that they can be defended against as if they were external dangers. She suggests that this theory

> seems to furnish an explanatory model of all psychoanalytic dissidences that to varying degrees, they tend to reduce the conflict, that is, the dynamic aspect of psychism, to a battle between the purified pleasure ego and a threatening and invading outside; to evacuate the internal conflict and replace it with constraints or, as we say today, repression. All dissidences seem to me to be Rousseauesque, to varying degrees. The purified pleasure ego is the good man of Rousseau. The collective unconscious of Jung that transcends the individual unconscious, the patriarchal society of Reich, the language and the desire of the Other of Lacan, the psychoanalysts linked to capitalism of the authors of the *Anti-Oedipus*, are all as many phases or mishaps of society, instigator of private property that comes to pollute the natural goodness of man for Rousseau and more profoundly of the hated external world, contemporary of the state of the purified pleasure ego. According to dissident theories, man arrives into the world like an empty container that is being filled and invaded by external formations conceived as totally foreign to the subject, that is, to man himself, as if all these formations, which are after all human manifestations were born out of nothing, without roots within the instinct. [pp. 14–15]

In this respect, Chasseguet-Smirgel agrees with Jones, who said that there is no danger that analysts neglect external reality whereas there is always a possibility that they will underestimate the Freudian doctrine of the importance of psychic reality.

Grunberger and Chasseguet-Smirgel (1976) attempted to show by means of the example of Wilhelm Reich that there are specific factors inherent in psychoanalysis that lead to its recurrent problems. "The paradox of Freudian analysis is that while always fighting against illusion, it contributes toward its activation. The unconscious fascinates especially those who have the most intense nostalgia for their primitive completeness. They want to put its forces at their own disposal, become fused with its omnipotence" (p. 11). They add: "We think that psychoanalysis has a particular propensity for converting itself into an ideology" (p. 113), and "Many analysts want to deny illness itself; this is a denial of castration. For them, becoming an analyst means to take a hold of the mysterious forces of the unconscious, to tame them, and to become stronger than death" (p. 238). In the judgment of these authors, therefore, the seduction to excess is inherent in the fantasies psychoanalysis induces. In their view, the problems in psychoanalysis attain the status of inevitability which they analyze in terms of psychic manifestations that can have political ramifications.

Despite the great interest in dissidence that led to the many studies from which I have quoted, Grunberger and Chasseguet-Smirgel offer no solution. On the contrary, their writings have a tone of the inevitability of conflict which no course of action can counter. Instead they are convinced that only an understanding of the dynamics underlying the recurrent distortions can help the individual analyst distinguish between the genuine and the perverted forms of psychoanalysis. In this, they probably express the point of view of most of the senior analysts of their society.

In keeping with their interest in the biological underpinnings of psychoanalysis, they regard many of the deviations as evidence of narcissism. Therefore Grunberger, in particular, turned to this phenomenon that attempts to transcend man's physical reality: narcissism, the subject of the next chapter, the disease of our age, the pathology that thrives on illusion, excess, and seductions by the unreal and immaterial.

Notes

[1]Bär (1974, p. 473) says that the linguist Mounin claims that Lacan's understanding of Saussure is always wrong. This is quite an indictment considering Bär's fairness and the extent to which Lacan's theory is based on the linguistics of Saussure.

[2]Turkle (1978) suggests that "Lacan stresses that the ego is formed by a composite of false and distorted introjections" and that he "taught the French analysts to see the ego as the distorted reflection of mirrors within mirrors" (p. 103).

[3]According to Roudinesco, (1986) "*Lacan fait du* Phallus *l'objet central de l'économie libidinale, à condition toutefois de le dégager de ses connivences avec l'organe pénien. Le phallus devient ainsi un* insigne *c'est à dire le pur significant d'une puissance vitale, partageant à egalité les deux sexes*" (p. 519). Or, to translate, "Lacan makes out of the *Phallus* the central object of the libidinal economy, on the condition that it is freed from its complicity with the penis. The phallus becomes in this way an insignia, that is the pure signifier of a vital power (potency) divided equally within the two sexes." Roudinesco thinks that Lacan took Freudian theory out of its paternalocentrist equivocation.

[4]Roudinesco (1986) also points to the ambiguity of the idea of a subject, especially one's being the subject of the unconscious or subjected by the unconscious. This leads us from the Cartesian "I think" to the Lacanian "it speaks." Or, to quote Lacan (1966, p. 517): "*Je pense où je ne suis pas donc je suis où je ne pense pas.*" ("I think where I am not therefore I am where I don't think").

[5]Whether or not the title was related to the book *Anti-Oedipus* by Deleuze and Guattari, and if so how, is not entirely clear, but the fact that such an attack on the central concept of psychoanalysis could achieve popularity played a part in the thinking of the participants. Schneiderman (1983, p. 29) thinks that *Anti-Oedipus* was an attack on Lacan.

PART II

THE EVOLUTION OF CLASSICAL ANALYSIS

8

Narcissism

If Freud's achievement consists of the discovery of the laws governing the unconscious and the mental representations of instinctual strivings, future generations were left with the task of integrating these aspects of his work with his theories concerning those forces that oppose the instincts, whether within the ego by means of the defenses, or in the form of the death instinct or narcissism.

In this country, the continuation of Freud's work resided in ego psychology, an interest which few members of the Paris Psychoanalytic Society shared right after World War II. During the 1950s, when the ego, the reality principle, and the problem of adaptation were studied here, French psychoanalysts remained closer to drive theory. They turned to the clinical and theoretical problems posed by the actual neuroses, psychosomatic disturbances, and narcissism, and they explained them by means of the dynamics and the economics involved. They did this to the exclusion of the structural hypothesis that appealed to their American colleagues.

Problems Inherent in the Study of Narcissism

Grunberger studied the issues around narcissism before the subject reached popularity here. The reasons prompting this interest are related to the fact that the French analysts faced a problem in the fifties that closely resembled the one that Freud faced in 1914, when he wrote his introduction to narcissism. The French had their own Jung in the person of Lacan, and they were equally motivated to save the biological implications of drive theory from Lacan's attempt to take psychoanalysis completely out of the realm of biology. Therefore they wanted to update Freud's theory so as to obviate the need for a totally new way of analyzing.

In Chapter 7, I discussed how Lacan studied the development of the self and the origin of identity without basing his explanations on drive derivatives. In 1936 he suggested the existence in human development of a mirror stage during which the mirror image is supposed to attain the function of an imago, "which is to establish a relationship between the organism and its reality—or, as it is said, from the Innenwelt to the Umwelt" (1966, p. 96). No reference is made here to introjections, objects, or zonal gratifications: according to Lacan, an important part of identity is predicated on a visual image that comes from the external world, enters into the constitution of the I, and has a complex and sometimes alienating relationship to the subject. From these few clinical thoughts, Lacan takes off into existentialism, society, and his belief in the universality of schisms. It would be difficult to refute him on this last point, since it is impossible to deny the internal conflicts created within the individual because of narcissistic strivings; but Lacan's explanatory model was so far removed from the libido theory to which most French analysts were attached that they turned to a further elaboration of drive theory in order to remain closer to Freud's original ideas.

Freud himself expressed his dissatisfaction with his theory of narcissism in a letter to Abraham dated March 16, 1914. He knew that it threatened his dual instinct theory in that it abolished the old antagonism between ego instincts and sexual drives. If narcissism is defined as the libidinal cathexis of the ego, the ego becomes the seat of the libido, and therefore the conflict that was once explained as being between libido and the ego no longer held true: there was libido on both sides of the conflict. His solution, to devise a more fundamental and biological instinct theory, retained the notion of two primordial antithetical forces at work, but it did not further the study of the relationship between the object instinctual strivings and the aims of narcissism. The alternate solution, which places narcissism on the side of the death instinct, does not correspond sufficiently to clinical observations.

Freud defined narcissism as an aspect of libido even though the quality of that love and the nature of the libido remained a problem to be solved at the time of his death. He did not reconcile two important aspects of narcissism: its anti-instinctual nature and the fact that it is one of the manifestations of libido. Its position within his last instinct theory (1920) is also unclear because the postulate that the libido cathects the ego in health or in pathology does not explain the fate of that libido. Clinically, we see narcissists who are exhibitionists and sexually hyperactive and narcissists who are withdrawn and inaccessible to erotism. They present themselves as realistic or dreamers, and contrary to Freud's assertion that narcissists cannot form a transference relationship, they can have very powerful attachments to objects provided that these objects fulfill certain requirements. Concomitantly, the question of how narcissistic investment can be related to object libido, which had hitherto been defined according to psychosexual development, remained unanswered. There also was as yet no theory to account for the evolution of narcissism from pathology or immaturity to maturity and object love.

In the United States, the theories of narcissism sprang up well after Hartmann's addition of self-representation to the analytic vocabulary. As Pontalis (1977) observed, the self that is so common a reference point in English-language parlance and psychoanalytic literature is relatively meaningless to the French. Therefore a theory elaborating the notion of self could not have occurred in France. Perhaps this is due to their own greater investment in psychosexual pleasures or to their greater concern for tradition; perhaps the reasons are too culture-determined to fathom, but the fact is inescapable that the French have not shown any inclination to discard the old drive theory in favor of self psychology. So, when Americans began to study narcissism in the 1970s, they were concerned about the influence of narcissistic pathology on the sense of self; but when the French approached the same issues, they were concerned about the body pleasures that were being sacrificed for the sake of—what?

There are a multitude of theories of narcissism—eleven according to Cremerius (1982), a German analyst. The parallels between the problems of narcissism and the fate of psychoanalytic theory as a result of the problem of narcissism is striking. It almost seems as if anyone tackling the issue would have to give up some important aspect of psychoanalytic theory, and I imagine that each of the eleven theories Cremerius counted eliminated one aspect of the total personality. In Freud's case, his theory of narcissism threatened his dual-instinct theory, which it was supposed to save, nor was it properly integrated into libido theory. In America, Kernberg focused on pathological narcissism with the idea that it can be analyzed and yield to health, and Kohut ignored the psychosexual phases. Neither adhered to both the idea of a development of narcissism as well as a connection between it and the psychosexual phases.

In France, too, there evolved a study of narcissism that

concerns a relatively limited province, that is, physical survival. The *psychosomaticiens,* Marty, Fain, de M'Uzan, David, and others, about whom more will be said later, attributed the psychic depletion and impoverishment they observed in patients suffering from psychosomatic illness to problems of insufficient narcissism. In their opinion, there could be an excessive outflow of libido in infancy leaving the individual prey to the death instinct, which decomposes living tissues, before the time when narcissism, the libidinal cathexis of the self, stems the discharge of the life force. In other words, infants who are insufficiently or poorly mothered are left in a condition that depletes them libidinally and physically.

The *psychosomaticiens* use Freud's theory of Eros and Thanatos not as speculation but as an explanatory model. In their writings the life and the death instincts are given the meaning of biological entities, and these analysts define narcissism as the libidinal investment that keeps the subject physically alive and well. Therefore they devised a theory of narcissism that attempts to throw light on conditions that are life threatening because of psychic phenomena that lie outside the realm of mental representation. Since they link Eros to life and survival, whereas Freud initiated the study of narcissism to explain love, they are approaching the question of exhaustion of libido from the angle of self-preservation. Because of their observations of states of depletion in infants, the *psychosomaticiens* do not assume the existence of an innate primary narcissism that can bind the work of the death instinct. The fact that infants die of psychic neglect is proof to them that the assumption of inborn narcissism or erotogeneity is incorrect, and they attempt to give a metapsychological answer to the question: why do infants die of psychic neglect?

By taking themselves out of the realm of psychic representations, the *psychosomaticiens* have added an important dimension to psychoanalytic theory, but their view of narcissism must of necessity be considered very partial and its application particular, that is, restricted to psychosomatic problems and character disorders. It is quite unrelated to self-love or self-esteem as we think of it, and refers only to the investment by a biological life force.[1]

Béla Grunberger's Work on Narcissism

Grunberger, who devoted his major efforts to the study of narcissism as it appears in psychoanalysis, aimed at a more inclusive theory. In his book, *Narcissism* (1971, English trans., 1979), which comprises his work from 1957 to 1971, he recognized the threat narcissism posed to psychoanalytic theory and suggested that the essence of narcissism consists in its attempts to discard the body and material reality in favor of some disembodied or idealized entity. When Grunberger speaks of depletion, he attempts to answer the question originally posed by Freud: if the libido is not here where it should be, keeping the individual loving himself and objects to a normal degree, where has it gone? For whose sake or for the sake of what ideal is this individual killing himself, denying himself pleasure, or just suffering?

I know of two attempts to bridge the chasm that separates narcissism from psychosexual development. Both theories, Fenichel's and Kernberg's, equate narcissism with a fixation at the oral level. The objection to rendering narcissism so phase-specific is that such a theory denies it any kind of evolution of its own. This is not the case in Grunberger's theory. He prefers to think of narcissism as an element that evolves through a process leading to its integration and partial reconciliation with object love.

As I see it, the essential value of Grunberger's approach is its inclusiveness. What it lacks, and this is true of all French psychoanalytic literature, is an attempt to speak the language of the natural sciences. This does not trouble me because I think that a psychoanalytic theory can be useful by becoming part of the listening process and take its place with all other elements that make up the analytic hour. Validation lies in the realm of that nebulous area we call progress. It exists, but can we define it, in view of the fact that there are transference cures, and flights into health that mimic it? I do not believe that the criteria of a natural science can be applied to psychoanalysis, and it must be reiterated that those looking for evidence of scientific methodology will be very frustrated by the work of the French. Their contributions can only broaden the way we think about a problem if we allow a meeting of the minds to take place.

Grunberger listens to and for a narcissism that is silent by definition. He thinks that it is silent because it has a bad reputation and therefore hides in shame. Those patients who are narcissistically vulnerable wish away questions of self-love and think that they solve their problem by means of denial.

I am reminded of my own experience with a psychiatrist who was at a total loss during one of his sessions when he was ill and in pain. He suffered greatly, could not stop focusing on the pain during the analytic hour, but could only reiterate that there should be nothing wrong with him. He found it extremely difficult to obtain treatment for his ailment and to prevent the condition from getting worse because he regarded it as something that should not be and therefore to be ignored. His thoughts were only about his inability to concentrate during the analytic session, and this failure compounded his self-depreciation. The patient cannot love himself when he suffers. His narcissism prevents him from loving a body that is less than perfect, and therefore his ability to help himself is paralyzed due to his lack of libidinal investment. He does not say: "I don't love myself, please help me love myself better." He says: "I can't believe that I am sick again," and bemoans the fact over and over. What differentiates these words from an expression of pain or physical discomfort is the fact that the patient may actually engage in activities that might cause him greater discomfort. He denies his infirmity and continues to love some thing that is not real and does not require care and attention. He acts accordingly, and the narcissistic injury is the pain that he cannot deny during the analytic hour.

What does this patient love? He loves an imaginary, ideal body that does not correspond to the real (temporarily sick) one, and he acts in accordance with that wishful image. Not self-love, not self-hate; this is what makes narcissism so complicated and so hard to define. In this example, the narcissistic factor prevents the libidinal investment of a sick body. The body is temporarily treated as if it were excrement, an anal object, as the French tend to call this, to be forgotten, discarded, and ignored. Love in this case is not the libidinal component of egotism as Freud suggested; the patient does love, only his love invests an image, and when denial fails and reality no longer corresponds to the image, there is only hatred for the reality that does not conform to the beloved image. This hatred that is the opposite of the love of the ideal attributes to reality an excremental nature that is ignored in polite society.

Grunberger does not interpret the self-hatred of the patient mentioned above as a death wish; he does not believe that man is ever motivated to die. Conforming to Freud's notion that there exists no negative in the unconscious, Grunberger suggests that in the unconscious, death corresponds to some positive goal such as the return to an embryonic condition. He thinks of narcissism as being ubiquitous, and follows Freud (1923) when the latter postulated that there was a third type of energy within the ego, reinforcing libidinal or aggressive aims.

The content of narcissistic strivings is predicated on the individual's history through a process that has interested Grunberger from the beginning of his studies. He thinks that the aim of narcissism remains unchanged despite the fact that the quantity of narcissistic strivings that are absorbed, or as

Grunberger would say *egotized*, varies. The factor that adds the weight of its energy to the ego's strivings is the derivative of the original narcissism that can undergo a long and complex evolution starting with the prenatal state. It adds value to instinctual strivings in adulthood because narcissism can evolve to the point where mature and adult functioning can act as gratifying derivatives.

Grunberger postulates that there are memory traces dating from prenatal bliss motivating the individual, and that the wish to return to that state never changes.[2] Whether it is the Garden of Eden, nirvana, or the mother's womb, narcissistic strivings aim to achieve a state in which all our needs are satisfied and we are accepted for our uniqueness. This is the goal of narcissism: whether or not everyone retains the memory of a state when this wish was gratified and whether this state was before or after birth seem quite unimportant to the theory.

According to Grunberger, value is the key concept for the understanding of narcissism. Value is subjective and is surprisingly difficult to explain considering that man's life is filled with it and propelled by it. Grunberger says that the greatest value is attributed to God, who says, "I am who I am." This statement imputed to God depicts such unquestioned value, such an affirmation of existence, that no other reason is given, and believers accept this as a confirmation of their faith. On the human scale, I have heard a woman say: "Wherever I am is the head of the table." She did not explain why, and any listener who might have asked the reason for her statement would have injured her narcissism. Such a statement of self-evaluation is not to be questioned, and the requirement of proof for such an assertion is considered an insult. Narcissists interpret questions concerning value as devaluations, and even the search for narcissistic confirmation has to be concealed because a lack constitutes a narcissistic injury in itself. These are the extremes to which narcissistic vulnerability can go.

Grunberger does not consider the overestimation of oneself pathological; rather, he calls it a vital necessity. Other derivatives of the original narcissism, such as fantasies of immortality, invulnerability, and the feeling of infinity, can take their proper place in man's thinking or lead to ego distortions and character difficulties, depending on the integration that has taken place. But essentially they derive, according to Grunberger, from the experience at the beginning of life and therefore have their underpinnings in biology even though in their content they tend to express the wish to go beyond the flesh.

Remaining within the language of biology, as Grunberger does, gives his thinking an advantage. He has postulated, for instance, a mutually antagonistic relationship between narcissism and anality, and this enables him to think of the split between the all-good and the all-bad as corresponding to the split between the spiritual and the material world based on the body process in which food is converted into what is useful and worthy of retaining, but as such disappears, and what must be eliminated and treated with contempt and fear of contamination. Grunberger demonstrates the fantasy of objects being turned into feces and treated accordingly by reminding us that Auschwitz was called "the anus of the world." Fecal matter is the opposite of value.

I shall not describe Grunberger's developmental approach in any detail, because his book on the subject contains his theory. I do think, however, that a brief overview is desirable so that his contribution can be properly assessed.

According to Grunberger (1971, 1979 ed.) narcissism is:

> That elative and megalomaniacal impression—with its memory of supreme harmony and omnipotence, which will never fade—will form the *narcissistic nucleus*, a specific source of psychic energy, an early and permanent acquisition that remains active from birth to death and—if one takes any sort of mystical approach—beyond. [pp. 20–21]

Grunberger observed narcissism and its derivatives and found that narcissism consists of a number of identifiable elements. It involves the memory of a unique and privileged state as well as the elation and the well-being derived from the omnipotence attributed to this memory. In addition, there is the pride from having experienced the uniqueness attached to one's life as a fetus. Grunberger thinks that the notion of value is derived from the memory of this early existence. It leads to the search for certain object relations, splendid isolation, merger ties, or mirror-type relations. Furthermore, there is the quest to refind the lost paradise along with the superego's prohibition against this wish, forbidden, as the identification with God is forbidden.

Eventually, these wishes are either integrated into a person's instinctual activity or there is the attempt to bypass reality and to fulfill the narcissistic quest by vicarious or fraudulent endeavors. Narcissism can lead to the contempt for the real, and we know of the narcissistic loss or injury that comes from disappointments or from the inability to live up to the demands of the ego ideal. Finally, Grunberger refers to the narcissistic mortification alluded to by Eidelberg, which consists of the shame of not having been able to master in a more active way experiences that were suffered passively.

For Grunberger, the aim of narcissism is unchanging. Only the ego and the way it regulates the narcissistic investment vary. Narcissism exists behind each experience but independently of it, and it remains a constant component of each stage of development, only in increasingly modified form.

> The role that narcissism plays in this continual restructuring is . . . a silent one, which often leads to error when it comes to identifying the narcissistic factor, for narcissism, lacking specific somatic support, can act only through other agencies, and to express itself, it must even borrow their machinery. Thus narcissism utilizes libido,

> but is not one with it, and this process, which is a movement of the self and which libidinally invests objects and the ego as well—its development, its activity, its instinctual satisfaction—is what I call *narcissistic cathexis*. [p. 24]

A large part of Grunberger's work is devoted to the study of the many ramifications of the interplay between the two sectors of the personality, the object instinctual and the narcissistic, their antagonism and their integration. His reexamination of the psychosexual phases to demonstrate the role played by the narcissistic factor in each has greatly enhanced the understanding of the task to be accomplished at each stage of development and maturation. He has shown by means of many examples how biological or psychosexual needs disturb the narcissistic universe and represent the first narcissistic injury. This idea enlarges upon Freud's thinking that hate "derives from the narcissistic ego's primordial repudiation of the external world with its outpouring of stimuli" (1915, p. 139) and suggests that biological needs constitute a similar outpouring of stimuli and therefore meet with the ego's repudiation until they have attained a narcissistic cathexis. The case of the psychiatrist discussed earlier illustrates clearly the problem of the narcissistic repudiation of needs. Another example is that of the patient who woke up thinking that she wanted a cigarette. She then thought that this meant that she had to have it, whereupon she became ashamed of the conviction that she could not do without it. Here a wish had been reinterpreted as a need which was injurious to her narcissism because she knew that she could not control it.

Grunberger stresses that man does not accept readily the states of need and limitations imposed upon him by his biological reality and his mortality. It is in conformity with all experiences that the drives are not only in conflict with superego restrictions but also with those dictated by the demands of grandiosity or omnipotence which do not tolerate tension.

Narcissism and Its Relation to the Drives

Grunberger thinks that orality has an equivocal structure since it is linked to objects but also devoid of them. Therefore, he prefers to think of many manifestations of orality apparent in analysis as pertaining to a more advanced mode of functioning and not to a simple regression to the oral phase. This is in keeping with the maturation and ego development that we can attribute to an infant and also Lewin's (1950) concept of the oral triad. At this stage, there is such confusion between subject and object that the two must be considered as one, that is, fused rather than introjected.[3]

Only anality ushers in the dimension of precision, and Grunberger prefers to think that in normal or neurotic conditions, the oral period survives only as a structural element, that is, the movement toward drive gratification, the underpinnings for the representation of a need and its abolition. In Grunberger's theory, the instinctual gratification of the orally fixated person, even if it uses the genital zone, is in the service of becoming one with the object.

Grunberger's definition of the oral phase corresponds to something akin to the pleasure ego ("The ego-subject coincides with what is pleasurable" [Freud 1915, p. 135]) that surfaces again in narcissistic regressions. His equation between oral phase and fusion appears more in line with the infant's mental structure than the Freudian notion of oral incorporative aims, which, like the Kleinian model, presupposes greater differentiation between subject and object.

The advantage to Grunberger's theory is that it can give greater weight to one of the main characteristics of primitive narcissism: its antagonism to the drives. If we conceive of the infant as Ferenczi did, as an organism still steeped in the aftermath of its postnatal, narcissistic universe, then hunger does not immediately lead to a wish for incorporation but rather for some precursor of the wish that the hunger go away. In other words, hunger or need does not lead to the object-instinctual fantasies, no matter how rudimentary, but to some sensory manipulation that attempts to get rid of the tension. Grunberger calls the impact of the physiological needs on the psychic organization the first narcissistic injury. Therefore a process of maturation is required to render experiencing them acceptable, regardless of whether they can be gratified. The analysis of narcissistic patients demonstrates that a frequent source of resistance rests in their inability to formulate a transference wish in analysis because, they say, it cannot be gratified. It requires great analytic tact to help such vulnerable patients to experience their wishes, the *sine qua non* of analytic progress. Patients frequently have to learn to accept the instinctual apparatus: this is the precondition for the ability to obtain gratification. In view of this, orality, that is the idea of incorporating the object, presupposes a development in which the zone has been accepted as well as an object whose separateness is recognized at least on some level. Grunberger's greatest merit lies in pinpointing the developmental task necessary to bridge the gap between narcissism and the wish to incorporate an object orally in order to be one with it. The aim of narcissism in which fusion to attain oneness occurs by magical means does not require the acceptance of the instincts.[4]

Grunberger classifies the instinctual aims that were enumerated by Freud as part of the anal phase or beyond. He thinks that genuine engagement by the instinctual apparatus is dependent on a change in the mode of obtaining satisfaction. Here Grunberger chooses to combine the concepts of dominant erogenous zone with concomitant ego development, which, like every other theoretical approach, has certain advantages and certain disadvantages. Because of it, Grunberger classifies oral aggression among anal phenomena, which is awkward, but it postulates a theory of a dialectical relationship between the oral and the anal mode of satisfaction that explains many clinical phenomena. On the oral level, satisfaction is obtained by magical thinking and fantasies of merger. At the anal level, the lost narcissism is recovered by means of mastery. It constitutes the point of departure for the later development of attaining gratification through body activity, and engages the subject in designs for gratification instead of fear of action. Compared to this, orally fixated persons do not demand gratification since it is difficult for them to formulate such a claim; they can only complain in a vague way. Oral characters generally cannot use aggression to satisfy themselves and therefore cannot make up for a sense of frustration other than through fantasy.

The following quotation from an article by Luquet (1962) illustrates further the condensed way in which many French theorists approach psychosexual development. It can be seen here how the erogenous zone is made unimportant compared to the aim and the maturity of the ego:

> The anus is certainly first 'oralized' and functions during the oral movement in the manner of the mouth. The laws of expulsion themselves are those of immediacy, of the all or nothing, of destructive rejection. But during the anal movement of the ego it is likely that it acquires sphincter properties. The anal movement seems to me centered on selectivity linked to sphincterization. It is the means used by the obsessive, it is without a doubt also because the fantasized sphincter activity seems to him to be more apt to filter and control the introjection of the object. [p. 217]

In Grunberger's formulations likewise, the anal phase is the pivot of all psychic organization. In addition to mastering the environment, it sets the stage for turning certain derivatives of anal sadism toward the ego in the service of controlling discharge and building psychic structure. Retention, a derivative of libido originating during the anal phase, is also advantageous to structure since it inhibits immediate discharge. These are the two ways in which the anal phase contributes to structure and reduces the need for an ego psychology: one emphasizes the derivative of a libidinal pleasure whereas the other stresses the anal-sadistic element.

According to Grunberger, the pleasure derived from the newly acquired control during the anal phase compensates the infant for the narcissistic injury imposed upon him during the oral states of helplessness. It concerns a newly evolved narcissism that engages the body and its musculature in order to achieve mastery and brings the infant out of a magical, fusional, and fantasy-oriented universe. During the anal phase, action becomes the means by which the feelings of narcissistic omnipotence are restored. Thus the wish for omnipotence persists but the means by which it is accomplished evolves during the anal phase to encompass the attempt to master reality, and to gain control over the body. These skills attain value in normal development which they lose when there are serious regressions in the narcissistic realm.

The oral relation to objects is distinguished from the anal by the fact that the latter is characterized by the control exercised over what is emitted from the body. Retention is at the basis of anal mastery and motor development. In this perspective, the fecal mass is both narcissistic and part-object, and it permits a sense of mastery in a universe that, for the first time, has limits and dimension as against the diffuse and immaterial world of the oral phase. Grunberger suggests that pregenitality consists of a dialectic between these two trends, but that, of course, it is the anal component that permits satisfaction in relationship to reality.

Clinically, I have found it interesting to observe that there is a type of eating that aims at control much more than at oral gratification. I am referring to patients whose aim is to fill their digestive tracts with bulk, who need to feel full, or who eat in order to insure against loss. Filling the abdominal cavity without concern about what fills it can be considered part of an attempt at anal mastery. I would like to illustrate this point with an incident that happened to a woman who was invited to a place where pie was served. She loved the pie and could barely keep herself from asking for a second piece, but she was ashamed to appear so voracious. After she left the home of her friends and the unfinished pie, she bought a box of cookies and ate them without leaving a crumb. By means of displacement she gained control over the pie. Or, to quote the inscription on the tomb of Sardanapalus, a Persian king: *Haec habeo quae edi* (I have what I ate). The inscription goes on to mention that he had to leave all other goods behind when he died.

Grunberger does not support the idea of primary masochism. He considers it to be the reversal of the active anal impulse which turns "You are my thing and I am going to dominate you" into "I am your thing and you can do with me as you wish." (There is disagreement among the French around this issue, and Braunschweig and Fain postulate a theory of primary masochism along with the notion of a death instinct.) According to Grunberger, masochism is secondary and consists of turning against the self aggression that was deflected from an object. In clinical practice the guilt underlying masochism relates to the anal introjection of the father's penis, a concept Grunberger has used for the interpretation of many phenomena, including the resistance to terminating an analysis successfully.

I am aware that the use of such an unusual construct requires some justification on this side of the Atlantic, and this is difficult. Grunberger does not discuss it anywhere nor does he defend or define its usage. He writes without awareness that the assumption of a phase during which there is a fantasy of the anal introjection of the paternal phallus is not a commonly shared theoretical approach. In attempting to trace the origin of this concept, I was beset by difficulties that are undoubtedly common to any foreign reader of French psychoanalytic writings, that is, the sense of an agreement between themselves that is spelled out elsewhere. Yet no agreed-upon definition for the anal introjection of the paternal penis existed before Grunberger adopted it, and it was difficult to assess the origin of the idea. I came across two references: one, a passage in which Abraham (1924) alludes briefly to the assumption that anal as well as oral introjection can take place; the other by Fenichel (1945), who mentions that "Objects may be treated exactly like feces. They may be retained or introjected (there are various types of anal incorporation)" (p. 67). Later Grunberger applied the idea in a challenging way to the explanation of certain clinical phenomena.

I think that McDougall (1974a) describes best the issues that determine the fate of the "anal introjection of the paternal penis" or the "anal castration of the father." McDougall says that the fantasy of absorbing the highly valued penis into one's body is typical of the anal phase of libidinal development. In this stage, children of both sexes imagine the possession of phallic power as an anal incorporation of the father's penis. The outcome of the child's fantasy depends to a great extent on the unconscious attitudes of the parents and the child's relation to them. McDougall cites two possibilities: "The wish may be felt as permitted, in which case it will become integrated within the ego and its identificatory system, thus opening the way to secondary identification and genital sexuality. But such wishes may also be regarded as dangerous, forbidden, and frought with the risk of castration—castration of the father, of the mother, or of the child himself" (p. 297).

Accordingly, the process by which the father's penis is introjected anally is part of normal development and takes place at the end of the anal phase, ushering in the phallic phase with its emphasis on phallic supremacy. The fantasied incorporation enhances the separation from the mother and represents a victory over her. Therefore it signifies a phallic-narcissistic gain for both sexes. Eventually it results in the acceptance of sexual impulses. I think that this derives from the idea that sexuality belongs to the man; therefore an identification with the father allows an identification with a sexualized being. In this way the introjection provides the underpinnings of sexuality which both sexes must transcend in order to accept the immaturity of childhood, their inability to gratify their oedipal longings, and in the case of the girl to take pleasure in feminine receptivity. For these reasons the anal castration of the father is the *sine qua non* of sexuality, yet it constitutes only the first step in a long development. It does not determine sexual identity as such but constitutes a gain toward acceptance of sexuality for each individual. While pertaining to the anal phase with all that it connotes, it is also an essential step toward sexual maturity.

As I became more familiar with this concept, I saw the usefulness of postulating a drive component that bridges the anal and the phallic phases and that leads to the change of object from feces to the penis and from the mother to the father. Still, I do not wish to place myself in the position of defending such a highly speculative concept. I can only attempt to convey its helpfulness in understanding certain situations within the analytic process and demonstrate its potential for relevance to phenomena that are often ignored. I found it helpful in understanding a man who had great anxieties about accepting money from other men. This hampered his business dealings tremendously, and each time he had to be paid, he was afraid that he was hurting the man who paid him (in accordance with the connection between money and feces, it can be assumed that he was afraid to castrate anally the men from whom he accepted money). It is as if the payment were an injury. His defense against this fantasy is that he himself can pay, for instance for his analysis, and consider the money as an investment that comes back to him the way one can withdraw money from a bank. He once attempted anal intercourse with a woman and became so anxious that he had to move to another city (he was afraid that he was going to be castrated anally by her). He is extremely careful with the objects that he inherited from his father, wants to make sure that no harm befalls them, while being convinced that his mother squandered his father's inheritance instead of keeping it for him. Homosexuality fills him with the greatest anxiety and cannot be mentioned to him. I think that these problems can best be understood in terms of the fantasies of his father's anal castration either by his mother who squandered his money or by the son himself, who therefore does not want to receive money from other men for fear of destroying them.

Grunberger's work on anal castration also sheds light on the fears of progress in analysis. In this country, we tend not to focus on the aggressive fantasies accompanying growth although Schlesinger has recently drawn attention to the undesirable aspects of what are generally considered positive gains in analysis. In a paper he read at a meeting of the Freudian Society in 1984, he referred to problems arising in analysis when the analyst or the patient fails to attend to the patient's fantasies of leaving. He stressed that these fantasies are often ignored by both partners in the analytic process, yet they may occur throughout the course of the treatment and do not necessarily involve the issue of real termination. Even though Schlesinger draws attention to the phenomenon that has interested Grunberger, his interpretations of the same issue are different. Grunberger stresses that progress can be experienced as an act of aggression toward the analyst; that the patient may actually fantasize like the child that he is castrating the analyst anally by depriving him of sustenance, potency, beauty, among many other assets the patient thinks he is taking.

Grunberger went so far as to suggest that some treatments falter because of the inability to tolerate this anal castration of the analyst, and that sometimes treatments have to be terminated by a second analyst because of the resistance to working through the problems aroused by this fear of anal castration.

The Role of Narcissism in the Psychoanalytic Process

Grunberger thinks that narcissism is the propeller of analysis. Most other theorists, including Freud, consider it a hindrance to the analytic enterprise or a condition requiring a specific approach that pertains to a well-defined group of patients. Grunberger, however, thinks that narcissism plays a prominent part in all analyses and that the analytic situation constitutes a narcissistic gratification in that the patient gives himself a gift when he submits to the process. Especially at the beginning of treatment, the analysis unfolds because the regression within the narcissistic sector of the personality creates a state of euphoria. Grunberger considers the honeymoon part of the treatment motivated not by historical transference factors but by narcissistic ones.

Grunberger has referred to a gift that the patient gives himself by being in analysis and also to the "gift" that the analyst occasionally gives to the patient. He does not mean a present, or the fulfillment of a wish, but a question such as "why not" when the patient declares that he is not worthy or something similar. In his review of Grunberger's work, Richards (1984) picked this up for criticism as well as Grunberger's failure to include clinical examples that would confirm his assumptions. It must be remembered that French psychoanalytic literature is particularly poor in clinical examples, but also that one clinical example can actually illustrate a number of theories. As to the "gift" of the analyst's words, it is important to know that the French tend to remain more silent than American analysts, so that a question shedding doubt on the need for self-abnegation by a French analyst is doubly received as a gift. Although American analysts are less silent (this is an impression I have had and which was confirmed to me by Colette Chiland who is quite familiar with American psychoanalysis), any patient who is asked why he cannot permit himself something that according to his account others can do, would consider such a question as a present. It is this kind of gift that Grunberger refers to as being narcissistically gratifying.

Grunberger is emphatically opposed to any gratification of a formulated request, since it introduces the analyst as an object before the patient is ready to have him be one. The intolerance of object relations must be respected in the treatment because the analyst gratifies the patient's narcissism by frustrating him instinctually. This is not as contradictory as it sounds when one remembers that narcissism is antagonistic to reality and the give and take of real relationships. An analyst who gratifies the patient instinctually frustrates the patient's narcissism. More often than not, the narcissistic patient does not even want to formulate wishes; he wants his wishes to be anticipated and gratification imposed upon him.

This observation explains one circumstance that seemed at first rather puzzling: a patient reported that she never forgave her previous therapist for his response to her when she told him she wanted to seduce him. He said: "You don't have to worry because I won't respond." I could not understand that the patient marked this incident as the beginning of the end of their relationship because this therapist had previously engaged in behavior that seemed much more out of line with good practice than this remark. According to Grunberger's thesis, the therapist's response to the patient's fantasy placed their relationship on the level of object-instinctual gratifications instead of leaving it on the narcissistic level in which no response is necessary. She felt it apparently as a major breach that he considered himself a real object in her life.

Outside the field of analysis, Grunberger's view of the difference between narcissistically and object-instinctually motivated behavior can be used to explain the effect of the reforms instituted in the 1960s in religious orders. Frustrations that nuns and priests bore with pride and humility as long as the church interpreted them as the will of God became onerous when the church changed its attitude and no longer sanctified them.

Many members of orders that previously were devout and submissive left the orders, became hostile and rebellious, and wanted more gratifications. The deprivations lost their narcissistically gratifying aspects when the image of what God wanted for man changed. Therefore the renunciations became intolerable for many who had previously derived pride from them.

In analysis, too, patients tolerate the frustrations imposed on them by the process for the same reasons that the nuns tolerated their deprivation: because of the expected fulfillment of the narcissistic quest. Analysis constitutes an important source of narcissistic gratification while avoiding all drive gratification. The patient has the analyst's undivided attention and thereby is transported back to a blissful state when he believed himself to be the center of the universe. To be in analysis becomes very meaningful even during periods of negative transference, since the aggression only involves the analyst and not the process, which remains highly invested.

The frustrations imposed by analysis are not experienced as such at the beginning, but the tolerance depends upon a certain minimal narcissistic investment of the process or the analyst. Altman (1975, pp. 187–197) describes a patient who lacked such an investment, and he ascribes the failure of the treatment to the patient's narcissistic pathology. I remember a similar futile effort with a patient whose investment in his treatment was continuously jeopardized by a girlfriend who insisted on being his authority. She mattered greatly to him, and his analysis could not withstand her denigrations. The treatment process was not sufficiently valued.

Grunberger says that the withdrawal of the anal-sadistic component, that is, motility, causes the narcissistic regression induced by sleep as well as the partial regression in analysis. The analysand looks at himself in a mirror, held up by the analyst who is out of sight. This reality distorts the transference situation in such a way that it does not generally correspond to a reproduction of a historically experienced past. Grunberger, like many of his compatriots, tends to think of treatment based on the analysis of dominant fantasies and imagos that organize or hamper the subject's pleasure rather than based on a thorough working through of an actual historical past.

Grunberger also suggests that oedipal situations can have a strong narcissistic component and therefore should not be analyzed exclusively in terms of the triangle. In certain regressive constellations, the castration threat or guilt toward the rival are not the principal components of the conflict. Grunberger calls attention to the nature of the narcissistic injury suffered by patients who have had a premature oedipal triumph over the rival-parent. In these cases, the main problem resides in the child's immaturity to consummate such a victory and not in the oedipal guilt as it is generally assumed. The two issues are quite different in that anxiety involves the presence of a parent who is considered strong enough to carry out the punishment. Situations in which the child fantasizes that an oedipal triumph will go unpunished encourage the child to think of himself and the object of his or her oedipal fantasies as a couple frustrated only by the child's immaturity and inability to consummate the union. The response to this is shame, not anxiety.

Grunberger's formulations apply particularly well to a situation with which I am familiar. A man related how, as a boy, he periodically experienced an illness that his mother treated by administering enemas. She collected his feces without moving him. As far as I know, the father never protested against the mother's handling of her school-aged son on such an intimate level. There was apparently no guilt linked to these scenes with the mother. Thus the patient achieved intimacy with the mother, but was, of course, mortified because the rear end was the focus of the mother's interest. I think that the level of body contact made him feel almost the equal of his father except that the organs of contact predicated on his phallic immaturity made the scene a source of narcissistic injury. Humiliation is this man's greatest fear, and in analysis he fantasized that all other patients had privileges that he did not enjoy because there is something wrong with him. He is beset by grandiose expectations of himself and berates himself for his failures, for when he fails he sees only his own shortcomings, not prohibitions. Cases such as this one are seen with increasing frequency. They demonstrate that unfortunately not every oedipal situation involves a reliable prohibition, and therefore Grunberger's distinction between the object-directed components and the narcissistic ones is most important. Freud had already begun to delineate the two factors when he spoke about the narcissistic investment of the penis for the sake of which the strivings toward the parent are given up in the classical situation. Thus where the oedipal object is not given up because of castration fears stemming from the prohibition by the father, the narcissistic problems concerning personal defects dominate.

The role of the ego in analysis is another one of Grunberger's important ideas. He points out that a well-organized ego is not necessarily a strong one since its organization requires attribution of value in order to gain strength. This explains why very accomplished people, whose ego is well organized, can be very depressed: they cannot attach a sense of value to their achievements.

Grunberger thinks that analysis can only be undertaken by those who long for the reestablishment of the narcissistic universe, and the ego's fear of the analyst reflects the attitude toward the omnipotence that has been attributed to him as the representative of the narcissistic unit. In essence the self applauds the defeat of the ego, which is impoverished since it is deprived of the narcissistic component and left only with the anal derivatives as a result of the union established between the oral drive and the analyst through analysis. The existence of the union explains why a patient in the midst of a strong resistance will be punctual and reliable in keeping appointments and attending sessions. According to Grunberger, this phenomenon reflects not a therapeutic alliance but oral narcissistic nostalgia.

With this, Grunberger confirms one of my long-held beliefs that no one enters analysis for the right reasons, that a thoroughly rational and detached attitude toward analysis can work against the process instead of with it. The ability to regress is essential. Grunberger postulates that the regression is a narcissistic one. Within the treatment the narcissism is invested in the analytic situation, whereas the real accomplishments of the patient are denigrated. The ego actually becomes the seat of resistance. It is reluctant to give up its organization, whereas the narcissistic factor is cooperative with the analytic enterprise.

None of the French analysts whose work I know have any regard for the idea of a therapeutic working alliance between analyst and patient. Grunberger objects to it on the grounds that the ego cannot have a prop, and he thinks that on the contrary, the ego works in the direction of resistance and not in the service of health.

This state of affairs highlights an important paradox: why the ego is willing to preside, so to speak, over its own defeat, as it does when it submits itself to the work of analysis, which represents a challenge to its work of defense. Grunberger believes that it is the autonomous force of narcissism that leads the way. The difference between a neurotic who has decided on the need for analysis and the one who attempts to remedy his difficulties through other means lies in the fact that the one who opts for psychoanalytic treatment has made the decision that the ego has failed in its task and has to be replaced by another one. Grunberger says that the ego itself is conservative and retentive. The ego is modeled partly in relation to outer reality and is the seat of both integration and defense: this explains why the ego cannot be relied upon as the motor for analysis. Furthermore, the ego is a product of the anal phase which sets itself apart from the oral universe established between patient and analyst. According to Grunberger, the relationship between analyst and patient must appeal to the patient's wish for a limitless and ill-defined union and therefore runs counter to the ego's need for organization. In this way, the dialectic between orality and anality is brought into the analytic process, and the interplay between compliance and resistance is established.

The work of analysis helps to integrate the narcissistic factor into the ego to the point where the ego can love itself, its frustrations as well as its gratifications. Grunberger (1979) points out that all definitions of a strong ego fail to include the concept of narcissism, or the self. Integration of the instinctual drives alone, even if achieved at an advanced and socially adapted level, is not the doing of a strong ego, but of a realistic and well-organized ego that is anal and static. Such an ego will seek and obtain its simple physiological satisfactions without cathecting them narcissistically. He adds:

> It will not be able to ennoble them, as it were, to enrich them, or to release them and use them for its own narcissistic ends. The psychology of pleasure needs to be revised; to the notion of pleasure as physiological détente resulting from the combination of a sadistic superego and a predominantly anal sadomasochistic ego, there must be added a fundamentally different concept based on a collaboration between narcissism and the id, the first dominating the second and drawing from it specific hedonic satisfaction. [pp. 116–117]

In my opinion, not enough has been said in this country about the possible sterility of a well-organized ego. I attribute this lack to cultural factors that have led to a tendency to overlook the deficiencies in a well-organized personality. Grunberger suggests that it is based on anality that is not enriched by narcissistic investment.

Grunberger holds to the notion of the dominance of the pleasure ego in the narcissistic sector of the personality. Like Freud, he does not have much to say about the reality ego: it is an area that Braunschweig studied because of her interest in the problems of self-preservation. But if psychoanalysis concentrates on the libido, which, according to Freud's definition, resists the impact of reality and tries to retreat into fantasy, then Grunberger has enlarged the scope of what we know about that part of the psyche that has little use for reality, adaptation, and even the body as a vehicle for pleasurable discharge. I think that he has made the silence of narcissism more discernible and has exposed the invisible that is hidden behind a screen of shame.

Notes

[1] Laplanche (1970), who is not a *psychosomaticien*, suggests that self-preservation is derived from secondary narcissism according to the formula, "I eat for the love of myself."

[2] I tend to reject the notion that actual memory traces of the prenatal existence are the motivating force, but I think that fantasy can easily be substituted for memory in Grunberger's theory of narcissism without losing its explanatory value.

[3] Fain and Marty (1959) state that most frequently the demand for everything hides a wish for something quite specific. This can be verified when very regressed patients can at times be made to become more specific if the analyst maintains a questioning attitude toward their global assertions.

[4] I think that Piera Castoriadis-Aulagnier (1975) has a similar problem in mind, when she proposes another process antedating primary- and secondary-process functioning. She calls it *le processus originaire*. It sets the psychic apparatus in motion in that it makes both the function of representing, as well as that which is represented by the function, acceptable to the subject.

9

Phallic Monism and Female Sexuality

Chasseguet-Smirgel called Freud's theory of psychosexual development "phallic monism." She is critical of Freud's postulating complete ignorance of the female genitals and their significance until the oedipal phase, but she tackled the problem in her own particular way: the tradition of textual analysis and reverence for the past precluded her simply saying that this is where Freud went wrong. Instead of dismissing Freud's theory, she analyzed his writings and her clinical experience to understand the underlying reasons for his theory. In this way, she found the basis for Freud's error and integrated it into the theory.

I think that in France, the need to refute Lacan also played a part in the study of phallic monism. Lacan defended the centrality of the phallus as a signifier, to use his term. He based his view on the mother's desire for the father's phallus, which, inasmuch as the child is also desired by the mother or wishes to be, becomes the child's object of identification. This supposedly causes the primacy of the phallic identification. *Phallic* and *castrated* are terms that are widespread in Lacanian literature and suggest that, unlike Freud, Lacan believed them to be descriptive of a universal phenomenon rather than way stations toward the fully mature ideas of male and female. Lacan adhered to the notion of psychic phallocentrism, as well as to a theory involving universal castration, and he makes fun of Jones as the champion of feminists because the latter said in effect: "to each his own genital" (Lacan 1966, p. 555).

Since the need to refute Lacan often led French analysts back to the question of a proper interpretation of Freud's writings, his theory implying phallic monism, or ignorance of the vagina by preoedipal children, stimulated Chasseguet-Smirgel to devote some major studies to the issue. She interpreted Freud's formulations as the description of a psychic reality that is not based on ignorance but on denial of the existence of the vagina. She thinks that much can be gained from Freud's ideas. In other words, Freud's theory is not necessarily regarded as the ultimate statement of truth, which most agree it is not, but as the description of a defensive stance stemming from the (permanent or temporary) regression to the phallic-narcissistic phase. Many others consider this aspect of Freudian theory a bit of an embarrassment to psychoanalysis, especially because of the attacks it has provoked from feminists. But from Chasseguet-Smirgel's perspective, the theory of the founder of psychoanalysis has a broader relevance than simply to reveal his blind spots.

Chasseguet-Smirgel studied Freud's reasons for the theory that excludes the knowledge of the existence of the vagina before the resolution of the Oedipus complex. She demonstrated that Freud's character and its defensive structure can stand as an example for the denial of the vagina, a more prevalent problem than our enlightened age would like it to be. She thinks that his thinking is not as far off the mark as we, with our twentieth century ideology, would like it to be and that Freud's error consists in interpreting the absence of the vagina in children's minds as ignorance, when in reality it is denied.

The Dark Continent: The Vagina and Female Sexuality

In a careful analysis of Freud's 1909 text, Chasseguet-Smirgel (1976) demonstrates that Freud ignored the evidence for Little Hans' knowledge of the existence of the vagina. She shows that Freud overlooked both the case material that he himself presented and the fact that the ignorance of the existence of the vagina, as he postulated it, is contrary to common sense: there would be no reason for the little boy to compete with his father and compare his own organ with that of a man if he were unaware of the organ's destination in sexual intercourse. If Freud persisted in maintaining that children do not know about the female genital until late in their development in the face of the logical inconsistencies and the clinical evidence that contradicts it, he had powerful defenses against the assumption that the vagina is known from early on. Chasseguet-Smirgel thinks that the defenses are directed against the image of the vagina as a part of the archaic mother's devouring qualities. She hypothesizes "that the theory of sexual phallic monism corresponds not to the lack of knowledge of the vagina but a splitting of the ego or to the repression of an earlier piece of knowledge" (p. 279).

This earlier piece of knowledge, Chasseguet-Smirgel asserts, is the mother as she is known in the unconscious. It is an image that is both threatening, engulfing, and narcissistically injurious, and to which the theory of sexual phallic monism (and its derivatives) represents an antidote. Freud's theory represents not only his own defenses against the knowledge of a powerful and negative image of the mother but, according to Chasseguet-Smirgel, it is a view shared by the rest of humanity.

Green (1980) also analyzes Freud's 'error': "Actually, Freudian intuition is not altogether wanting, as we shall see. One could put it this way: something that derives from women or is related to them and that 'passivizes' gives rise to active rejection in both sexes" (p. 120). Green relates this phenomenon to the fact that the mother is the first seducer and therefore sexualization recalls for both sexes the elements that she introduced: fusion, dependence, and passivity. He thinks that the attempt to deny women's special identity erects a defense against the problem of passivity.

Chasseguet-Smirgel (1964, 1970 ed.) postulates that the denial of the existence of the vagina is never complete. Here she disagrees with Braunschweig and Fain (1971) who theorize that there is a stage during which the vagina is unrepresented. She prefers to think that in the unconscious there is a terrifying image of the maternal vagina from which separation becomes most urgent and with whom identification is most hazardous. Possession of a penis becomes the fantasied vehicle for the separation.

Chasseguet-Smirgel stresses that if the mother is fantasized as having an organ capable of devouring, the girl, were she to identify with the mother's sexuality, would be forced to acknowledge that she, too, is equally equipped with such a menacing organ. Men also fear the power of their mothers, and women become accomplices to this fear by limiting their own power and anality. Therefore, the fantasy of possessing a phallus or its equivalent avoids the identification with the destructive organ of the mother and can help the girl attain a sense of separateness from the mother as well as support the fantasy that she can return to her, which is modeled on the fantasy of a negative Oedipus. For these reasons, the phallic phase of the girl attains a primary importance.

Clinically, the problem of woman's sexual identity in relationship to separation from the mother is quite common, even though it is not customary to express these difficulties as inherent in the threat the mother poses to identification. However, the results of a statistical study (Oliner 1958) support the hypothesis that men and women have different ways of identifying with the parent of the same sex. The answers given on a rating scale in which adults rated themselves and their parents on questions that generally discriminate between men and women placed the women at a greater distance from their mothers than the men from their fathers. In my opinion, the data support the thesis that men's identification with their own phallus allows them to identify with other men without being threatened. Women, on the other hand, appear to have to compensate for their sense of deficiency by creating greater differences between themselves, their mothers, and other women. Men apparently do not need the dissimilarity that lends a sense of uniqueness and narcissistic confirmation in the same way women do.

I believe that this study suggests the importance of a phallic identification in the process of separation. Exactly how the knowledge of the penis can be conceptualized at such an early stage is difficult to spell out, but I also believe that it is important to consider separation as a very gradual process that tends to be wrongly inserted into the developmental scheme as if it happened at one particular time and were resolved after that. For these reasons, I fully accept Chasseguet-Smirgel's view that the boy's penis enables him to free himself more easily from the mother and to sustain the fantasy of a possible return to her in the future. When all goes well, he can rely on fantasies of the phallic potency he hopes to acquire as a vehicle for an eventual return to the original object. The way back to the mother is simply not as easy for the girl, at least not by the same route. Seen from this perspective, the penis is of central importance because it can lead to the fantasy of a mature version of the return to the womb, which is not accessible to the girl.

Chasseguet-Smirgel believes that there is a primary genitality, that is, the existence of some foreknowledge of the function of the genitals from infancy on. I am more inclined to think that in adult analyses one phase blends into the other sufficiently so that the function of the penis, about which children learn at a later time, influences retroactively the way earlier issues are resolved, and that experiences with the mother also support the girl's notion that her individuality would be less threatened were she a boy.

The image of the mother who possesses a penis has been used in various ways by Chasseguet-Smirgel as the basis for certain interpretations. She believes that this image results from the denial of the mother's vagina. At the most primitive level the wish for a penis is addressed to the mother as the possessor of all power, including the phallus.

Chasseguet-Smirgel (1964, 1970 ed.) suggests that the wish for a penis at a later stage of the anal phase constitutes an attempt to eradicate the narcissistic injury inflicted by the mother. The girl wants a penis in order to have something that the mother lacks, the implication being that the image of the mother has progressed to the point where she is not considered phallic. That her penis belongs to the father and is therefore only borrowed is a fantasy that enables the daughter to think that she can obtain it from the father, too, and thereby triumph during the latter stages of the anal phase. This fantasy opens the way to heterosexuality and the wish to possess the father's penis. In itself, it is an aggressive wish directed at the mother's power and in the service of winning the competition in the anal phase. It is accompanied by fear of the mother and guilt toward the father and constitutes the basis for the oedipal triangle. If the wish to possess the father's penis is eroticized, it leads to the negative Oedipus complex. But this determinant of penis envy can result in a specific difficulty that Chasseguet-Smirgel has studied extensively and that will be discussed in the next chapter along with her work on creativity: the girl experiences every narcissistic gratification as usurping the paternal power.

If the mother continues to be experienced as phallic and there is no change of object in the psychosexual development, a homosexual situation can set in forever.

The problem of homosexual women was studied by

McDougall (1964, 1970 ed.). This extremely valuable work distinguishes between homosexual and virile women and highlights the essential differences between those women for whom the father does not constitute a desirable object and those women who have changed their love object from the mother to the father but desexualize and idealize him.

It must be stated at the outset that whereas one group, the virile women, are neurotic, the homosexual ones belong in the category of perversion. This distinction, which is crucial, will not be taken up in the present context. The present discussion will focus only on the difference in the identification patterns of the two types of patients.

According to McDougall, there is a failure in the identification with the genital mother in both cases, but whereas one tends to idealize the father, the other denigrates him. "Although the father [of the female homosexual] played an important role in the psychic structure, he had never been accepted as an object of sexual desire" (1964, 1970 ed., p. 180). This is due to the repression of his early seductiveness that made it necessary to exclude him and to keep him perpetually outside the self. The homosexual woman keeps the penis of the father, which was refused her and granted to the mother, outside her own psyche. Therefore "she castrates the father of his penis and his rights over the mother, she castrates equally the mother through her wish to possess the virility of the father, and at the same time she steals from her mother her own femininity in order to attract the father" (1964, p. 295). The mother is idealized and therefore, ipso facto, desexualized, and the stolen sexuality is restored to the homosexual partner in order to reconstitute an ideal unit. In other words, the desexualization of the mother is undone by means of the sexual pleasure given to the woman lover. Treatment must aim at giving validity to the vagina, feminine desires, and penis envy, and it must dispel the notion that the girl deprived her mother of that which could have attracted the father.

In this respect, there is no similarity between the homosexual woman and the virile one who idealizes everything masculine and cannot identify with the wish of men for sexual contact with women. Virile women idealize a desexualized masculinity that can only lead to attempts to identify with men but not to desire them sexually. The desire to repair the primary object that was mentioned in conjunction with homosexual women is absent for virile women, and this is what McDougall suggests is the important factor that differentiates the two groups.

McDougall's study is enlightening because it demonstrates the process of desexualization of the idealized parent. This enables McDougall to refer to a process of castration inherent in the idealization, highlights the desexualization of the phallus which Braunschweig and Fain (1971) discuss with an eye to the absurdity of such a notion and provides yet another important facet of the role of phallic narcissism in the problems of female sexuality.

McDougall's study also suggests that the difference between the attachment to the idealized mother, as in female homosexuality, and the fixation on the idealized father, as in the case of the virile woman, has important consequences. The difference in the objects can go hand in hand with the difference between perversion and neurosis, which suggests that the change of object normally brings about a change in the level of ego functioning. This confirms Chasseguet-Smirgel's assertion that normally there is more than displacement from one object to the other in the true change of object. There is a qualitative difference between the love for the mother and for the father, and if the investment of the mother is only transferred onto the father, the father is imbued with the mother's frightening qualities. Normally, the change in object entails a lessening of aggression that does not require as much defensive idealization.

Luquet-Parat (1964, 1970 ed.) studied the problem of the change of object. She emphasized the difficulty in assuming the passive-receptive aims toward organs on which aggression has been projected, be they the breast or the phallus. She proposes that a phase designated as anal-phallic be inserted into the developmental scheme. This phase would describe phallic strivings that are still predominantly anal. Eventually further psychosexual development of the girl causes aggression to be transferred to the mouth, whereas the passive ones invest the vagina as a result of further psychosexual development of the girl.

Chasseguet-Smirgel views the phallic phase of the girl in light of the anal phase that precedes it, overlaps with it, and affects its fate. Anal-sadistic drive derivatives present a particular challenge to the woman whose aggression cannot be channeled as directly into sexuality as the man's because its aim is not active. Because of this, her sexual relationships confront her with a particular set of problems concerning activity and aggression. This problem is compounded because the girl is at a disadvantage in freeing herself from the archaic mother, and therefore she has to do so more aggressively than the boy, although her sexual aim cannot necessarily discharge the aggression. This aggression could be considered dangerous when it is directed against the father in an attempt at incorporating his phallic qualities during the process that was described as the anal introjection of the paternal phallus (see the previous chapter on Grunberger's theory of narcissism).

Chasseguet-Smirgel (1966) states that since Freud, psychoanalytic literature seems particularly rich in studies of masculine fear of the vagina, on which men project their pregenital aggression (oral and anal). However, the literature seems singularly poor in references to the position of the female superego, with regard to her own aggressive impulses toward the penis. Everything is explained as if it were understood implicitly, that this aggressive position either is not conflicted or that it is only defensive. This would mean that it is a matter of perversion (a perverse sadistic component), or that normal genital female sexuality, unlike male sexuality, does not necessitate integration of aggressivity.

Chasseguet-Smirgel thinks that Freud's notion of the

woman's wish for the penis was too narrow and that his bias with its emphasis on phallic narcissism ignores the fundamentally feminine wish to incorporate the paternal penis in order to be impregnated by it. "One must remember that during sexual intercourse, the woman does actually incorporate the man's penis. Although this incorporation is only partial and temporary, women desire in fantasy to keep the penis permanently" (1964, 1970 ed., p. 102) in order to be impregnated. Chasseguet-Smirgel points out that Freud did not study the woman's wish for a child as a primary wish, one that is derived from the wish to receive and to be penetrated. He analyzed the wish for the penis only from the dynamics of the frustrated phallic narcissism that will accept the child for lack of a penis even though in the study of the transformation of instinct he inserted a more direct derivation from feces to baby. But this derivation, which contributes to a more primary femininity than that which derives the wish for the baby from the wish for the penis, typically has been ignored because it has to contend with the defenses against such a primary view of femininity. The use of the penis obtained in an aggressive way so as to produce a baby, according to Chasseguet-Smirgel, also signifies for the unconscious its fecalization and finally leads to the fantasy of holding on to an anal penis.

This fantasy generates guilt that often leads to a reversal whereby the woman becomes the content of a menacing container. Chasseguet-Smirgel considers this to be a specifically feminine guilt concerning the anal-sadistic component of sexuality, that is, the wish to incorporate the penis is considered an act of aggression that can result in the punitive fantasy of a reversal whereby the woman identifies with the content of a menacing container. The defense against such fantasies might be the woman's idealization of her father, which tends toward the defusion of instincts and leads to the repression or countercathexis of aggression toward the father and his penis.

Problems of Female Identity

In her 1966 study concerning a similar fantasy found in both paranoia and phobia, Chasseguet-Smirgel highlights one of the vicissitudes of the defense against the aggression implied in the incorporation of the penis, that is, the turning of the aim against the self. It entails the idea of a trap, in which one is the endangered content of a menacing container. Analytically, this reverses the situation of the aggressive incorporation of the penis in intercourse, which constitutes the anal-sadistic fantasy of female sexuality. Because this is considered to be dangerous to the partner, it is sometimes turned against the self and leads to inhibition and an identification by the woman with the threatened penis. Chasseguet-Smirgel stresses that the fact that the woman in reality incorporates the penis of the man in intercourse has the potential for many disturbing fantasies, which she documents in her study. These fantasies lead to sexual inhibitions as well as to the fear of being trapped. By means of the reversal she can have the wish as well as the punishment. She becomes the content that disappears in the container. Therefore, according to the author, every conflict around introjection has its consequences in female sexuality.

In paranoia, "the anal introjection of the penis is that drive component whose gratification will always be desired and always feared because of the intensity of the aggression projected on the object experienced as threatening to body integrity" (p. 135). The passive homosexual desire remains, whereas the aggressive aspect is projected, making any approach dangerous. The wish to attract the object in a trap in order to control it is reversed into the passive component expressed in the thought of being caught in a trap, in an attempt to master the fear of being penetrated. The anus becomes the world, and content and container are reversed. The anal sphincter has been projected.

According to Chasseguet-Smirgel, the wish to have a penis and the wish to be penetrated are not necessarily antagonistic;

rather, penis envy and normal femininity are complementary in the sense that a woman does not necessarily want to be a man but rather wants to be free of her mother in order to be a woman and autonomous.

She thinks that Freud's description of female development renders women into little girls whereas the real female Oedipus complex entails intense rivalry with the mother and is no more comfortable than a boy's competition with his father. The pressure to resolve it is as great for the girl as it is for the boy.

Chasseguet-Smirgel differentiates between the identification with the autonomous phallus and the identification with the father's penis in which the little girl would remain the complement of her father. The latter fantasy would lead to the idea of becoming the thing of the other, in order to circumvent the guilt attached to the incorporation of the penis on an anal mode. It is as if the girl had the need to say: "I am your thing, you can do with me what you want." This attitude leads to "extreme submissiveness in women" as described by A. Reich (1940, 1973 ed.). The identification with the autonomous phallus could lead to the image of the body as phallus, which results in impenetrability and narcissistic pathology.[1]

André Green approached the problem of female development from a more theoretical point of view, emphasizing the problem of identity, even though he does not call it that. His (1975b, 1980 ed.) study examined the problem of the identification with the mother in terms of the special dilemma it represents for the girl. In separating herself from the mother she has to declare herself to be other, which deprives her of an object for identification and therefore constitutes a narcissistic deprivation. Although mother and daughter are of the same sex, an identification with the mother is hazardous during the early phases of development because it threatens the girl's separate identity to a greater extent than it threatens the boy's.

Green (1975b) highlights the problem of the significance of the aims of female sexuality. He considers the rejection of femininity by both sexes as universal and attributes it to the collaborative relationship between the presexual and the sexual in the girl as against the antagonistic relationship between these two factors in the boy.

If my own interpretation of Green's point of view can be trusted (he is one of those writers who is sometimes difficult to understand), he emphasizes the problem of the narcissistic devaluation of passive-receptive aims. Because psychosexual development leads to a repudiation of the passive aims, the continuity between the phases causes the pleasure in receptivity and retention that dominates female sexuality to enter into conflict with pleasures of the phallic phase. This conflict appears to take the child back. In the United States, Kestenberg views problems from this perspective. She suggests that both sexes give up the passive-receptive aims of the oral and partly the anal phase, to which the girl has to return subsequently. This return of the previously repudiated aims, now located in a different erogenous zone, is troublesome because of both the seeming regression and passivity involved. Green focuses on the fact that feminine genital pleasure resembles pregenital pleasures now transferred to a new zone, rather than on the problem of the aggression implicated in the passive-receptive attitude, which has been the focus of Chasseguet-Smirgel's studies.

As for masturbation, Green (1975b, 1980 ed.) thinks that "while the boy seeks external discharge in pleasure, the girl finds it easier to forego that pleasure since it involves a more threatening penetration of her internal space" (p. 118). He suggests that sexualization plays less of a delimiting economic role in women, since their erogeneity is more diffuse and more easily satisfied even without discharge. I would add that it is for this reason that female receptivity tends to be undervalued and conflicted when compared with the more externalized and newer aims introduced by the phallic phase.

Green does not refer to an earlier article by Grunberger (1964), although the latter stresses the same point: women do not seek instinctual gratification as much as men do. His conclusion is based on his understanding of the pregenital antecedents of heterosexuality that provides the boy, but not the girl, with a heterosexual object. Therefore the boy's pregenital impulses receive gratification and narcissistic confirmation, which means that the drives are more satisfying even though there is frustration during the oedipal struggle. "The pregenital stages are much more frustrating to the girl because the maternal object is only a substitute for a truly adequate sexual object. I believe that this uniquely feminine situation is itself the cause of many disturbances" (p. 72). The girl does not have to change objects for the desired narcissistic confirmation since she does not have a sexual object to begin with. She has to give herself the narcissistic satisfaction, that is, women tend to be more narcissistic because of a restricted notion of the nature of an adequate object during the pregenital stages.

"As man's sexual life is focused on immediate instinctual relief, woman's love also is located in time, but she dreams of eternity and thereby suppresses the material elements, the real instinctual derivatives, of her love. On the whole, women's sexuality is narcissistically oriented . . . ; love bears the marks of this orientation, especially because it is the central interest of her life" (p. 71). Love is a more serious business for the woman than for the man, and the man who takes love too seriously risks looking a little ridiculous.

Grunberger stresses that instinctual satisfaction is more important to men than to women, whose need to be loved and valued dominates their emotional ties to objects. Women introduce another dimension, the narcissistic element, into their love life. Since Grunberger does not believe that this has to be abnormal he thinks that it is either integrated or it can become an obstacle. In normal life, narcissism increases with object love, whereas in neurosis the two run counter to each other. The narcissistic phase that comes between the pregenital and the genital phases can act as a bridge or as an abyss. Thus the clitoris, a narcissistic organ, can either induce further genital contact or inhibit it, depending on the integration between the two.

Grunberger's views, which are reminiscent of the differentiation Freud (1914b) made between the male and female model of love, have not been favorably received because of the negative value attached to narcissism. However, Grunberger bases his ideas on the assumption that phallic narcissism does not have to constitute a barrier to mature object love, even though in cases of pathology it certainly does.

Phallic Narcissism: Its Desexualizing Aspects

Braunschweig and Fain (1971) espouse the opposite point of view. They are convinced that narcissism and erotism can never be integrated. As a matter of fact, in their study *Eros and Antéros* the role of *antéros* falls to phallic narcissism. In this rather fanciful work, full of references to culture and quite devoid of clinical material, they do not differentiate between normal and abnormal development. Instead they highlight the implications of phallic narcissism and conclude that it is the antithesis of the potential for mature love.

Like McDougall, they discuss the relationship between idealization and desexualization, but they express this idea in terms of the murder of the father as it is described in *Totem and Taboo* (Freud 1913). The death of the father that Freud placed at the dawn of human history is avenged by the brothers through the cult of phallic narcissism. This cult, which can take the form of hero worship, becomes most apparent in the psychology of groups, which, as Freud suggested, limit human sexuality. Braunschweig and Fain enlarge the scope of these observations when they differentiate between the groups formed by men and women. They think that men form groups that are capable of sexual aggressivity because men can draw it from their identification with each other, whereas women cannot. By contrast, women have greater sexual audicity alone.

Braunschweig and Fain (1971) appear to devalue groups because of their relatively asexual character, and they express themselves rather forcefully on the subject of groups formed for women's liberation: they do not consider them genuine groups because the women who form them are not interested in genital relations with men. "The official women's groups, especially those that demand sexual equality, have a lugubrious and miserable character. . . . Whereas sparkling femininity . . . gives men the feeling of the existence of their penises, the spectacle of militant feminism exhibits a castration behind which is outlined a masculine devouring anus" (p. 19).

Braunschweig and Fain suggest that in normal development women appreciate on some secret level that the submission to phallic narcissism is only one aspect of reality and that they hold the key to another one, one that is revealed as well as concealed by the father. The silence that is imposed on the erogenous zone of women is incomplete. They believe it is in the order of things for the mother to silence in the name of paternal law that which the father can reveal. "This is why the counteroedipal position of the father is so revealing of the sex of the little girl while being bridled and forbidden" (p. 84).

Virile women, according to Braunschweig and Fain, accept phallic supremacy, even though they, too, know that it is an illusion. Nevertheless, they would also like to be recognized as having a phallus. This wish is the source of their dissatisfaction and leads to the continuous need to be recognized. Knowing that their own sex had to be subordinated due to phallic narcissism, they would like to be endowed with the same recognition as that accorded the boy. Despite the apparent masculinity of this endeavor, it is nothing but the submission to phallic narcissism, for it does not lead to a better acceptance of themselves as women.

There is something slightly offensive in the author's depiction of the clever woman who knows men, keeps her wisdom to herself, and makes the man feel masculine. But their description of the dynamics that brings men together into erotic groups that have not been reliably genitalized is equally uncomplimentary to men. The latter are portrayed as tending to follow the Don Juan principle, according to which the oedipal failure is denied. Just as modern women's groups exhibit their contempt in order to hide their inhibition, those men who form an erotic group want to satisfy themselves on an object that is inferior. Don Juan dishonors women.

Braunschweig and Fain (1971) state that members of the men's groups are united by an intense homosexual bond that is incompatible with feminine satisfaction. On the contrary, they say, femininity disappears when the father image linked to the individual ego ideal is eclipsed. Even passive homosexuality does not truly represent masculine femininity. Its practice implies the conservation of the penis. It concerns the overinvestment of a kind of anal-erotism, "as if to say, wouldn't it be interesting to accomplish the irreparable, to let oneself be castrated, and then light in the eye of the father this troublesome gleam that comes out when he takes his little girl into his arms?" (pp. 42–43).

In Braunschweig and Fain's interpretation, there is a juxtaposition between the father and the oedipal triangle on the one hand and the imitators of Don Juan on the other. The law of the father is linked with interdictions; most specifically it breaks up the unit formed between the mother and her son, which, according to them, is the forerunner of the hero-leader. The hero may protect against castration anxiety in group formation, but within the family, he threatens the father's power and therefore should not be identified as representing it. "Paradoxically, we think that every time the hero appears in a crowd, he eclipses the image of the father in favor of that of mother and child" (p. 48). They further state: "If the mother has not broken up the narcissistic unit with her boy in order to make him into an erotic object by virtue of his sex, it is the whole of the body that tends to take on a phallic value at the same time as the feminine tendencies are reinforced" (p. 93). The fantasy of the hero always involves a beautiful physique.

The views expressed by these authors are often controversial; they have a certain shock value and are purely anecdotal. In their own peculiar way, however, they drive at points that are frequently overlooked. One is, of course, the question of what women really want for themselves. The other is the special place given to the father, in whom the idea of masculine genitality is embodied, as against the hero, who represents phallic narcissism and behind whom lurks the image of the mother-son unit of early infancy.

Braunschweig and Fain want to avoid any tendency to confuse erotic heterosexuality and phallic narcissism. They seem to imply that phallic narcissism is the order of the day for both sexes and that further development toward heterosexuality is dependent on a shared secret in which both sexes learn to accept the fallacy of the cult and the existence of the female genital. But it is the best-kept secret in town.

Their view is not widely accepted, as far as I know. Their approach is not at all normative; therefore they highlight the manifestations of phallic narcissism within the culture at large and tend to place it side by side with genitality. They consider the manifestations of phallic narcissism so prevalent in social organization that they unapologetically continue to highlight the role it plays. In this respect their attitude is devoid of the moral judgment many theorists now bring to bear on any theory dealing with fantasies of male supremacy.

Chasseguet-Smirgel maintains that phallic monism represents a prestage of sexuality, one that is overcome in normal development and is less inclined to accept its manifestations in the culture at large as inevitable and possibly a bit amusing. In this respect, Chasseguet-Smirgel's approach is more normative, and she stresses the contribution of phallic monism to problems in female sexuality as well as to ego-ideal pathology and perversions.[2]

The studies concerning the role of phallic monism in the development and pathology of ego ideal and its relationship to perversion will be taken up in the next chapter, which is separated from the present one only for the sake of organization.

Notes

[1] The problem of the link between the subjects integrity and damage to the object, which leads to the belief that gratification can only be obtained at the object's expense and is therefore his prerogative, has been a frequent theme in Chasseguet-Smirgel's studies. She thinks that it is a problem for men and women alike, and in 1962 she recounted the treatment of a man whose body experience closely paralleled fantasies concerning drive derivatives stemming from the anal phase. Here again the emphasis is placed on the conflicts around anal introjection. In later studies, she links creative efforts with fantasies of doing damage to the object, also because of the conflict around the introjection of a capacity that is considered phallic and therefore the father's prerogative.

[2] As I stated at the outset, this review of female development is restricted to the conflicts between its aims and a phallocentric outlook. Therefore, I shall not review the recent work of Chasseguet-Smirgel in which she studies female development from the aspect of a component that she and her colleagues had previously neglected, that is, the possibility of a positive identification with the mother than runs parallel to the phallic identifications described above. In her more recent studies she adopts the point of view that it is possible for the girl to "return to the mother" by means of an identification with the child she herself will one day bear. The potential identification of the girl with her mother's childbearing ability may well be a positive factor in female development, one that counteracts the importance given to her phallic identification and the theory of phallic monism in psychoanalysis. But this point of view has received considerable attention in the United States and does not need to be reviewed here. In general, the originality of the work of the French on female sexuality centers on its relationship to the supremacy of the phallus. The fact that it may not tell the whole story of female sexuality has not prevented the French from devoting considerable attention to it.

10

Perversion, Idealization, and Creativity

According to Martin Bergmann, a respected psychoanalyst, Chasseguet-Smirgel and McDougall have revolutionized the way we look at perversion. Both women studied perversion as a result of clinical experience, and their theoretical approach to the subject constitutes an outgrowth of their previous studies on female sexuality. Taken as a whole, their work provides an important addition to the literature about the unconscious fantasies that motivate perverse sexuality, or *neosexuality*, as McDougall prefers to call it. They approach the problem through a different conceptual framework than others studying the same phenomena, even though there are no contradictions in the conclusion they draw. Each theoretician remained consistent within her own point of view; therefore McDougall's approach differs from that of Chasseguet-Smirgel, and the two theories cannot be integrated with each other. Clarity and respect for the originality of each demands that each contributor's work be studied separately.

Both emphasize that perversion entails more than fixation on an earlier phase of development. Perversions are more complex than a positive, to which neurosis would be the negative, as Freud thought early in his writings. Chasseguet-Smirgel thinks that perversion entails the idealization of an instinct, a process to which Freud referred in a footnote (1905). McDougall stresses the denial of the hatred of the pervert, who uses a partner in order to keep love and hate separate and in order to fulfill the unconscious wish to castrate and kill. The fact that the sexual organs are involved in these neosexualities has recently seemed less important to McDougall than the internal deficit underlying perversions. This brings them closer to addictions.

Chasseguet-Smirgel treats phallic monism as foremost among the concepts overlapping the studies on female sexuality, perversion, and idealization. She has found the idea of one genital, the penis, as applicable to the study of perversion, idealization, and creativity as it was to the study of female sexuality, and it therefore has a prominent place in this context as well. At the risk of repeating what was said previously, it should be stressed that phallic monism implies a prestate of sexuality. The belief in the existence of only one sex organ, the penis, is typical for a fixation point because it negates the difference between the sexes and asserts that the female gender is the equivalent of the castrated male. Idealizing the male organ diminishes the narcissistic investment of the real genitals of both sexes, and the resulting deficit influences the constitution of the ego ideal.

The Idealization of Anality in Perversion

Chasseguet-Smirgel, whose theory will be discussed first, thinks that perversion must be understood as one of the vicissitudes of the idealization process and as the result of a pathological development of the ego ideal. This in turn manifests itself not only in perversion but also in problems of creativity. She has been interested in the ego ideal almost from the beginning of her published work, and she has amply demonstrated the relevance of this early interest to her understanding of perversion and creativity. She postulates a particular relationship between the mother and the future pervert that gives his ego ideal a specific character. Paraphrasing Chasseguet-Smirgel, it can be said that the mother of the future pervert seduces him into thinking that there is no gap between his ego and the ideal. This prevents him from maturing but encourages him instead to realize the fantasy that he can rely on his wishful thinking.

Chasseguet-Smirgel theorizes that the task of dispelling illusion is the work of the ego ideal. Theorists on this side of the Atlantic subsume this function under self-observation and often attribute it to the ego. Chasseguet-Smirgel justifies including the function of dispelling illusion to the ego ideal by pointing out that the time at which the concept of the ego ideal was formulated straddles Freud's two important works: that on narcissism (1914b) and on the structural theory (1923). Therefore the tendency to treat the ego ideal as if it were a mental structure is not supported by anything but a tacit convention.[1] Chasseguet-Smirgel does not think that a clear-cut decision as to Freud's intention is possible, and therefore she formulates the function of the ego ideal in her own way.

Ever since 1967 she has stated repeatedly that it is the ego ideal that monitors the process of maturation. "We have to set the long road that leads the subject to the Oedipus and to genitality against the short road that fixates the subject to pregenitality. These two roads define the two forms of the ego ideal" (1984b, p. 111). This constitutes a condensed formulation that encompasses both the content of the ego ideal and the level of ego development caused by its degree of maturity.

Freud (1914b) said that the development of the ego consists in a departure from primary narcissism, giving rise to a vigorous attempt to recover that state, and that this departure is brought about by means of the displacement of libido onto an ego ideal.

This conception justifies, according to Chasseguet-Smirgel, a view of human evolution based on the idea of a nostalgia that propels man forward in order to regain that which he has lost. The ego ideal plays an important role as a guide in this, and when the ego ideal and the ego coincide, as they do in pathological states, it is experienced as a fusion with the primary object. Otherwise the ego ideal implies a project.

Chasseguet-Smirgel, who has given her book *The Ego Ideal* (1975b) the subtitle *la maladie de l'idéalité* (the illness of idealness), equates the ego ideal with the longing to return to or advance to the fusion with the primary object. She perceives a universal, lifelong striving to achieve that which was lost at the outset and only the mode in which one regains it evolves with development. It depends on a process of maturation that she has called the evolution from the short road to the long way of recapturing the original fusion. Therefore the wish is actually unchanging, and the evolution of the ego ideal depends on the ideas concerning the ways in which the wish is to be gratified.

In order to differentiate between the complete and the incomplete process of maturation, Chasseguet-Smirgel (1967) studied and reinterpreted the examination dream presented by Freud in *The Interpretation of Dreams* (1900). The dream suggests that an examination has been failed in order to portray the dissatisfaction of the ego ideal with the ego that did not fulfill another developmental task. She points out that the professor who played a part in the dream reported by Freud had only one eye, symbolizing, therefore, the ego that let itself be duped in the process of defense. In this sense, the examination dream reveals the denial of a failure in the maturational process that occurred in an aspect of life connected with the examination that indeed had been passed. In this early work she postulates that the ego ideal works against the defensive maneuvers and holds up a mirror to the ego's attempt at self-deception.

With regard to the psychoanalytic process, Chasseguet-Smirgel thinks that this aspect of the ideal supports the wish to be analyzed and constitutes a positive force toward health that is generally not attributed to it. The normal ego ideal refuses to idealize the primitive merger fantasies that the regressed ego ideal tolerates and contains the wish for an orderly resolution of all developmental phases.

Chasseguet-Smirgel has described in many papers the evolution from a regressed ego ideal to the level that causes it to reject illusion. What follows therefore depends to some degree on my own integration and interpretations of her statements regarding the fate of the ego ideal. In the interest of clarity, I have organized her ideas, taken certain liberties with the translation of concepts, and attempted to present a faithful rendition of her thoughts. I have introduced the idea of the "pleasure ego" because I think that it fits the processes that are being described. I have referred to other, competing developmental models in order to create links between the phenomena described by Chasseguet-Smirgel and others. There is always a hazard in such interpretations, but in my judgment they place her thinking in a larger context, one that is perhaps more accessible.

This developmental scheme condenses the study of sexual aims with ego development and narcissism and traces psychic evolution from the beginning, starting with the close relationship between primary narcissism and the fusion with the mother. Freud postulated such a state at the dawn of human consciousness, a state from which the pleasure ego evolves, that is, the structure that conceives of pleasure-giving sensations as "I" and pain as "not I."[2] During this early development, the object does not exist as separate from the matrix of the pleasure ego; nevertheless, the earliest psychic structure is generally defined around elements of the mother-infant universe.

The undifferentiated phase that evolves into the state in which the pleasure ego dominates has been variously described as primary narcissism, the oral stage, the symbiotic phase, or the fusion with the primary object (Chasseguet-Smirgel 1975b). Even though most would agree that the mother per se does not exist, the need for verbal expression generally implicates the mother. "I stress that I conceive of the primary object as being that which has not yet been differentiated from the ego and which is only experienced as 'object' a posteriori" (1975b, p. 61). From the point of view of the psychosexual phases, the drive, if it is postulated to exist at this time, aims at the object's disappearance: she is swallowed, incorporated, internalized; in other words, where the formulation entails an object, the aim is described as the mother's disappearance and her absorption into the body or ego.

This early phase, therefore, is either conceived of as being without an object or as the instinctual drive aims that seek to abolish it outside and put it inside. Nevertheless the stage is formulated in terms of some kind of mother-baby unit by all but the most devoted Kleinians, who do not accept the notion of an objectless state, which they call defensive, because their concepts involve the existence of an object at the dawn of consciousness.

When Chasseguet-Smirgel (1975b) speaks about a wish to return to the fusion with the primary object, this is what she has in mind. She points out that if the sexual union with the mother constitutes the possibility of refinding the primary narcissistic state, the difference established by Freud in his 1914 text between narcissistic object choice and the anaclitic object choice tends to diminish. From the beginning, both choices strive to recapture the narcissistic completeness that existed before the defusion with the primary object.

In her most recent work, Chasseguet-Smirgel has begun to refer to an archaic matrix of the Oedipus complex. She refers to the fusion with the primary object in terms of the return to the "universe without obstacles, without roughness or differences, entirely smooth, identified with a mother's belly stripped of its contents, an interior to which one has free access. Behind the fantasy of destroying or appropriating the father's penis, the children and the faeces inside the mother's body . . . [can] be detected a more basic and more archaic wish, of which the return to the smooth maternal belly is the representation" (1986b, p. 77). The empty container represents unfettered pleasure whereas the contents represent reality.

The regressed ego ideal prompts the individual to believe that maturation is not necessary and that this ideal state can be achieved by means of illusion. Normal development, on the other hand, leads the child to project his ego ideal on the father. This advance to the phallic phase signifies that the return to the original object is possible only by means of an identification with the father who has access to the mother through his penis.

The anal phase, which draws the individual into the real world and its mastery, separates the two phases during which the return to the original object constitutes a central motivational force. If the accomplishments of the anal phase are maintained, that is, the phallic phase does not lead to an ego regression, we speak of a normal developmental scheme, and the fact that during the phallic phase the body is invested sometimes at the expense of objects is considered as another stage toward growth and not a sign of pathology. Exhibitionism, shame, concerns about intactness and potency are all accepted as normal problems if they are accompanied by the acceptance of the need for mastery and not a return to the magical universe of early childhood, in other words, a return to the first narcissistic phase.

The gains that are made in the anal phase have often been taken out of the realm of psychosexual development and examined in the light of ego development and thereby separated from the dominant instinctual drive concerns. This is a drawback stemming from compartmentalization in psychoanalytic theory that the French like to avoid. They have implicitly assumed that the anal phase acts as a dividing line between the oral and the phallic phase, and that if it has been allowed that function, the narcissism at the phallic level has a different quality than if it involves only anality in phallic disguise (for instance placing value on money and power as a substitute for potency) or a regression to the earlier narcissism of the maternal universe.

The end of the anal phase ushers in a shift of the projection of the ego ideal upon the father. This is of utmost importance to Chasseguet-Smirgel's theory because the dominant idealization concerns an object rather than the idealization of the drive. Any interference with this process through fixation or regression leads to an idealization of anality under the guise of phallic narcissism.

Many of her interesting and important studies demonstrate the consequences of such regression to or fixation on the anal universe.

Whether or not the evolution of the individual is based on an illusion, on the identification with a glorified anal product, or on the identification with the father on whom the ego ideal has been projected, depends, according to Chasseguet-Smirgel and some of her co-workers, on the introjection of the paternal phallus. (See the two previous chapters for a more detailed exposition of this fantasy.) Chasseguet-Smirgel has always maintained that the idealization of the paternal phallus is a developmental necessity. To her way of thinking, it does not become the underpinning of phallic monism; on the contrary, it ushers in the acceptance of the father's role in procreation which leads to the acceptance of the complementarity of the two sexes. If the idealization of the father is impossible, there is an attempt on the part of the child to substitute his own immature genitals for those of the father and to bypass the importance of the difference of the generations and the sexes through a process that idealizes his own phallic equivalent. When the father becomes the object upon whom the ego ideal is projected, the primitive fantasies of fusion with the mother are relinquished.

In a passage that depicts how she conceives of the integration between some Freudian and Kleinian concepts, Chasseguet-Smirgel says that she does not think that the dissolution of the fusion with the primary object is followed by a projection of this narcissism upon the mother. She maintains that the first object is born in hatred and therefore invested with a bad omnipotence. She thinks that at least part of the lost narcissistic cathexis is projected on a second virtual object (the good mother) of whom the child will expect the restoration of the lost state, or rather the affect that accompanied it. A second object, according to Chasseguet-Smirgel, is there to minister and to reestablish this state, that is, if we adhere to the idea of the good and the bad mother being split off from each other. If the experiences with the real mother have been good enough, the search for another object to idealize will be less pressing. It is disappointments in the breast that lead to the premature search for an *objet pénien* (penislike object), the second form of triangulation, the first one, the one consisting of the good and the bad breast, having failed. She regards Schreber as an example of a case in which the idealization of the father occurred prematurely, and the father eclipsed the mother and made triangulation impossible (1975b).

Chasseguet-Smirgel believes that the ego ideal of the pervert is deformed. She thinks that there has been an insufficient idealization of the father's penis and his role in procreation and that instead the future pervert has idealized his own pregenitality as a child, usually with the mother's connivance. The perverse structure coincides excessively with self-idealization, and therefore, as Braunschweig (1971) said, "the pervert wants nothing from analysis" (p. 655).

Chasseguet-Smirgel is unequivocal in her conviction that the bedrock of reality resides in accepting the difference between the generations and the difference between the sexes. Accepting the generational difference prevents the child from remaining his own ego ideal for very long and therefore mitigates ego ideal and narcissistic pathology. Accepting the difference between the sexes is related to drive development but is dependent on the prior acceptance of the difference in generations.

Chasseguet-Smirgel reiterates that in perversion the underlying fantasy consists of not having to envy the father and considering the infantile anal-sadistic erotism as equal or even superior to mature genitality. She cites many examples supporting her conviction that perversion aims at destroying and leveling differences so that the prevailing laws are abolished and substitute rules are created. Through her study of the writings of the Marquis de Sade she demonstrates that perversion entails the idealization of an anal, homogeneous, and undifferentiated universe. Destruction is subsequently idealized and reality is reconstructed by artificial means according to those fantasies that serve the needs of the pervert. Therefore the histories of many cases of perversion highlight the fascination with the use of orthopedic devices that replace or imitate absent body parts or deficient functioning: these fantasies allow the belief in the possibility that growth can be supplanted by a manufacturing process. These fantasies, according to Chasseguet-Smirgel, are an attempt to fantasize the manufacturing of an anal phallus having a fetishistic role. The anal penis aims at maintaining the illusion that denies the father's procreative capacity.

Chasseguet-Smirgel (1981) says that if psychosis creates a new reality by means of delirium, if neurosis tends to substitute the fantasy world for the real world, perversion generates a transmutation of reality by means of the idealization of anality. When the hatred of reality prevails, the subject tries to destroy reality and to create a new one, that of the anal universe, where all differences are abolished. The pervert attempts to replace genitality with a glorified anality, the symbol of falsehood. Genuine genitality, however, causes the breakup of the original union between mother and child. Genitality also mitigates against the projection of the ego ideal on anything but a project, in and of itself unattainable. The ego ideal should pull us ahead.

To illustrate the foregoing theories, a clinical example might be helpful. A patient was struggling with the wish to deny his father's superiority. During one session, he touched upon the following themes that illustrate some of the dominant ways in which the son tried to maintain the illusion of his superiority over the father: He referred to people with accents, the newcomers, who are doing better than people born here. To this way of thinking, seniority does not count. He spoke about Christianity, the religion of the son; the God of the Old Testament, who is vengeful (he starts to cry for his dead father); and finally about the Wizard of Oz with the machine he manufactured. Coming as they did in one session, these associations follow the chain relating to the loss of the Almighty, his dethronement by the son, the meaninglessness of seniority, and the machine that can be made by magic or wizardry. They confirm Chasseguet-Smirgel's contention that there is a close relationship between the wish to render the father's seniority meaningless, the illusion that the son can be superior to the father, and the idea of an artificial creation that permits this reversal of nature.

Chasseguet-Smirgel stresses the mother's role in the development of the future pervert, and the help she gives him in maintaining his illusions. She cites Braunschweig and Fain (1971), who mention the father's failure to help the mother return to her role as a lover after she has given birth to the child, but her own studies concentrate on the mother who allows the son such a dominant place in the family. From Chasseguet-Smirgel's case material there emerges a father who himself cannot embody adequately an ego ideal that encompasses genital procreation and phallic potency. Otherwise, her theoretical formulations tend to stress the mother's role in the maintenance of the boy's illusion concerning his own immaturity as well as the role of the denial of the existence of the vagina. She credits McDougall with the recognition that the mature female genital reminds the pervert of the father's role in procreation and his own inadequacy to function in the same way. By maintaining the illusion, the future pervert is saved this narcissistic mortification as well as the oedipal defeat. According to Chasseguet-Smirgel, the fetishist who thinks that his mother has a penis can render the father useless to her and in that case his own pregenitality can be thought of as sufficient to satisfy her. In order to add greater weight to this fantasy, the pervert has to idealize his pregenitality.

Chasseguet-Smirgel has mentioned two reasons why she thinks that women are less prone to develop perversions. One is that as a child, the girl cannot maintain the illusion that she herself can bear a child, whereas the boy can fantasize himself to be the husband of his mother. Consequently, the girl learns that she has to wait for maturity. The second reason concerns the severity of the superego. Chasseguet-Smirgel thinks that the superego of women is more restrictive, and therefore they are more inhibited in expressing their instinctual urges. Because of this, Chasseguet-Smirgel studied the problems that lead to perversions exclusively in men.[3] However, she also relates these to inhibitions in creativity where they have an important role for the pathology of both sexes.

According to Chasseguet-Smirgel, true creativity is possible as the relationship to the ego ideal becomes desexualized and therefore more impersonal. In her major 1971 work, she makes the important distinction between that which is engendered and that which is manufactured, the latter being a product of anality and therefore a derivative of the fetish, itself being related to the false. Genuine creativity depends on a genuine identification, one that is acquired through assimilation and not magic. Genuine creativity depends on the evolution of anality beyond reaction formations: anality must be transformed in order to result in sublimation. Chasseguet-Smirgel also disagrees with Klein who regards the basis for creativity to be the need to repair the object whose retaliation is feared. She thinks that this would base the creative process again on reaction formation against sadism, whereas it must rest on sublimation. If indeed we can refer to reparation, it can only be of the ego, as Freud postulated in his paper on narcissism (1914b).

Chasseguet-Smirgel illustrates her point of view by means of a clinical vignette of creative inhibition. The patient whom she describes complains of vagueness, fluidity, and fogginess in her thoughts and in her body experience. At the same time the patient dreams of men who are mutilated and cut in pieces at the bottom of a cave. In the following part of the dream she obtains her doctorate. She is always depressed during examination periods, but in contrast to this inhibition, she learns Hebrew with an amazing facility. Her father made considerable sacrifices for her studies. The patient, who is not Jewish, considers Hebrew to be the language of unhappy people and during examination periods she pretended that her degree did not interest her and that only Hebrew mattered. (I have been able to confirm this tendency by many observations. In one, a patient, who is the child of survivors of the Holocaust, read about the war during college examination periods. In another, a woman wrote her doctoral thesis with a knitting in her lap.) In Chasseguet-Smirgel's case, the inhibition is linked directly to the dream and the attack on the father, his penis, in order to introject it anally (the mutilated parts in the grotto). The inhibition concerns the seizing of the words and allowing their penetration.

Such a deficiency is also described in Chasseguet-Smirgel's study centered on anality and the anal component in the body experience (1962). Chasseguet-Smirgel demonstrates how each time the subject's integrity is too closely linked with damage to the object, it is experienced as if it could only be obtained at the object's expense. In the clinical example, the study of Hebrew is considered a reparation of the object; the secondary creative activity attenuates the feared destruction of the object. It is an "alibi" creation that assuages guilt (1971, p. 94). The author says that authentic creativity aims at giving the individual the feeling of narcissistic completeness, which results in the representation of one's own phallic body. But creativity implies creating one's body and one's ego from material borrowed from the object which is integrated and introjected by the subject. The phallus of the father represents for both sexes the privileged object whose introjection is necessary to build both body and psychic ego. She suggests that among the causes for creative inhibition appear to be the guilt attached to this process if it is experienced as an act of aggression against the object.

The preceding statement contains some of the main points of Chasseguet-Smirgel's thinking. It focuses on the individual's fantasy world, which, when it contains more aggression than can be integrated, results in excessive guilt, denial by means of idealization and illusion, or inhibition in functioning. The point of departure is always the fantasies that are symbolic of sexual objects or part objects of instinctual drives or drive derivatives. In this sense her approach constitutes an enlargement of classical theory.

Perversion As a Way to Gain an Identity

When McDougall approached some of the same issues, she added to the study of the content of fantasies her interest in the function of fantasy. In many aspects her early work parallels but does not duplicate that of Chasseguet-Smirgel. In other respects the influence of Winnicott's attention to psychic space as well as the focus on the role of fantasy in mental economy stemming from the *psychosomaticiens* can be felt in her work. McDougall seems to be more consistently Kleinian in her formulations on the early relationship to the mother; therefore her notion of the separation from the object takes on a different coloring. She does not concentrate on the regression to the anal-sadistic phase. She is concerned with ego identity and the problems of defects in structure and the impact of disturbances in the mental life in cases of addiction, somatization, or acting out. Her work therefore provides an excellent bridge between those French theorists who remained with the classical psychoanalytic concerns and those who evolved a theory of developmental defect *à la française*.

One of the great virtues of McDougall's work for Americans is its accessibility. She bridges two cultures, and the ease with which she presents her often very touching clinical observations makes further comment superfluous. She does not need an interpreter, but she definitely deserves a place.

McDougall (1964, 1970 ed.) believes that the difference between neurosis and perversion is twofold. Firstly, perversion involves action, but neurosis involves only fantasy. Secondly, perversion involves reparation, whereas neurosis does not.

I think that there has been an evolution in McDougall's thinking and that her idea of reparation has evolved to the point where she thinks that it is not only, or possibly not even, the object who is being repaired in the sexual act but the subject himself or herself. She (1982) says that perversion involves a druglike sexuality used as much to flee from certain painful states and fill the gaps in one's sense of identity, as to gratify instinctual wishes. This attempt at self-cure has the advantage of permitting the subject erotic contact with himself and with others, while avoiding affective explosions that might lead to acts of destruction of self or others. If perverse sexuality serves the function of an addiction, its nonsexual aspect, comprising the staging of the enigma of desire and otherness, resembles a creative act. As long as reparation remains, albeit manic and illusory, perverse sexuality avoids a psychotic solution to some of the conflicts it resolves and does its duty: Eros triumphs over death. She adds that perversion protects against the return of aggression directed against the self and triumphs because of the erotization of this lethal drive. Her conclusion is that "perversions are only a manifestation of a condition in which depression, anxiety, inhibitions, and psychosomatic symptoms are mixed. . . . It is not a simple deviation but a complex organization that must respond to multiple demands, which endows it with a particular compulsivity" (1982, p. 210).

In one of her earliest studies, she observes that in perversion there is an anonymous spectator who must be deceived, whereas the partner's enjoyment validates the sexual game. This validation addresses itself less to castration anxiety, which is abundantly present, than to the denial of the differences between the sexes, which guarantees the identity of the player. The mother who supposedly possesses her father's penis guarantees the subject's identity. The father is the voyeur, the spectator, replacing the child who was the onlooker in the primal scene.

Such a patient once described the issue in the following way: he was having a fantasy of having intercourse with his wife under him, a position he never takes, and thought that anyone looking on could just imagine the scene flipped over upside down. This was a fleeting thought upon which he could not act because in his actions he still has to satisfy the spectator who only allows him to be a man on the condition that he assume the woman's place.

McDougall thinks that the sexuality of the pervert is compulsive because it expiates unbearable guilt and attempts to make castration exciting. In this, she considers it a manic defense against depression or persecutory anxiety. It is part of psychic stability based on an unconscious restructuring of the primal scene. It consists of an "external pursuit" of the father and attempts to repair by means of the interaction with an object a failure in symbolization. This failure is caused by the wish not to assign the proper place to the paternal phallus and to attribute the appropriate meaning to the primal scene. The individual who seeks pleasure in a perverted sexuality needs to believe that he has the better recipe for pleasure. In the case history there is always the moment of revelation of the secret for this particular sexual pleasure which, among other things, has to prove that castration does not hurt. Castration anxiety has to be mastered over and over in a compulsive acting out.

Whereas the lack of an internal representation of the father is a threat to identity, the magical sexual act gives the illusion of refinding the paternal phallus. This is what distinguishes perversion from psychosis. In order to distinguish perversion from neurosis, McDougall evokes the differentiation between disavowal and denial through fantasy. The neurotic builds his fantasy around the idea that "there is nothing there, but . . . ," with regard to the missing penis of the mother. The perverse solution implies an avowal followed by the "dis," that is, the destruction of meaning by cutting the associative chain. McDougall thinks that it conveys the violence hidden behind the challenge to reality better than denial, which suggests merely reshaping reality by means of fantasy. The pervert's perception of the empty sex of the mother as well as the meaning that should have become attached to it are examples of Bion's notion of representations that have been denuded of their meaning. This lack of significance leads to the devaluation of the paternal phallus that also loses its significance through this operation of disavowal.

The child can relieve his anxiety by creating a substitute fantasy in which the primal scene that signifies the parents' sexual desire for each other can lose its meaning. In this, the denial of the mother's vagina acts as the primary defense against the reality that is deemed unacceptable because it is narcissistically so injurious. According to McDougall, it invariably constitutes the defense that underlies the scenario of perversions, which attain their compulsive qualities from the need to replay the primal scene in such a way that it eliminates those parts that cause anxiety.

In perversion, the primary anxiety still concerns the absence of the object; therefore it has many aspects of psychosis. There is a hatred of reality fostered by an object who could not tolerate psychic pain; therefore the perverse subject tries to recover from outside his own psyche what he has lost inside by means of the illusion which he controls and limits. By attacking his own ego he protects his parents from his fantasized attacks. The reinvented primal scene, replayed indefinitely, a privileged form of the manic defense, is a creation that is preferable to madness. Anyone coming in contact with such cases can confirm the validity of those observations.

McDougall stresses the continuity of the issues of individual identity and sexual identity; thus bisexuality not only means that the other sex does not have to be recognized, it also can reach into the refusal to recognize the other in general. Separation is often called primary castration to mark it as the precursor of the fantasy of the separation from the penis because of oedipal fantasies. First there has to be individual identity before there can be sexual identity, otherwise sexuality will be used to repair a fault within the ego. McDougall thinks that development depends on the ability to maintain the split between the good and bad mother as postulated by Klein because it alone guarantees the internalization of the good breast. Without it oral avidity is too great and too threatening to the object.

In my introduction to McDougall's work, I said that she bridges various aspects of French psychoanalysis. Thus, in her article on the antianalysand she raises issues that lead her to study those conditions that lack a psychic dimension. She describes the person who enters analysis, adjusts, and makes no links to any kind of inner world, the past, or other nonfactual matters. In these cases, the links between past and present, idea and affect, and conscious and unconscious do not emerge from the patient's associations. The patients are like robots. She calls the relationship they form *a-transferential* and distinguishes this from the obsessional need to keep the analyst at a distance. They disavow otherness. They know rules but no laws. These patients are angry against certain groups or people, but their defensive system that denies otherness manages to keep them alive by keeping away pain. They share with the patients suffering from psychosomatic illnesses, described by Marty, deM'Uzan, and others, the tendency to use and manipulate reality to keep it unconnected with unconscious fantasies; but they differ from psychosomatic patients because the latter can die. They lack the libidinal investment in a body that is alive.

McDougall has studied extensively the various conditions

in which fantasy is lacking. In this respect she comes close to the French *psychosomaticiens* who are interested in the problem of a deficient rather than a conflicted internalization. She has found that even in sexuality there can be a shallow and manipulative behavior pattern that does not link up easily with an internal object world. But she has always retained the vantage point of the analytic setting and has always maintained a complete openness with regard to the issue of the degree of symbolization present in psychosomatic symptoms. In this respect, therefore, she differs from the group devoted to the study of psychosomatic phenomena to whom the next chapters will be devoted. McDougall remains within the classical analytic framework even when treating those conditions where fantasies seem almost impossible to elicit, partly because, unlike some of her colleagues, she has been struck by the meanings that can be attached to somatic symptoms that eventually yield to interpretation.

Because of the wide variety of body reactions to emotional situations, McDougall has attempted to define the place of the body in the various pathological conditions. She points out that classical psychoanalysis describes states in which there is mind-body unity, which means that the body and its various parts have received psychic representation. In conversion, certain body parts can be used to convey repressed ideas, but Freud also used the notion of actual neurosis to describe conditions in which the body suffers from a surplus of energies that have never attained psychic representation. These can make a person sick and place him on the side of *anti-life*, as McDougall calls it. The psychotic, on the other hand, does not inhabit his skin. He does not have his own limits and there is no internalized, coherent body image that corresponds to his sense of a physical existence.

McDougall's studies move easily from analysis of the conditions in which the absence of an emotional mental life causes the body to become ill as a response to stress or prompts actions that manipulate reality in order to eliminate stress to examination of the compulsive sexuality that has to confirm and affirm the existence of something that is missing within the symbolic universe of the person practicing it. She sheds doubt on whether perversion should be considered an aspect of the sexual instinct. She suggests rather that it is a triumph over sexuality in which the individual can manipulate his object world in order to confirm his existence in a way similar to that in which patients suffering from psychosomatic disorders, or those who are prone to act out, manipulate their environment in order to deaden their internal reality.

In all these cases, McDougall thinks that there is a fundamental gap in the internal psychic world, and in the case of perversion there is the search for the ideal phallus in the external world to take the place of the missing symbol of the father's penis and its role in the parents' sexuality. The fact is, according to McDougall, that the perverse act does not constitute denial by means of fantasy. Instead, it owes its success to disavowal by which it acts as a defense against an anxiety-arousing reality. This brings it closer to conditions of early ego pathology, but in this case the breach is repaired through the sexual act.

With her interest in character disorders, behavior disorders, and neosexuality, McDougall bridges two segments of the Paris Psychoanalytic Society. Her work, which focuses on sexual drives and reaches over into the unsexualized factual dialogue of "operational" thinking, frequently introduces the same concerns as are introduced by those who call themselves *psychosomaticiens*. In an article entitled "Psyche-soma and the Analytic Process" (1974b), she expresses some of Fain's theories in a more lucid fashion than he does himself, so that even though she has remained within the practice of classical analysis, her work reflects her awareness and interest in those conditions that will be the subject of the next chapter, that is, those in which the body reacts to stress while the mind remains unaffected.

Notes

[1]In a most enlightening 1966 article devoted to the subject of self-observation, reality, and the superego, Martin Stein demonstrates clearly and meticulously that self-observation is derived from parental evaluation leading to self-evaluation and from there ultimately to mature self-observation. His approach is clinical and developmental, whereas Chasseguet-Smirgel justifies her theory on the basis of Freud's writings.

In reality, Freud left its status unclear, and A. Reich (1954, 1973 ed.), one of the most lucid students of ego ideal pathology, equates narcissistic desire with an ego ideal. She refers to the regression "from the superego to primitive structures which I would prefer to call narcissistic 'ego ideals' "; she uses the plural to suggest that a person can have more than one ideal. Her statement that "frequently, the ideals show bluntly unsublimated sexual features" (pp. 228–229) demonstrates that the status of the ego ideal as a structure is not assured.

[2]Regarding the "not I," Fain, whose work will be discussed in a later chapter, suggests that it might be better to consider it as not organized at the beginning of life rather than bad, as Melanie Klein would have it. The "not I" is not included in the primitive ego organization, therefore disorganized or not egotized.

[3]Recently (1987) Chasseguet-Smirgel has written about the "perverse conduct" of a female patient. In this case, she thinks that the patient's attempt at a perverse solution ended in failure, because of her, and perhaps all women's, inability to idealize the fecal stick.

PART III

A HEALTHY MIND IN A HEALTHY BODY

11

The Psychosomaticiens

Psychosomaticiens is the name given to a group of analysts who work in a general medical setting or in clinics uniquely devoted to the treatment of psychosomatic problems, including the treatment of cancer patients by means of psychotherapy. When these analysts function in the hospital, they are far removed from the traditional consulting room, which most of them maintain alongside their hospital activities. They are convinced that their psychoanalytic training is essential for the work they do, although, as we shall see, it is not psychoanalysis in the strictest sense. It is an application of the knowledge acquired in one setting to a field that has traditionally been the domain of the general physician or surgeon, and in most cases it still is.

The question as to the degree to which the findings of psychoanalysis are applicable to the interpretation of phenomena beyond the couch is as alive in France as elsewhere. The popularity psychoanalysis has recently enjoyed in France and the widening audiences it continues to reach have accentuated concerns about the appropriateness of its application outside the consulting room, but this does not prevent many respected, analytically trained professionals from using their knowledge and writing about it.

Racamier (1973, 1979) has described his work in psychiatric hospitals, thus enlarging the scope of the application of psychoanalytic knowledge. Laplanche has examined the role of analysts within a university and has defended it by suggesting that traditional psychoanalytic settings run the risk of seeming to be secret societies. He wrote a multivolume work encompassing his lectures on the fundamentals of psychoanalysis, thereby bringing psychoanalysis into the academic world and making it accessible to those not initiated by their own experience on the couch. In this way psychoanalytic texts become documents pertaining to the general cultural heritage. Anzieu and his group of collaborators have made extensive studies of the dynamics of groups, drawing inferences based on interpretations of unconscious processes. These are some of the ways in which French analysts have taken their knowledge beyond the consulting room and applied it.

Psychoanalysts in General Hospitals

It has been a little different for the group of analysts who have used their training as classical analysts to understand psychosomatic illnesses. Working in general hospitals as consultants for the treatment of psychosomatic disorders, they underwent a more radical development. Not only have they applied what they have learned during their training as analysts, but they have found it necessary to reformulate some basic tenets and to enlarge psychoanalytic theory itself in order to account for their findings. Their work has had a determining effect on a sizable number of French analysts, including those who are not directly engaged in the treatment of psychosomatic patients.

Continuous reference to these analysts as a group requires

some explanation. Michel Fain, one of their main theorists, thinks that it is wrong to suggest the existence of a psychosomatic school of the Paris Psychoanalytic Society. The name by which they are commonly referred to applies to a group whose friendship ties are much more important than a communality of views. Nevertheless, it is certain that the group started by focusing on the economic aspects of problems emanating from the psychosomatic patients. Some members of the group, such as Pierre Marty, have never strayed far from this central concern, and he has written extensively both on the general question and on specific illnesses. When he turned to theory, which he did less often than Fain, he focused on the topographic division of the mind. Fain's approach is genetic, with an emphasis on regulatory principles. Others, like Braunschweig, David, de M'Uzan, and McDougall and Green to a smaller extent, have been stimulated to examine various aspects of the mind-body problem.

Similar issues have been examined by Laplanche, who is not in any way affiliated with this group. He did so in the context of his peculiar reworking of Freud's writings. He found it useful to return to concepts such as the instinct of self-preservation, narcissism, and erotism in his own academic way. Returning to the relevance of the instinct of self-preservation, he tackled the problem of the detachment of the sexual drive from the instinct of self-preservation and the problem of the nature of the sexual object as distinct from the need-gratifying object. These problems also play an important part in the studies made by the *psychosomaticiens* for the understanding of the mind–body issue. Laplanche's work is strictly parallel to rather than a part of that of the *psychosomaticiens.* His interest was prompted by the need to reconcile that which appealed to him because of his leanings toward Lacan with the classical theory concerning the role of the body that was lost when language assumed an all-important place in Lacan's theory.

Despite the wealth of their contributions, the provincialism of the *psychosomaticiens* is also spectacular. They do not quote Laplanche, and no one refers to Schur's concept of resomatization, even though this is the focus of their interest. This fact illustrates the separation that exists between the two major organizations. They tend to keep themselves uninvolved with each other's work. Furthermore they tend to use the concept of the death instinct as if there were no problem with it, mostly unself-consciously, and as if it were not in need of definition: in short, they see the death instinct as that which causes death and that which reigns when the life instinct is exhausted.[1]

The degree to which psychoanalytically trained physicians are practicing in general hospitals seems to be unusually high in France as compared to other countries. They are available for consultation in cases where the etiology of the medical condition is deemed to be psychogenic. Patients suffering from cancer are sometimes referred to them in order to ameliorate the condition and to prolong life, and the treatment that is instituted is aimed at the cause rather than at the symptom. A study done in 1983 by the Laboratoire d'économie sociale de Paris compared the estimated cost of the patient had he not been treated by the hospital with the actual cost including the psychotherapy and found that it was economically sound to reimburse the fee for psychotherapy because it brought about savings in other medical costs. This, it seems to me, is a strong endorsement of the work of the *psychosomaticiens*.

In a 1984 article bearing the descriptive title "Survey of Psychosomatics in the Light of Symptoms or on the Passage from the Sick Body to the Erogenous One," Régine Herzberg-Poloniecka describes analysts' activities within a general hospital. They are concerned with patients who have exhausted the resources of the medical profession. It is true that a consultation with a psychoanalytically trained professional is an innovation much to be applauded, but the author stresses the resistance, which is always great and causes extreme delays in instituting such consultations. Because of this resistance, the *psychosomati-*

cien treating hospitalized cases is often confronted with extremely grave situations. The physicians are called to the bedsides of persons hooked up to tubes and often on the verge of death. The situation described by Herzberg-Poloniecka is therefore so far removed from the leisure of the analytic office that comparisons cannot be made. As a result, the nature of the intervention is also quite different, considering the state of urgency that exists.

According to Herzberg-Poloniecka, the effect sometimes borders on the miraculous. Contact with a psychoanalytically trained physician can and does save some of these patients by nonmedical means, whereas sophisticated modern medicine has failed, and the patient is considered lost.

"The [physical] symptom plays a revealing part, like a magnifying glass in its role of apprehending mental functioning," says Herzberg-Poloniecka (1984, p. 89). The symptoms have no meaning, and patients cannot be compared to their symptoms, except for the fact that the mental functioning of these patients has certain underdeveloped qualities, unrelated to intelligence or general sensitivity. The symptoms often create a sense of urgency, which has been described in reference to anorexia but which also involves patients suffering from Crohn's disease, hemorrhagic colitis, diabetic coma, and other ailments. At their bedsides there is no leisure time for theorizing since patients must be helped to summon their powers of self-preservation immediately. Patients are approached basically by means of the physician's interest in attempting to arouse their interest in themselves and in the possibility of recovery.

Herzberg-Poloniecka has often commented on the apparent lack of concern these patients have for the severity of their condition. She thinks that this must have been preceded by an insufficiency of the mother that now manifests itself in an insufficiency of anxiety in view of the danger to their own lives. These patients neither ask for help nor do they complain. Frequently, they do not refer to their symptoms of their own accord and have to be led to it by the interest of the visiting helper. This reluctance is paralleled by that of the referring physician who views with understandable ambivalence a patient who puts into question his whole medical education. Therefore, he may appeal to the *psychosomaticien* only as a last resort, which accounts for the gravity of the condition which the *psychosomaticien* often meets.

Some patients are seen at outpatient clinics either because they are ambulatory or because they are in hospitals where there are no facilities to treat psychogenic disorders, in which case they are sometimes brought to the clinics by ambulance. Describing contacts with these patients, Marty, de M'Uzan, and David (1963) write:

> The investigator cannot stop being struck by how little interest in relating is aroused in the patient by the contact and by the very unmodulated character in which he, the investigator is being apprehended. The patient tends to react mechanically, without waiting for anything but the play between stimulus and response. Unconsciously the patient wishes to reduce the object to the level of his somatic reaction. One could say that he is absorbed by an internal somatic object, but it is distinguished from the internal object of the neurotic in that it does not have an identifiable sense, resists interpretation, and lends itself poorly or not at all to a mental elaboration either in fantasy or through an intellectual effort. The orientation is practical, operational, and does not correspond to an effective libidinal investment. There is an absence of a relationship to an internal living object; instead, there is a blank: the subject is present but empty. There is a lack of introjection. [pp. 11–12]

At first these patients are approached in a very simple fashion that does not pretend to be a psychotherapeutic interview. This is due to the fact that the initial meeting often takes place in the rooms of hospitalized patients and also due to the patients' lack of awareness of psychic processes and feelings. The task of making contact with whatever interests the patient the most, even if it is the weather, is of utmost concern since the contact itself is more important at first than the issue around which that contact is made. Nevertheless, Herzberg-Poloniecka stresses that psychoanalytic training is indispensable for this work since the nuances of relatedness have to be assessed properly, and sensitivity for what is missing in the dialogue is as crucial as the listening process itself.

The patient may not be interested in any kind of activity, yet this activity must sometimes be speedily brought about and, according to Herzberg-Poloniecka, it cannot be random. It must aim at identifying the traumatic causes underlying the present condition and opening the way for them to be talked about. In order to achieve this, the patient needs considerably more response from the analyst than would be provided in conventional interviews, both because of the nature of the patient and the gravity of the situation.

In the actual treatment of the patient, the physician is alert to the slightest weakening of mental functioning, to the least looseness of associations, to the slightest recourse to facts, to the smallest loss of interest in himself, or on the contrary, to a great excitement that does not abate in reaction to every external stimulus. Each could signal the oncoming of a relapse. The therapist must immediately attempt to bring to the patient's mind the cause, such as a trauma, to which only the slightest allusion has been made, but which has not been sufficiently recalled and verbalized. At times, the close cooperation with other treating physicians is required. The detachment from the patient's life that is usually appropriate for analysts cannot be maintained. Here the analyst is a member of a treatment team, and the patient at first responds to this pool of treating individuals as an amorphous entity in which the components are assimilated to each other.

Despite the lack of insight or interpretations, the condition improves when this relationship has been established. It is fragile and always prone to relapses, but it is apparently the beginning of what can eventuate in a full recovery.

This role of miracle worker gives Herzberg-Poloniecka cause for reflection, for it colors the relationship of the doctor to the patient, to his colleagues, and ultimately to himself. It creates countertransference problems of which she is acutely aware, and the possibility of improving the technique leads her to further reflection. She asks: since when have psychoanalysts been in the business of actually saving lives?

Herzberg-Poloniecka tends to maintain a questioning attitude and points to the countertransference danger causing the physician to remain stuck in his attitude to the patient and to not to respond adequately to the moment when the patient is ready to move from concerns of self-preservation to the area of pleasure and the psychosexual drives.

Lastly, she questions the relationship between pain and lesions, and she asks, what does it mean that a severely ill patient does not complain of pain, whereas that same patient later finds her menstrual cramps so uncomfortable? Is it the difference in pain or the difference in the stage of development within the patient?

Herzberg-Poloniecka thinks that in order to assess the problem in the detail that it deserves, the generations preceding the patient would have to be studied, with the possible hypothesis of a memory within the somatic system.

The Dynamics of Psychosomatic Illness

Their ability to help physically ill patients by means of a new relationship has been described with many clinical examples in *L'Investigation Psychosomatique* (Marty, de M'Uzan, and David 1963). It has led many of these analysts to review the basic tenets of psychoanalysis and to return to its beginning when it was itself so closely linked to the treatment of physical symptoms.

Within the history of psychoanalytic ideas, the interest of the early psychoanalysts in mental phenomena began to supersede interest in physical symptomatology as soon as the symptoms were found to be bodily expressions of repressed mental conflicts. Conversion symptoms were understood as pathogenic fantasies using the body as a vehicle, whereas the realm of the actual neuroses, that is, the field in which the symptom lacks a symbolic value, was divorced from the mainstream of psychoanalytic endeavor and left virtually neglected. "Early on and thereafter the development of psychoanalytic thought was more enlightening for its discoveries of continuities among manifestly different phenomena than for its accounts of their differences" (Kaplan 1984, p. 298). The evolution of the theory depended on the elucidation of those disturbances in which verbal development was assured and in which conflicts were expressed symbolically by means of words, actions, or identifiable conversion symptoms.

The interrelationship between the realm of the physical and the psychological, which preoccupied Freud only briefly at the beginning of his career, has been taken up by the *psychosomaticiens* at great length and constitutes in effect their attempt to broaden and enlarge psychoanalytic theory. Marty and de M'Uzan (1963) suggest, "Fundamentally, and for the first time, psychosomatic medicine, by rejecting the most important aspects of the responsibility of external factors, postulates that the individual himself is capable of destroying his body" (p. 355). In other words, the cause of the illness is related to the personality of the patient, but does not symbolize it. Marty is convinced that it stems from those conditions in which there is a deficit in mental development or, perhaps more accurately, where the mental development is split off from the emotional affective underpinnings and therefore cannot serve as a vehicle for the discharge of tensions originating in the organism. In a recent personal communication, he says that he now thinks less of a psychosomatic personality type than of one with faults within the personality that lead to physical disorganization or malfunctioning.

The question as to how the body attains mental representation has led the *psychosomaticiens* to conduct repeated observations on adults and children. They have reached the general conclusion that the quality of mental life is related to physical health and that those patients who suffer from somatic reactions to stress tend also to reveal a particular thought pathology. Apparently, they are in the process of evolving their theories, and their conviction that there are psychosomatic personality types has been replaced by the idea that the psychosomatic symptom connotes a certain mode of functioning that does not necessarily encompass the total personality but constitutes a fault within an otherwise neurotic or normal personality. Herzberg-Poloniecka recently described a case in which severe, life-threatening psychosomatic symptoms were found along with what she calls *islets of neurosis*. Thus their thinking increasingly concerns what Schur has called *resomatization*, but to my knowledge, they do not use this term nor is there any similarity to Schur's explanatory model. Their interest led to theories on the function of the preconscious and economic factors involved in its mediating role; the structure of the unconscious, sleep, and its implications of object dependency; and the structuralization of fantasy. As usual, the French were ambitious in the scope of questions they attempted to answer.

Concerning psychosomatic conditions Green (1970) says that "the body takes part in the conversation" (p. 1041). This does not play the same role as that played by the drive, since the drive is the measure of the work of the psychic system as a result of its link with the body. The drive is, in itself, work already effected on the body. The more its psychic representatives reflect this work, the more language can come to terms with them. Language can only work on material that has previously been articulated and is therefore powerless when a structure establishing a link between the body and language has not been built; that is the case, according to the *psychosomaticiens*, in persons who react with disease to psychic stress.

These considerations have led to a renewed interest in some of Freud's earliest work on dreaming; the differentiation between dreams as to their function of giving pleasure; and the role of words in the maintenance of the secondary process, which formerly had been linked unquestioningly to maturity. With attention to words that are compatible with external reality but are detached from a thing representation in the unconscious, these theorists reexamined the role of secondary process in a light that challenges its one-to-one relationship to the quality of psychic functioning. They have removed the automatic stamp of approval that tends to be attached to the secondary process, and they have studied dreams that do not serve the pleasure principle adequately. Keeping the history of French psychoanalysis in mind, one might say that they found a new and better way than their artistic predecessors for questioning the role of rationality.

Fain (1962) in his own inimitable way, says that when the secondary process is imposed at all cost, it is a function that has become an object, the object being the subject in action. In his own words, "the individual becomes the instrument, the penis, of the other" (p. 375).

Contrary to the tendency of some French analysts who push subtlety to the point of obtuseness, Marty's approach is very direct, clear, and highly systematized in a manner that originated with him.

For him, the central issue is, and has been for many years, the study of factors leading to resomatization. But whereas Schur, Cremerius, and McDougall studied this phenomenon as part of the total picture of regressions, Marty stresses the premorbid character structure of patients undergoing psychosomatic disorganization, thereby placing the patients themselves in a group apart. (It must be added that this is how his early work reads; now he might not stress the total personality involvement as much as he did previously, but he has not otherwise changed his approach.) Marty has remained close to clinical issues and observations and has made repeated attempts to differentiate between those character structures that allow a regression on the mental level (*névroses mentales* [mental neuroses] as he calls them) and those that lack the capacity to absorb the shock of trauma and therefore react with somatic illness to stress.

Marty (1980) is convinced that the study of the disorganizations leading to psychosomatic illness adds a dimension to Freud's discoveries. He emphasizes structure, which he calls organization, but he uses the language of drive theory and topography. He omits the structural hypothesis of id, ego, and superego from consideration except for a brief reference, suggesting that he thinks of it as the result of a development later than the articulation between conscious, unconscious, and preconscious.

He links the concepts of organization and disorganization within the mental apparatus to quantitative factors and to the idea of the life and death forces at work within the organism. Again, taking as a point of departure the theory that Eros, the life force, binds, he considers the disorganization leading to psychosomatic illness evidence of insufficient libidinization or organization. Thus, the death instinct is allowed full scope within the organism and, in a sense, threatens the integrity of the physical being. He thinks that the life instinct stems from the first organized movements of matter whereas the death instinct comes from the *inorganization* that preceded life. Accordingly, he advocates that psychosomatic medicine not use the term *pathology* because pathology involves levels of organization that he considers the work of Eros, or the life force. He believes that it is helpful for the understanding of physical illness to think in terms of the exhaustion of life forces either through aging or through the disorganization that loosens ties. Therefore, he differentiates between disorganization and repression since the latter always presupposes an anterior stage to which the individual is returning, whereas in disorganization the life instinct is overcome by the disorganization of the death instinct.

Marty's (1968) developmental diagnostic scheme has received wide recognition in France, especially the concept of an *essential depression* which together with the *vie opératoire* (operational life) is the precursor of the breakdown. Essential depression "presents the picture of a crisis without a sound, which precedes often the assumption of an operational life, constituting a truly chronic depression into which it dissolves" (p. 596). Marty (1980) says, "The essential depression that regularly accompanies the *pensée opératoire* conveys the lowering of the tonus of the life instinct at the level of mental functions" (p. 59).

The *psychosomaticiens* postulate that these precarious types of organizations permit a certain normality that is insufficiently libidinized and therefore cannot prevent greater disorganization as a response to trauma. "The psychic apparatus (in these cases) is seemingly prisoner of a massive counterinvestment that has lost its individual qualities in favor of common social characteristics. We can establish that there no longer exists an ego ideal that intervenes, but an ideal self of primitive omnipotence. Detached from the supports of its personal basis, the subject becomes legalized" (Marty 1980, p. 23). The legalization that rules these patients, according to Marty, is a set of regulations they do not view within the context of rich social symbolism but from the reduced perspective of a meager fetishism of law. Here the author distinguishes the ideal self that comes from an infantile narcissism and that has gone through a primary identification with the omnipotent mother from the ego ideal he considers a secondary formation. Between the two there are complicated intermediary zones that are important for psychosomatic medicine. Marty considers it necessary to discriminate between the two since an inflated idea of narcissistic omnipotence can hide behind the ego ideal pertaining to the father. He thinks that the ego ideal can hide the ideal self which is insatiable and lethal, probably what Annie Reich calls the archaic ego ideal.

Marty stresses that neurosis and psychosis resemble each other in a certain sense more than either resembles the disorganization leading to physiological breakdown. Neurosis and psychosis are mental disorders and therefore the psychotic, who breaks with external reality in order to perceive his internal world in a distorted manner outside himself, is closer to the object world of his past than the reality-adaptive person leading an operational life. The latter does not give evidence of any opposing internal world meeting the external one. This type of patient experiences everything through the deadening of the inner world and comes closer to the object loss usually attributed to psychotics. Marty points out that in psychosis contact with outside objects is lost, but contact with the inner world is retained. In the cases he is studying, however, the concept of inner loss is applicable. He contrasts regression with disorganization, showing that whereas mental neuroses lead to regression in analysis, character neuroses can easily result in disorganization, that is, resomatization. Therefore, inasmuch as essential depression can slowly lead to death, it resembles the anaclitic depression described by Spitz and Wolf (1946). Furthermore, the absence of preconscious content behind the observed adaptive reactions as well as the role of the ideal self contribute to the clinical picture of the psychosomatic personality.

Marty has pointed to the brittle nature of the secondary process in the absence of a well-functioning preconscious. Cournut (1975) called Marty's work a veritable rehabilitation of the preconscious, whose role of bringing to the conscious mind derivatives of the unconscious capable of working on the influx of excitations stemming from the external world has recently been neglected. But even before Marty's "rehabilitation" of the preconscious, it was studied mainly in its function of taming the force of the derivatives of the unconscious rather than as the source of energy that can bind the impact of the environment.

Marty's work demonstrates the usefulness of the preconscious as a theoretical tool for understanding the layer within the mind that optimally permits enough derivatives of libido to enter the conscious to nourish it and allow it to better protect itself against traumatization. Sufficient but not excessive libidinization of thinking acts like a cushion that absorbs the impact of stress. Marty and de M'Uzan (1963) say, "In obsessional thinking, words are overinvested; in operational thinking they are underinvested: they cover exactly the thing or the action, abolishing, so to say, the distance between the signifier and the signified (p. 353). The relationship to temporality is quite different because the obsessional regards thinking as a way of detracting from action in order to evolve infinitely during a time whose limits are very imprecise; however the subject who thinks operationally is locked into a limited time span, determined by the notion of succession. The sense of timelessness that the unconscious provides is missing in those personalities in which communication between systems is missing.

McDougall (1982) remarks that the body of the patient suffering from a psychosomatic ailment is represented as an external object that lies outside the psyche. This observation supports Herzberg-Poloniecka's finding that these patients show little or no concern for the suffering of their body, which is placed at varying degrees of distance from the self. The lack of elaboration of a body ego is accompanied by a similar paucity with regard to the object world.

Marty calls the mechanism at work *projective reduplication*, by which he means that the person tends to react to the world as if it consisted of individuals who are duplicates of each other. These patients experience the object world with a minimum of mental elaboration. They deny their own originality and that of others in an attempt to obliterate strangeness and difference.

Projective reduplication is an attempt by the subjects to recognize themselves in others.

Marty and de M'Uzan (1963) point out that the object world of patients who think operationally has a specific quality. It cannot be absent, because sensory stimulation is important for these individuals, but the object cannot assume the dimensions of a complex personality, because operational thinking is incapable of processing a multiplicity of qualities. Thus it is difficult for these patients to report their own histories and require continuous solicitation from the listener. Their account is generally restricted to barren facts that emerge as the response to the questions posed by the interviewer. It is devoid of spontaneous elaborations and does not suggest the presence of an inner fantasy object.

This view leads the *psychosomaticiens* to recommend that the therapist not try to establish his own individuality by going beyond what the patient brings to him. The patient's ability to respond to differences may be too limited because of the faulty mediation by the preconscious in response to outer reality. The personalities that are described remain excessively stimulus dependent in their responses. Thus the pathology resides in the mediation or its lack. This does not preclude the occurrence of impulsive acts such as inviting death without there being a fantasy to sustain it, but these are manifestations of the unconscious for which the preconscious does not provide a bridge during the operational life. The functional aspects of activities, including those leading to instinct gratification, can take place, but they are without pleasure or conflict.

McDougall (1978) thinks that the idea behind 'operational thinking' can be enlarged to encompass certain types of impulsive behavior linked to addiction and the search for screen experiences. She has named certain practices *sexualité opératoire* (operational sexuality) because they are geared to manipulations and devoid of fantasy.

Prompted by the observation that the unconscious is not

absent in the reactions of patients leading an operational life, that the issue instead resides in the fact that it is not mediated by preconscious representations while maintaining the capacity to respond to excitations, Marty has attempted to explain the irruptions of the unconscious in patients leading an operational life by presupposing both the failure of the mediating function of the preconscious and the existence of structure in the unconscious. The structure is assumed to be phylogenetic; therefore it is not subject to the vicissitudes of individual development. Marty suggests that it might be helpful to think of a "principle of sensitivity to excitations" that precedes the instinctual principle in the unconscious. Thus, in disorganizations such as the operational life, the principle of response to excitations subsists, whereas the instinctual responses might be disturbed. "The clinically established rupture between mental organization, behavior organization, and somatic organization on the one hand, and the unconscious on the other, would only pertain to a layer of the unconscious that is acquired later in development than the layer of the unconscious that regulates functioning" (Marty 1980, p. 104). Automation, reiteration, and the principle of repetition can maintain functions, even if only in a relatively stagnant way, whereas the principle of programmation, which is established later, could be thought of as opening the road to different linkages, functional associations, hierarchization, sexualization, in other words, to the development of organization and reorganization. The principle of programmation introduces the dimensions of the future, whereas the more primitive principle constitutes repetitive function. In this connection Marty cites David, who refers to an innovative impulse as opposed to the repetition compulsion. Both concern the life instinct, but clearly one constitutes a higher level of complexity. Conceived in this way, the unconscious would consist of a level that corresponds to the existence of wishes of various degrees of complexity plus a more primitive level that parallels need gratification of the simplest and most elementary kind.

These are challenging and interesting concepts, and they reveal the extent to which those who have studied resomatization have been stimulated to rethink some basic psychoanalytic tenets in a different way. By placing the onus on the structure of the unconscious rather than on the level of ego development, Marty creates his own version of developmental arrest. By thinking that the ego's lack of supplies stems partly from a layering of the unconscious that antedates ego formation, Marty accounts for the brittle and delibidinized nature of the ego by referring to factors outside its organization. The psychosomatic ego, that is, the ego that is organized from a superficially adaptive point of view without being resilient to stress, breaks without being able to shield the soma from excitations. This view contrasts with that of Schur (1955), who interpreted resomatization (in the context of analysis) as an ego regression.

The Wish to Survive and the Striving for Pleasure

Fain and Marty (1965) link the failure of the "narcissistic psychosomatic investment" to a narcissistic undoing due to the insufficiency of the early environment. They stress the reality-adaptive nature of the ego and superego of psychosomatic patients, structures that are defective because they have been deformed. This deformation results in the anti-instinctual and death-dealing agencies responsible for the serious disturbances that manifest themselves in their clinical practice. The assertions of the *psychosomaticiens* are reminiscent of Grunberger's statement concerning the fact that a well-organized ego devoid of narcissistic cathexis is not a healthy one.[2]

Fain distinguishes between those discharge processes that are motivated by the search for pleasure and involve delay of gratification, as well as the pleasurable building up of tension, and those that seek only to relieve unpleasure and aim at exhaustion. Most fundamentally, he tries to examine in this way the underpinnings of the sick body as against the erotic one. In other words, Fain, sometimes in collaboration with

Braunschweig, tries to distinguish qualitatively between various aspects of what Freud called the pleasure principle: the wish to discharge tension, the wish to avoid unpleasure, and the wish to obtain the maximum degree of enjoyment by means of building up tension that is then subsequently released.

Fain (1962) attempts to account for the dearth of libidinal investment in psychosomatic conditions by suggesting that the pleasure principle can be the origin of the need for discharge only when the discharge takes place in an eroticized manner and does not lead to depressive manifestations. When an individual feels fundamentally poor because of the lack of narcissistic supplies, "every discharge manifestation becomes a hemorrhage and an object loss" (p. 375). Fain is referring to a vicissitude of the libido to which Freud did not address himself: exhaustion. It is a fate different from repression, regression, or discharge through sexually appropriate or inappropriate means. Libidinal exhaustion in infants requires modification of the dual instinct theory on which Fain bases so many of his assumptions, in that the discharge seems to have ascendancy over the binding and can only be stemmed by what Fain calls the censorship derived from the influx of maternal libido derived from the mother's maternal narcissism. He thinks that at first the mother provides the libido that stems the outflow. This is compatible with the idea that organ pleasure may after all not be innate and that proper autoerotism itself is dependent on good mothering. The revision of the theory leads to a recognition that Eros and libido are not synonymous.

There is undoubtedly no one theory that completely satisfies, and this one falls short in that it does not take into account the postulate of an innate force binding excitations and working against discharge. Freud's original idea of the primary process that aims at immediate discharge never questioned the channel through which the energy flowed. He assumed that the organism would not be threatened in its very structure by the loss of libidinal energy and that discharge of tension leads to the satisfaction of sleep, which is replenishing. Fain's theory questions this assumption because he was struck by psychosomatic disturbances in infancy that challenged the notion of an innate reservoir of libido that binds energy to the organism and therefore provides a biological shield against illness.

Fain (1971) states that "there exists for everyone a threshold beyond which, despite all our efforts of representation and verbalization, our flesh is endangered. . . . When the world is nothing but exaggerated stimulation, no erotism can develop, only soothing inducement" (p. 333). Therefore, his frequent collaboration with the *psychosomaticiens* has opened for him the possibility of a wider application of their findings, but I am not aware that he ever published any account of the other fields to which his theory applies.

Being acquainted with studies of the pathology encountered in former concentration camp victims, I find a striking correspondence between descriptions of some survivor syndromes and the lack of structurization favoring psychosomatic reactions to stress. Krystal (1978) describes the need for quiescence noted in those who have survived the extreme trauma of incarceration plus the loss of their world and their loved ones, and he attempts to clarify its connections to other known syndromes. He notes that Stern (1951) called the freezing, immobile, inhibitory response the "catatonoid reaction" and pointed out that its cognitive and expressive form may be considered a primal depression. This demonstrates the similarity between descriptions by Americans studying the reaction of survivors of World War II and references by Marty and Bergeret to essential depression, including the similarity of terminology.

The state described by Krystal entails cognitive restriction and progressive blocking of mental functions such as memory, imagination, associations, and problem solving as well as the tendency to deanimate the animate and to create a monotonous round of unnecessary duplicates (reminiscent of Marty's projective reduplication). Krystal also estimates that this regression accounts for the high incidence of psychosomatic disorders, disturbance of affectivity, and regression in the capacity of survivors to verbalize. The patients cannot identify feelings or use them as signals, since their emotions are undifferentiated. Similarly the author alludes to the general impairment in fantasy life and the preoccupation with mundane details of the external environment, which, as he says, Marty and de M'Uzan (1963) have termed operational thinking. Krystal considers this condition descriptive of the shallow adaptiveness of some concentration camp survivors who manage to reestablish contact with everyday affairs by suppressing and abolishing the past without integrating it emotionally. Therefore, the adjustment is fragile and subject to periodic disintegration.

Krystal (1981) says that survivors who had problems integrating the trauma they lived through tended to fall into the categories of those who were impaired in (1) affect tolerance, (2) capacity for self-care, (3) hedonic capacity, and (4) affective functioning. He uses the diagnostic term *alexithymia*, which involves a regression in affects (dedifferentiation, deverbalization, and resomatization), so that affects are much less suitable as signals.

In the face of the enormity of the trauma of the concentration camp experience, some of the survivors had to leave the past unrepresented in consciousness and to attempt to live in the present on a level that is relatively shallow and reality adaptive, aiming more at manipulating life to survive than at reacting affectively to it. When indeed the affect breaks through, it is in a manner that is disorganizing and traumatic, and when the affect can be held in check, reactions to stress may evoke resomatization. Kestenberg points out in a recent private communication that survivors are often unable to evolve wishes. She thinks that they tend to stay closer to need gratification tied to issues of survival than to instinctual gratification leading to pleasure. Very often, they curtail fantasies, and they link gratification to deprivation and compensation for it, rather than to wishes that are the personal property of an individual and his private history.

The similarity between the description of psychosomatic

patients and that of survivors of the concentration camps shows the validity of a return to Freud's earlier formulations that encompassed pathology not caused by the sexualization of secondary process functioning. The examples of the traumatized survivors and the patients suffering from psychosomatic illness validate the necessity for some reformulation based on self-preservation. It is clear once more that if a trauma has a sufficient degree of intensity, it can have the same effect as a fault in the individual's development. The experience of being incarcerated under inhuman conditions can have an effect similar to that of being raised by a mother who showed inadequate response to her children's physical well-being. Marty and de M'Uzan (1963) suggest, however, that those who adopt this operational mode of thinking as a result of external circumstances demonstrate that they do not enjoy this way of living and eventually complain about it.

Implicitly, these studies constitute a return to an aspect of the actual neuroses identified and labeled by Freud, in which the symptom does not have a meaning but stems from the inability to represent a conflict psychically. McDougall (1978) points out that this deficit deprives the individual of the capacity to repress the conflict, and since the introjected object is missing, sensorimotor contact with the object world replaces the relationship with inner objects.

There are those who see a danger inherent in the fact that emphasizing operational thinking and life-styles might lead to finding it, whereas further probing might lead to the discovery of an active fantasy life. Herzberg-Poloniecka herself warned that the therapist must be sensitive to the moment when the patient is ready to move away from the sick body to an erogenous one. Even Marty now speaks of a disorganization within a personality organized along normal or neurotic lines.

Cremerius (1977), a German specialist in psychosomatic medicine, expressed his concern about the equation made by the *psychosomaticiens* between the type of functioning and the symptoms. In his view, the level of thinking they describe is typical for the lower socioeconomic milieu rather than for patients suffering from psychosomatic illnesses. He gives examples from his practice of interviews in which probing led to the uncovering of rich fantasies in patients referred for psychosomatic difficulties, and he juxtaposes these findings with some of the interviews published by Marty and his colleagues.

Cremerius and others (1979) concluded that the structure of the interview leads to some of the results that they obtain. Cremerius thinks that the passive wishes do not emerge in the interviews with the patients described by the *psychosomaticiens*, and therefore they interpret the patients' detachment as a fundamental disturbance rather than as a defense. Cremerius (1977) suggests that what they describe as the psychosomatic structure seems to stem from the pathology of pregenital disturbances or schizophrenic diseases and may also be a function of belonging to a lower social class. He recalls that Federn reported a case of the analysis of an asthmatic patient in the meetings of the Wednesday group and that it was suggested that the term fixation-hysteria be used for the organically preformed, abnormal, somatic reaction. Cremerius concludes that defense theory is adequate for explaining the phenomenon of resomatization.

In a personal communication to this author, he mentions that he does not oppose the study of deficient structurization within the personality as long as it is not connected as intimately to physical disorganization as the *psychosomaticiens* do. "I am not against alexithymy; it exists quite generally as a severe disturbance of the cognitive ego. I am only opposed to its being specific to all psychosomatic illnesses. I cannot view Freud, with his great sensitivity for emotional processes, as an alexithymic patient, which he would be, based on his many psychosomatic disturbances, in accordance with the assumptions of the French school" (translation from the German by the author). This disagreement parallels, at least to some degree, that which divides those espousing the conflict theory from those who stress developmental arrest.

It is not necessary to take a position in this controversy.

The *psychosomaticiens* themselves have recently taken the position that resomatization is frequently one aspect of a personality, therefore becoming less involved in the diagnosis of a total personality type. Regardless of the controversy, the diagnosis, categorization, and treatment of psychosomatic disorders are only one aspect of the work of the *psychosomaticiens*. They share with their other colleagues the French penchant toward theorizing, so they soon depart from the consulting room and question the underpinnings of psychoanalysis, reformulate the theory of sexuality and the role of the instinct of self-preservation in defense, and leave us with many challenging thoughts. Whether ultimately the psychodynamics they describe can be applied to the study of the survivor syndrome, normopathy (McDougall), faults within the personality, a totally new personality type, severe behavior disorders, or the dynamics of certain social milieus does not influence the importance of their contribution.

Notes

[1]Green, who stands at the periphery and is more aware of the wider picture, takes some pains to define the death instinct. He does not represent the norm of those using the concept. Green (1970) spells out what the *psychosomaticiens* imply: it is wrong to think of the death instinct in terms of anal sadism. Anal sadism is the consequence of the death instinct, not its expression. This implies that the primary work of the death instinct is dissociation and defusion. It is because the death instinct succeeds in defusing aggression from libido that aggression can result in this second expression of the death instinct, that is, the destruction of the fantasy object. Once the aggression is devoid of its libidinal component, it can express itself as the aggression that the ego psychologists have adopted as the second of the two instincts.

Fain suggests that the death instinct can produce a silencing action that erases memory traces. Therefore, forgetting does not necessarily stem from repression. He uses this conceptualization as if it were universally accepted and probably pushes Freud's formulations past his original intentions.

[2]Fain (1971), whose attacks on the existence of an autonomous ego were mentioned in Chapter 1, claims that the autonomous ego is precisely such a pathological ego because it is presumed to have been acquired through the neutralization of the lethal factor, leading to libidinal exhaustion. In his estimation, the vicissitudes through which a thing representation is linked to a word representation describes better than the structural theory the problems encountered with these patients and the lack of linkage between the two parts of the psychic system within their personality. Laplanche (1970, 1976 ed.), whose focus on the vicissitudes of psychoanalytic theory led him to suggest that the advent of the structural hypothesis threatened psychoanalysis in its essence, believes that the introduction of the death instinct to account for unbinding and discharge saved Freud's theory of sexuality but weakens the importance of the ego as an explanatory concept.

12

Life and Death in Psychoanalysis

The experiences with patients suffering from psychosomatic disorders led some French analysts to consider questions concerning life and death in psychoanalytic theory. With this topic as a goal, their intellectual ambitions reached new heights. Not content to effect the divorce decreed by Freud when he separated actual from psychoneurosis, hate from sadism, and then concentrated on the latter two because they dealt with the fate of the libido, they attempted to reintegrate and reabsorb into libido theory areas of the psyche that had been relegated to other explanatory models or disciplines.

Marty enlarged the concept of defense to include the immune system. In this way, the notion of defense is applied not only to the force that counters instinctual urges but also to that which counters somatic illness. His theory suggests that libidinized mental activity, especially affect, can be considered a defense against an attack on the physical organism as a result of stress. And from a different point of view, David and Laplanche, each in his own way, remind us that Freud conceived of the sexual instinct first as the perversion of the instinct of self-preservation. But foremost among those who worked on the enlargement of drive theory in order to bridge the gap between psychic and somatic phenomena is Michel Fain, who conceived of defenses as originating in the stimulus barrier and who traced their evolution from there.

A word is in order concerning the writings of this brilliant man. Frequently, he worked with a collaborator, yet when he wrote by himself he espoused the same ideas so that it is natural to attribute to him thoughts that may have originated with his collaborators, chief among whom is Denise Braunschweig. This may have led me to some inaccuracies that are unfair to Denise Braunschweig, who was generous with her time and enabled me to check my understanding of some of this material. The second source of inaccuracy may come from the material itself. Commenting on Fain's work, the Barandes (1975) say that the best texts in recent years owe more to the imagination, to inspired reveries that declare the inexhaustible character of the material, than to the methodological and theoretical rigor of an earlier period. They ask, "Could it be that psychoanalysis, after having acted upon the knowledge in its entirety and contributed to transforming the world in a way that is difficult to define, now undertakes a treatment of replenishment?" (p. 132)

In explaining their approach, Braunschweig and Fain (1975b) say that they feel free to "lend Freud latent thoughts that he is not here to challenge and that arise from our own associations of ideas." They consider themselves to be "more faithful in this way to the great living being that Freud was than by keeping a respectful and petrified distance from his brilliant thoughts frozen by death" (p. 11). Fain, with or without Braunschweig, has engaged in some fanciful writing which I have tried to convey through translation and interpretation. Because the nature of the texts makes reformulations mandatory, there may be inaccuracies in the interpretations, yet the only way to avoid this hazard would have been to omit some of the most stimulating and most original thoughts to emerge from Paris.

The Role of Fantasy in Maintaining a Healthy Body

Fain and Braunschweig's particular reassessment of the psychosexual phases was prompted in part by studies of psychosomatic reactions in adults and children. They also observed the shallow adaptive behavior and impulsive acting out of certain patients with character disorders whose ability to dream or to fantasize seemed to be almost nonexistent. Fain and the others influenced by the *psychosomaticiens* consider these conditions to be symptomatic of libidinal exhaustion, and in their explanations for this pathology they challenge the belief in an innate libidinal investment in the body or any of its parts because they think that the notion that the ego is primarily a body ego is predicated on a prior evolution. (There is undoubtedly a Lacanian influence in the theory that challenges the innate libidinal investment of the body.)

McDougall (1978), who has reflected on the difference in the investment of the body between various diagnostic groups, suggests that the patients under consideration have not invested their bodies with fantasies; on the contrary, they tend to treat the body as an object to be manipulated like an external thing. This is in contrast to "the neurotic [who] has acquired the right to experience his body as unified and his psychosoma as a unit at the cost of his sex as an instrument of pleasure and of the renunciation of the omnipotence of the wish. . . . The neurotic or normal subject has at his disposal an imaginary representation of his body as a body-container" (p. 204).

Fain attributes the pathology encountered and studied by the *psychosomaticiens* to the failure of the body to function as a container. Green suggests that fantasy acts as a container. The two notions come together in that they refer to libidinal investment in the body by means of (auto)erotic fantasies, which those analysts who have observed psychosomatic disturbances and anaclitic depression in infants are convinced cannot be taken for granted. The primary investment in the body, according to them, is not innate but subject to developmental vicissitudes.

To this way of thinking, fantasy attains a privileged position in explaining the libidinal investment in the body, more so than mental life in general because the latter encompasses the capacity to react adaptively and realistically to stimuli and therefore does not necessarily have the independence attributed to the ability to fantasize.[1] The *psychosomaticiens* think that fantasy underlies the development of the body's erotic potential, which they link to the binding of libido that in turn becomes an aspect of self-preservation: a fantasy in the face of stress is better than a sick body. It is a consideration based on the economic approach and on the notion that stress constitutes an excess of energy that cannot be represented adequately.

Of course, what they call fantasy here lies at the dawn of human consciousness and deals more with the constitution of instinct than with postoedipal fantasies. It is linked with later fantasies, partly because the same vocabulary is used. The supposition underlying this theory is that many of the precursors of fantasies are rendered unconscious through primary repression, but repressed fantasies become part of the psyche. Therefore censored and unconscious thoughts cannot be considered nonexistent. They must be sharply differentiated from the lack of mental content that comes from the persistent need to discharge excitations instead of retaining them. Repression maintains libido in the psyche, and this makes all the difference between it and that which has never been stored in any part of the mind. At its most extreme it is the difference between life and death from exhaustion.

Fain contrasts a reaction to excitement that involves fantasy formation leading to autoerotism with a reaction that involves recourse to the sensorimotor apparatus, and he stresses the beneficial aspects of the ability to retain and rework the excitement as against the need for immediate discharge. The recourse to immediate sensorimotor discharge or the search for sensorimotor stimulation prevents the beneficial containing of the libido. One of the preconditions for this capacity is the ability to decathect the sense organs as is done in sleep, and here Fain invokes the need for the faculty of censorship.

Fain's use of the term *censorship*, although typically never really defined, seems most in line with Freud's "opposing, inhibiting and restricting agency" (1933, p. 15) that is eventually linked to the superego. According to Laplanche and Pontalis (1967, 1973 ed.), "its effects are more clearly discernible when it is particularly relaxed, as it is in dreaming: the sleeping state prevents the contents of the unconscious from breaking through on to the level of motor activity" (p. 66). Thus, for Fain, censorship is the faculty that enables the individual to inhibit motor discharge, to decathect the sense organs, to suspend the search for stimulation that creates screen experiences, and to turn inward to sleep or fantasy. It is the prototype for the libidinized container that can retain tension instead of needing to eliminate it through motor release or the search for sensorimotor stimulation such as rocking.

Freud did not concern himself with the particular aspect of censorship that Fain finds so crucial because he believed that the libido investing organs innately guaranteed a retention of energy within the body. Since he considered organ pleasure innate, his theory of discharge according to the pleasure principle never dealt with the problem of libidinal exhaustion. Thus, his theory of libidinal development did not require the addition of an envelope to contain the libido and prevent it from flowing out in the process of discharge. Braunschweig and Fain treat this as a problem inherent in Freud's drive theory, but rather than discard it in favor of the structural hypothesis (from which they have maintained a critical distance) or reject drive theory as the Lacanians did because of their distaste for Freud's "biologism," they added to Freud's theory. These additions diverge from

Freud's tacit assumption about the innate character of the sexual drives and, as a consequence, treat the development that Freud traced in his *Three Essays on the Theory of Sexuality* (1905) as subject to a prior evolution.

The Development of the Capacity to Fantasize

This evolution is predicated on the evolution of the stimulus barrier into the faculty of censorship.[2] Fain does not go so far as to enlarge the concept of stimulus barrier into one that Freud specifically meant it not to be: a barrier working against internal stimuli; but he thinks of the libidinized stimulus barrier as the precursor of censorship. For this libidinization to happen, the stimulus barrier has to attain the capacity to screen out the external world without the help of what we have come to call screen experiences, that is, stimuli aimed at soothing and pacifying. It is around the stimulus barrier that the mother's function as an auxiliary structure comes in. According to Fain this maternal function supplies the necessary libido to the infant's stimulus barrier. This influx is necessary because the stimulus barrier works in the service of the death instinct: it attempts to destroy the excitability of living matter and thereby protect the infant from excitations that would threaten its integrity. Unaided, this stimulus barrier works in the direction of eliciting a sensorimotor response to stimuli that impinge on the organism. Only with the influx of maternal libido can there be a container that can retain excitations; this influx is perhaps the first that is absorbed by the infant and constituted into the autonomous function of censorship which contains libidinal excitations coupled with interdictions that bar their access to discharge.

Fain differentiates between the satisfying mother and the calming one, and he postulates that the continuous excitation produced by the soothing mother leads to a pathological dependence on sensory input. Ultimately this results in reliance on sensorimotor reactions as an aid to a brittle stimulus barrier designed only to ward off the excessive excitation of a reality that has no mental representation and is therefore potentially traumatizing.

Fain outlined the genesis of fantasy in a long and informative article entitled "Prélude à la Vie Fantasmatique" ("Prelude to Fantasy Life") (1971). Subsequently these ideas were reelaborated in *La Nuit, Le Jour* (Night and Day) (1975b), which he wrote in collaboration with Braunschweig. Fain starts with the premise that the stimulus barrier of the infant must gradually be transformed into censorship. The difference between the two, according to him, is best illustrated by describing how both guarantee sleep: the stimulus barrier would cause the formation of a dream that represents the events of the previous day without distorting them, whereas the faculty of censorship would transform these events through the intermediary of the dream work described by Freud (1900).

The function of censorship allows the outside world to be decathected and permits contact with reality based on memory traces that stem from the pleasure ego rather than reality. These representations are integrated with instinctual wishes to allow for hallucinatory wish fulfillment. In contrast, the lack of elaboration within the dream prompted by the stimulus barrier deprives it to a considerable degree of its wish-fulfilling function and suggests cathexis of the sensorium. It resembles the dreams associated with traumatic neuroses.

Fain thinks that this type of dream masters the excitations through the repetition compulsion and the Nirvana principle, whereas the other type of dream follows the pleasure principle and the libido economy.[3] Thus, according to Braunschweig and Fain, both the stimulus barrier and the censorship faculty might be adequate to keep excitations at a level compatible with sleep, but in terms of their capacity to absorb, screen, and transform excitations, they cannot be compared. Braunschweig and Fain (1971) say: "The wish to return rapidly to a state of quiescence by means of a specific excitation playing the role of stimulus barrier should be countered by the refusal of this impulse, constituted by the wish to obtain satisfaction in just as specific a way by means of the enjoyment of retention of the excitation and the representation of the satisfying object" (p. 203). This is available to a very limited degree to the infant as he decathects his sensorium (and we are not referring here to the infant who is being rocked to sleep) and turns toward sleep and possibly dreaming. Fain postulates that the inability to elaborate through dream work is related to operational thinking in waking life and that the representation of reality in the dream recathects the sense organs to a degree that renders the dream almost inadequate to its function.

I am well aware that everything that has been said does not address itself to an established time sequence. This is not due to my omission but to a trend in French psychoanalytic writings. The French do not generally attempt to pin themselves down to an identifiable time sequence; as a matter of fact, they convey the sense that they are describing mechanisms that continue throughout life and therefore should not be pinned down developmentally. For instance, when they write about states of exhaustion that precede fantasy formation developmentally, they are also assuming that these states can occur in adulthood when a person is traumatized, that is, when the ordinary capacity to fantasize is overwhelmed because of an important loss or threat. I have therefore come to think of their descriptions as statements of statistical probabilities: in early infancy, there is only exhaustion, and the mother must function as a container; later in the life of a reasonably healthy adult, the pleasure principle dominates until a traumatic event temporarily puts it out of action.

Freud's work implies that the pleasure ego, and concomitantly the ability to transform into a dream the excitement that threatens sleep, develop because of inborn tendencies. Fain and Braunschweig prefer to regard the capacity to dream as based on the ability to retain excitement and therefore subject to the development of a capacity that enables the infant to inhibit, delay, and thereby create a phenomenon that they equate with *latency*. This term is applied especially with regard to thoughts placed in latency in the same way as Freud spoke of the elements that prompt a dream. These thoughts placed in latency form a reservoir of excitation that eventually can lead to a fantasy in the form that we know it. However, first such a reservoir simply counteracts the need for immediate discharge through the senses or motor activity.

Because Freud named this need for immediate discharge the pleasure principle, Braunschweig and Fain think that it is important not to confuse it with the containment necessary for erotic pleasure. "The pleasure principle can only be at the origin of the need for discharge on condition that the discharge takes place in an erotized manner and does not lead to depressive manifestations. When an individual, because of lack of narcissistic supplies, feels fundamentally poor, every discharge becomes for him a hemorrhage and an object loss" (Fain 1962, p. 375).

Braunschweig and Fain think that the pleasure ego comes into being when the contact with the mother acting as stimulus barrier can be relinquished, censorship of the need for immediate discharge is established, and the tension that is produced by its absence can be represented by a pleasurable fantasy. States in which only contact with a brute and unsymbolized source of stimulation, such as rocking, leads to exhaustion are not constituted along the lines of the pleasure ego. They lead to consumption but not consummation, according to the authors. The ego remains excessively tied to outside stimulation and responses to it, and does not have the autonomy that only the pleasure ego can hope to attain. In adult life it leads to a way of being in which most mental life comes from an external apprenticeship and seems to follow a manual of instructions. This type of mental life is realistic, practical, and hopefully unexciting. The individuals who follow this pattern tend to use screen experiences in order to release the excitement that builds up despite themselves.

According to Fain, dependence on sensory stimulation—rocking in infancy, operational thinking in later life—is based on a fusion between the stimulus barrier and the death instinct, which aims at keeping excitations silent and leads to the search for screen experiences. This wish for soothing stimulation that permits discharge until exhaustion is reached is found in those infants who cannot create a link between representations based on memory traces and excitation caused by the mother's absence. They are traumatized by the excitement her absence causes, and as a result of the experience of trauma they cannot decathect the sense organs. Therefore the contact with the world outside is not sufficiently broken to permit a dream.

These calming incitations do not lead to a proper decathexis of the sensorium but rather depend on its stimulation for relaxation. That this stimulus dependency is different from the pleasure achieved in sleeping and dreaming was recently illustrated by observations made in the United States by Ferber (1985), a specialist in the field of sleep disturbances in early childhood. A filmed report showed how Ferber retrained parents of children with sleep disturbances to gradually permit these children, who woke up repeatedly during the night, to put themselves to sleep instead of rocking them. It was evident that the afflicted children had been rocked to sleep and that Ferber linked the frequent waking during the night to the dependency on the soothing movements. He demonstrated by means of a camera that had been placed in the room of the children that when the terror of being alone was overcome, the children started to use their own resources for self-comforting, something that the dependency on rocking had prevented up to then.

In this context, a recent case presentation by Ascher (1986) demonstrated the contrast in the responses of a little girl who was handled by both her mother and her grandmother. The grandmother rocked the child and therefore maintained her in a continuously quiescent state, whereas the mother did not rock and faced a hyperactive child who was unable to sleep.

In my opinion, another illustration of Fain's assertions comes from the culture at large when we consider the noise level associated with contemporary entertainment for the young. There seems to be no room for the contact between inner representations and outer stimulations in a situation that favors psychomotor responses and in which the stimulus quality drowns out the possibility for representation of derivatives of instinctual impulses. The pictures of contemporary dance halls represent frenzy.

Fain's warning against surrounding infants with an external world that consists only of stimulations is partly based on the assumption that excitement is generated not only from inside the child's body. It is a truism that every mother, who has tiptoed out of the room of an infant who has just dropped off to sleep and whom she does not want to disturb, knows. But psychoanalytic theory at times is threatened by abstractions that are divorced from everyday experience, and in some theories everyday events surrounding infants are not given their due place. Libido theory runs this risk at times. Fain attempts to reformulate instinct theory in keeping with the idea that the outside world is important in the psychic economy, in that an optimum dose of stimulation can be transformed into libido whereas excessive deprivation or gratification can lead to dependence on stimulation and screen experiences. Fain introduces into the theory of the libidinal economy greater object-dependency than is generally postulated, but he does not invalidate the economic approach. Laplanche (1981a) also adheres to this point of view. He advocates that "one should perhaps take seriously Freud's idea that any upheaval in psychic life (from shock or emotion) is accompanied by a new inrush, a true neoformation of libido. If these 'indirect sources' of sexual drive are at work during childhood, why couldn't they be effective during the whole lifespan?" (p. 88).

In Braunschweig and Fain's theory, the inrush comes in the form of "the censorship of the woman in love," that is, the mother desiring the father sexually. Here is a source of libido that is not biologically inherent: it comes in the form of a prohibition (censorship) that has the function both of exciting and of binding. The excitement transmitted to the child by the mother's erotic fantasies becomes transformed, according to Braunschweig and Fain, into exciting fantasies of the absent couple on the condition that the mother is able to divest herself sufficiently of her maternal function to create this breach in the contact between herself and her baby.

The infant's ability to retain the excitement, not to have to direct it toward the senses or motor activity but rather to deflect the flow inward toward the self, leads to what Braunschweig and Fain call the *double reversal* of the instinct. By this they mean that the direction of the flow of energy is changed from outward to inward, and the object is replaced by the subject. This was described as one of the important vicissitudes of the sexual instinct by Freud (1915), as a defense of sorts, and it has been tacitly assumed heretofore that it derives from the nature of the drive. Green (1983) calls it the first middle position between an impulse and repression.

Primary Masochism in the Evolution of Narcissism

Fain and Braunschweig do not consider this property innate. They treat the double reversal of the instinct as developmentally determined and dependent on the capacity to retain the excitation. It is instrumental in bringing about the narcissistic cathexis of the ego and can fail in that the need for immediate discharge of tension does not store the necessary energy to undergo this structuring and passivizing evolution.

Braunschweig and Fain link the malleability of the sexual instinct with this double reversal. Traditionally, the malleability of the sexual drive has been attributed to its displaceability with regard to zone and object, but there is merit in stressing the importance of the capacity of the instinct to be turned inward and away from the object in a crucial movement that permits its retention.

In this context masochism attains a positive value because it turns the drive around, places the ego in the position of an object, renders tension pleasurable, and thereby prevents the outflow of energy, which can become dangerous. That Braunschweig and Fain call this masochism may be considered unfortunate. The more widely accepted tendency is to think of the first cathexis that flows back upon the ego as that which constitutes its first investment by libido and not to stress the self-directed, inhibitory, and passive aspects. Not so for them, and their terminology agrees with Laplanche's schema postulating a primary masochism (1970, 1976 ed.).

Braunschweig and Fain justify their approach by linking the pleasure ego to primary masochism inasmuch as tension becomes a source of pleasure: this is how they see the structure of erotism. It is made possible by means of a representation of an initially painful excitement that leads to the double identification caused by the double action, that is, censorship and excitement, activated by the parents who exclude the child. It is desexualizing, and part of primary repression, as well as exciting, and therefore at the source of autoerotism. It implies a continuous interplay between the censoring and the sexual tendency, which their theory needs because censorship is the precondition for inhibition of discharge.

For the body of the child to attain erogeneity, the mother has to be both stimulated by her own oedipal fantasies and censoring them. The paternal superego of the mother's father will activate her concern for her real child; yet it is by becoming wife again that, in a conflictual way, she becomes mother.

Developmentally, Braunschweig and Fain take as their point of departure the mother's wish for her child to go to sleep. This wish is linked to her own sexual wishes with regard to her spouse and the unconscious fantasy concerning her own father. According to Fain and Braunschweig, this wish creates for the baby a source of excitation both because of the absence and the stimulating presence of the mother who is mentally absent. In order to retain this excitation, it has to be tied up with pleasurable fantasy. The censorship transmitted by the mother works in the direction of inhibiting discharge and aiding in this linkage between the unpleasant tension and the fantasy that can represent it and render it pleasant. It leads to the essence of primary masochism: tension linked with a pleasurable thought.

In Fain's opinion, the problem is related to the mode in which the mother resumes her role as the father's lover and gives up her mothering function while the infant sleeps. Good development allows for a compromise between the representations linked to the absent object and the need to censor the outside world with its influx of unrepresentable and therefore potentially traumatic stimuli.

The important element of this theory is the differentiation between mother and child caused not by loss but rather by the excitation caused by the mother's absence, which is then symbolized by envy for the penis that satisfies her. The theory departs in an important way from the more usual idea that a drive that was once satisfied by an object is frustrated. Braunschweig and Fain's view is compatible with that expressed by Laplanche and Pontalis (1964, 1968 ed.): "The 'origin' of auto-erotism would therefore be the moment when sexuality, disengaged from any natural object, moves into the field of fantasy and by that very fact becomes sexuality" (p. 16).

Laplanche (1970, 1976 ed.) arrives at a similar position by different means. When he interprets the history of Freud's thinking, he makes a distinction between need gratification and sexual excitement and he postulates that it is the loss of the need-gratifying object that leads to the search for a pleasure-giving object re-created in fantasy. He says:

> In the human infant, sexuality rests entirely on a movement which deflects the instinct (or self-preservation), metaphorizes its aim, displaces and internalizes its object, and concentrates its source on what is ultimately a minimal zone, the erotogenic zone. [p. 23]
>
> Sexuality appears as a drive that can be isolated and observed only at the moment at which the nonsexual activity, the vital function, becomes detached from its natural object or loses it. For sexuality, it is the reflexive (*selbst* or auto-) moment that is constitutive: the moment of a turning back towards self, an 'autoerotism' in which the object has been replaced by a fantasy, by an object reflected within the subject. [p. 88]
>
> A different derivation, a different genesis is revealed to us, in the course of which infantile sexuality frees itself from an entire series of nonsexual activities, emerging, so to speak, from the 'propping' [*étayage*] which has it first 'leaning' on the self-preservation functions. In the various moments of propping (*Anlehnung*), we constantly rediscover the guiding threads of contiguity and resemblance that cause the drive to emerge from the instinctual function. The two essential phases here are a metaphorization of the aim, which bring us from the ingestion of food, at the level of self-preservation, to fantasmatic incorporation and introjection as actual psychical processes, this time at the level of the drive—and, on the other hand, what might be termed, after Jacques Lacan, a metonymization of the object, which, substituting for milk what is directly contiguous to it (the breast), introduces that hiatus allowing us to say without contradiction that finding the object is refinding it, since the rediscovered object is in fact not the lost one, but its metonym. [p. 137]

Braunschweig challenges Freud's formulation further when she said in a personal communication that she does not think that the object is the milk, nor the mother, but the mouth. She is equating the source and the object of the drive; the mother is only the precondition for autoerotism.

Piera Castoriadis-Aulagnier (1975) also postulates a process by which in early infancy the erogenous zone and the object become indistinguishable from each other. In her theory, the originating process underlies the primary and secondary processes. The originating process is that which metabolizes the object into the representation of a body part "to incorporate it, and, owing to this to cathect the incorporator himself" (p. 50). Castoriadis-Aulagnier is a specialist in the study of psychosis in which the dedifferentiation between the subject's body and the object plays such an important part. This has undoubtedly prompted her interest in devising a theory in which the erotogenic zone and the maternal object are seen as one.

Laplanche (1981a) seeks to undermine one of the pillars of the importance of the external object: the need for self-preservation. Freud (1911), in his *Formulations on the Two Principles of Mental Functioning*, states that the reality principle supersedes the pleasure principle in all but the sexual sphere. Therefore the need for self-preservation led to submission to the reality principle. Laplanche suggests that self-preservation be regarded as part of narcissism, or, as he says, ego-love. "It is out of love and not out of survival instinct that the baby will soon take food: love for his object, the mother, and love for his own ego" (p. 86). But he does not spell out whether this love seeks its gratification by means of the reality principle or whether, coming closer to libido, it follows the pleasure principle. I am not sure that Laplanche, as lucid and admirable as some of his analyses may be, improves on Freud's original thinking in which reality played a part, no matter how equivocal.[4]

The Creative Potential of Frustration and the Mother's Absence

Absence, in Braunschweig and Fain's thinking, becomes the creator of an excitation that is not countered by sensory input and therefore has to be represented mentally by means of fantasy. There is, in effect, no real object at the outset but an absent one that is created in fantasy in order to represent the excitation caused both by the absent mother and by the stimulation caused by her fantasies of the forthcoming sexual encounter with the father.

The censorship that she imposes on her own incestuous fantasies as well as on those transmitted to her baby adds an additional sexualizing component, so that both stimulation and prohibition can be considered a source of sexuality. Since the baby's sexual excitation is not derived from a gratification that he has obtained but is, on the contrary, derived from a lack of gratification, and since the gratification that is realized in direct contact with the mother pertains more to the edification of a stimulus barrier and a dependency on sensorimotor stimulation, the mother is not in reality ever a sexually gratifying object. The first sexually gratifying object, as Freud (1905) showed with the example of thumb sucking, is the child's own body.

According to this theory, the failure to develop the ability to reach a modicum of autonomy through autoerotism and dreaming is related to the mother's incapacity to organize her maternal instinct. This accounts for the deficiency in fantasy formation by the actions of the mother who fails to regulate her role as the infant's auxiliary stimulus barrier. In a sense she negates herself by creating excitations such as rocking aimed at soothing the infant, but while soothing the infant through stimulation, she hampers the development of modes of screening out external reality by means of a mental effort. Rocking or similar sensory stimulation creates a brute reality that cannot be symbolized; it stimulates instead of allowing a total absence leading to a relatively greater decathexis of the sensorium.

Fain makes the daring assumption of a communication between the id of the mother and that of the infant that stimulates the link between his own autoerotism and the love life of the absent couple. In fantasy, autoerotism is represented in terms of the desire of others, and this is where the presence of the sexual father is essential for the underpinning of the fantasy life of the growing child at a time that precedes the Oedipus complex. Fain calls this primary genitality.

Fain thinks that autoerotism without representation is inconceivable, but equally inconceivable is the notion that all life's experiences are representable. Representability becomes the foundation of the libido economy, which is a position taken by Loewald (1972), and sexuality develops in response to some stimulus from outside with that which represents it internally, as Laplanche and Pontalis also postulate in their 1964 study on the origin of fantasy.

In Fain's opinion, there is also a primary reality that is met with "primary fetishism" in the constitution of the pleasure ego. But, to my knowledge, he has not elaborated this thought further.

Basically Fain thinks that what the pleasure ego does not encompass is nonexistent, thereby disagreeing with Klein who suggests that what is outside the pleasure ego is bad. The pleasure ego represents the good but does not have a representation for a *reality* beyond it. Therefore, that part that is excluded from the organization cannot be considered split off or bad, as in Klein's way of thinking. Fain thinks that Klein's model for normal development constitutes the blueprint for pathology. Therefore he conceives of a Kleinian and a Freudian model working in complementary fashion in such a way as to consider one the scheme for the regressed conditions in which the hallucinatory wish fulfillment is threatened. In keeping with this, he does not consider the depressive position as being based on the fantasy of the destruction of the object but rather on the loss of its representation. He feels that the Kleinians do not sufficiently take into account the silencing quality of the death instinct, sensitive as they are to its noisy manifestations.

Placing the accent on fantasies involving aggression, as Klein does, illustrates Braunschweig and Fain's criticism of a tendency that is equally evident in Freud's theories, where there is always something: in sleep there is the dream, at the sight of the female genital there is the fantasy of castration, and death becomes murder. Freud favored the active impulse over the passive one, and he suggested that notions of a void, death, or absence are not represented in the unconscious. The theory of the death instinct did not change that because it merely reiterated the striving toward inertia that hitherto had been ascribed to the pleasure principle.

With their usual audacity, Braunschweig and Fain call Freud's tendency *fetishistic,* and while I would be willing to quarrel with them about the use of the term, I think that their reasoning is difficult to fault. They reason that sexual excitement is tied to an absent object, which means that the drive has only a fantasy object. Laplanche (1970, 1976 ed.) reaches a similar conclusion by examining Freud's *Three Essays on the Theory of Sexuality* (1905) in which he says that the sexual component of the pleasure in sucking makes itself independent of the gratifying object, whereas the pleasure linked to the satisfaction of hunger remains tied to the object. This close link between sexuality and absence, which in turn leads to greater personal autonomy, seems to me to be most fortuitous. It suggests that the absence of the object per se does not have to traumatize and that presence is not necessarily beneficial. It remains for us to inquire into the quality of each, and the capacity of the erotic fantasies to transform each into a gratifying fantasy.

I think that the notion that there never was an object of the sexual drive could be a help inasmuch as it takes psychoanalytic theory back into the realm of individual fantasies rather than a reality that was. It avoids the danger that is often encountered in which analysts consider the frustrations by the parents to be the cause of the patient's difficulties rather than the fantasies that the frustration generated. Nor is object loss per se the cause for psychic disturbances, on the contrary, in this theory object loss can lead to the establishment of a triangular relationship in which the desired organ, the father's penis, temporarily wins the mother's attention. While one might want to take issue with the time sequence, that is, the notion of placing the triangle so early in development, there is also some evidence for the belief that in normal development the father has a formative place in early life that he lacks in psychotic conditions.

Since there is neither drive nor its gratification before loss, that is, the mother's return to the father, the fantasy that represents the exciting scene of the parents' sexuality, symbolized by the penis, never completely fills the gap that exists between the excitation and its representation, and the gratifying object can never be exactly the refound fantasy object. All attempts to deny the gap or to consider it inherently bridgeable tend, according to Braunschweig and Fain, toward fetishization and the avoidance of mourning. The presence at the heart of the pleasure ego of a little primary reality (not represented) adds some spice to the unreality of hallucinatory wish fulfillment. There should not be "a constant need for fetishistic denial or recourse to calming stimulations" (Braunschweig 1971, p. 783).

These assertions, in which the drive and its object never correspond but are linked by means of fantasy, are compatible with Freud's statements in *Formulations on the Two Principles of Mental Functioning* (1911) in which he postulates that the sexual drive does not follow the reality principle but turns away from it. It supports Braunschweig and Fain's notion that the representation never accounts for all aspects of the excitation as well as their preference for imprecision.

Another Approach to Narcissism

Braunschweig and Fain derive their notion of narcissism from the libidinal investment of the ego which requires the retention of excitation. There is nothing, according to them, in Freud's last instinct theory to account for this ability to retain the outflow of libido, and they propose the process of identification as the factor that interposes itself between uninhibited discharge and the constitution of a primary narcissism. It is the means by which an equilibrium can be established between the two instincts.

Braunschweig warns against confusing primary narcissism with the undifferentiated state since self-preservation is not part of the undifferentiated state until the maternal instinct that serves as a stimulus barrier becomes attached to it, and then it should be called primary narcissism. Thus the wish for death is not so much a return to the state of primary narcissism but the wish to return to the undifferentiated state in which self-preservation has not yet evolved.

In keeping with the differentiation between primary narcissism and the undifferentiated state, Braunschweig insists on maintaining the distinction between ego instincts and ego libido. Ego instincts are the continuation of the undifferentiated state in which some of the maternal stimulus barrier quality has been internalized, whereas ego libido pertains to narcissism (which Braunschweig and Fain link to eroticism via penis envy and the indefinite extension of phallic significants—ideas whose fancifulness is incompatible with an Anglo-Saxon need for clarity).

Because of their attention to the instinctual property of turning upon the self, Braunschweig and Fain return to the differentiation that Freud made in 1915 between hate and sadism. Freud was clear that hate, which belongs to the realm of self-preservation, pertains to the total ego and therefore does not have the capacity to undergo the fate of sadism, which can be turned into masochism.

Again, it is unfortunate that neither Braunschweig nor Fain has recourse to the felicitous distinction made by Freud between hate and sadism, which I consider most relevant here and most compatible with their formulations. They contrast the instinct that undergoes the double reversal, a sign of its sexualization, with something that they also call sadism, only it is of a different type that cannot be turned around and directed toward the self; but they do not call it hate, which would seem to be appropriate for what they describe.

Instead, they refer to a reactive type of sadism due to the child's inability to identify with the passive wishes of the mother. They think that it is difficult to attribute to it either erotism or pleasure and that it uses the path of the instinct of self-preservation to lead to the destruction of the object. It sweeps away all memory traces, leads to a masculinity that is not tempered with repressed masochism, and therefore acts as a fetish protecting the individual from disintegration. It is the kind of sadism that helps to firm ego boundaries and insures against the anxiety of being penetrated. Passive wishes can only be projected and are expressed in persecutory fantasies because they are not adequately represented even in the unconscious. In short, it is an instinct that lacks the malleability of what should properly be called sadism, which can undergo the two vicissitudes described by Freud.

I believe that their observation is extremely important and that their theory would have been enhanced if they had remained with Freud's original distinction between hate and sadism. I have become convinced that the distinction provides us with a good explanatory model for phenomena that I have observed and described previously in work on the psychopathology of children of concentration camp survivors (Oliner 1982a). I have come to the conclusion that sexualization can attenuate trauma and that hysteria deserves a privileged place among the reactions to trauma and their transmission, that is, hate that can be transformed into sadism can become masochism, and whereas it generates depression, it is still more ego building than hate that only thrives on discharge.

In general, the sexual drive has been known for its malleability and for the diversity of pathology it creates through displacement, condensation, turning upon itself, yielding to the pleasure principle, and ultimately being difficult to influence. To my knowledge, the sexual drive has not yet received sufficient recognition for the avenues it opens to the individual not only for providing pleasure but also for avoiding a rigidity in which life is focused only on problem solving, action, and surviving. The assumption here is that as painful as survivor guilt may be, it pertains to the realm of sexual fantasies and therefore allows for pleasure, no matter how perverted, whereas a hateful attitude caused by the trauma shows a complete absence of mental elaboration.

It is in this way that the deflection and retention of energy becomes crucial. It can make the difference between pleasure and exhaustion, or life and death. Braunschweig and Fain use a model of energy distribution without invoking the structural theory. Therefore they also fail to distinguish between libido that is repressed and that which is not. According to them, energies stored by means of primary repression are available to the psyche although they never elaborate on this. Stored energy provides the underpinnings of psychic life and structure, and is, of course, contrasted to that which is simply lost through discharge by means of the response to sensory stimulation. The stored energy can evolve into erotism, narcissism, and self-preservation, all of which underlie the loving mind in a healthy body, and the ability of the mother and child to tolerate the absence created by her return to the father is the cornerstone for this complex evolution, one to which Braunschweig and Fain return time and again.

Notes

[1] In this theory, fantasy is used in an almost Kleinian way. Nigel Mackay (1981, p. 194) says that in Klein's view, "Phantasy is not some mental activity opposed to reality-tuned perception: it is no 'escape mechanism.' Rather it is the mental medium in which experience is represented. As the 'mental corollary of instinct' it is fundamental to all psychic activity."

[2] Laplanche and Pontalis (1967, 1973 ed.) translate the word *pare-excitations* used by Fain as *protective shield against stimuli*, which is also Strachey's translation for the German *Reizschutz* used by Freud, but I shall use *stimulus barrier* for reasons of simplicity.

[3] A similar but not identical distinction is made by Green (1983) when he differentiates between sleep narcissism aiming at exhaustion and dream narcissism aiming at pleasure. Castoriadis-Aulagnier (1975) distinguishes between the Nirvana principle and the death instinct by postulating that the former pertains to the pleasure principle, which aims at quiescence, whereas the latter involves a reaction in which having to represent plays the part of disturbing a previous sleep in which everything was silence.

[4] In a similar vein, Castoriadis-Aulagnier (1975) postulates that the earliest representation, which she calls the pictogram and which is derived from the originating process, is the representation that the psyche gives itself of itself as a representing activity. It represents itself as that which engenders the erogenous pleasure of the body parts. It contemplates its own image and its own power in its engendered production, be it in what it sees, hears, or perceives, all of which present themselves as auto-engendered by its own activity. Just as these theorists attempt to create a theory that postulates an early fusion of zone and object as the drive constitutes itself, there is, in this last theory, an attempt to fuse the mind with its own productions at a primitive and constitutive level, so as to account for the thought disturbances in psychosis. "In psychosis the problem becomes that secondary process attempts to express or make sense out of experiences based on representations in which the world is only a reflection of a body that swallows itself, mutilates itself, and rejects itself" (p. 78). This describes the fusion between the mind that represents and its contents.

13

The Ubiquitous Triangle

In the previous chapter Braunschweig and Fain's theory concerning the origin of sexuality was discussed in the light of an early triangle with the mother, the father, and the baby, who is left alone to master the excitement created by the mother's absence and the couple making love. The focus was placed on the excitement created in the infant by the fantasy of this scene and the censorship which creates a libidinized barrier to the discharge of this energy. The ability to retain the excitation was seen as central to the internal structure of the instinct because it attains the capacity to turn from active into passive and from the object to the self. There is more to the theory as it attempts to account for phenomena other than the process of libidinization, and I shall return to it with all the mental reservations necessary for the exposition of such an early love triangle.

It is important, however, to state that Braunschweig and Fain are not the exception in their speculations about an early role of the father; on the contrary, most of the French analysts prefer to think of triangular relations, and they tend to postulate the existence of a triangle where others might only hypothesize the presence of two participants.

In the case of Braunschweig and Fain, this approach leads to oedipalization, as Lebovici (1982) calls it, in early infancy. As such, this theory uses Klein's interpretation and presupposes that preceding the classic Oedipus complex there can be a Kleinian-type of Oedipus (Fain 1971) corresponding to the fantasy of the mother who detains within her body the penis of the father. Fain thinks that this fantasy is indicative of pathology, and that in normal development we find a different version of the triangular constellation formed by the mother, the child, and the representation of the father's penis, leading to primary penis envy.

Lebovici (1982) is more cautious. He warns against the application of triangular situations to all kinds of mental functioning and advocates a clear distinction between pregenital aspects of the Oedipus and the Oedipus after the major pregenital defenses have been worked through. "To overlook this basic premise and to describe the Oedipus complex as a continuous process, originating at birth, is to forget that repression and the unconscious are consubstantial" (p. 211). He believes that the universality of the Oedipus complex "does not justify what I called the 'oedipalization' of psychoanalysis" (p. 213).

This warning does not pertain to triangulation, which he considers a preoedipal phenomenon upon which the Oedipus complex is built. Unfortunately, many of his colleagues do not adequately maintain the distinction between an early Oedipus complex, a precursor of the classic Oedipus, and triangulation. This criticism applies especially to Braunschweig and Fain, who leave room for doubt as to whether they are discussing the underpinnings in infancy for the normal Oedipus complex or an early Oedipus complex implying knowledge of the distinction between the sexes and its meaning.

Despite the fact that there has been much warranted

criticism of their theories, I have found many of Braunschweig and Fain's audacious speculations interesting, especially in their ability to shake up preconceived notions. The question of the retention of energy and the erotization of the body, already discussed, is an attempt to devise a better drive theory in order to update it and make it applicable to the explanation of the relationship between mind and body in a better way than it has done so far. Braunschweig and Fain did this by assuming that structure formation is best explained by means of distribution and retention of psychic energy, and contrary to the tendencies current in the United States, they do it by introducing a triangle along with the mother-baby dyad.

In this chapter, I intend to concentrate on their idea of the content of those fantasies concerning the absent couple, and again they raise some interesting questions especially about the mother's inability to put sufficient distance between herself and her baby, but also about the mother's involvement with her own father that threatens the role of the child's real father. In addition they attempt to shed further light on the role of idealization leading to desexualization. As usual, there are no clinical data. These two bright and fanciful clinicians, whose work would be inconceivable in this country, simply relate their thinking in order to make some sweeping pronouncements. These are expressed in a vocabulary that does not take into consideration genetic development. Instead it attempts to create a continuity between pre- and post-oedipal dynamics and differentiates between the two only by referring to the former as *primary* or *the first phase* of events that occur later in the generally accepted developmental scheme.

Braunschweig and Fain represent the extreme of what I shall present of the French tendency toward intellectual virtuosity. As I have indicated at the outset, I have eliminated some of their more extreme writings and omitted a whole body of literature that reminds analysts brought up in the tradition of Anglo-Saxon pragmatism of the Emperor's clothes.

The Preoedipal Triangle

Braunschweig and Fain's theory postulates an early development responsible for erogenization of the body, regulation of excitement, and mental representation, all derived from the same set of circumstances: the baby who is left alone while the parents are making love. There is great similarity between what they say and Castoriadis-Aulagnier's (1975) statement that "excitation, erogenization, representation" form an inextricable threesome: they designate the three qualities necessary to an object for it to exist in the psyche. They tie representability in with libido (p. 75).

According to Braunschweig and Fain (1975b), life is known because it is interrupted. They think that the mourning that accompanies the loss of the mother creates sexual excitement in the way that Freud suggested when he presumed that any stimulus of sufficient intensity will cause a sexual reaction. This reaction, consisting of diffuse energy, is further promoted and shaped by the mother's unconscious fantasies so that her absence is gradually converted into fantasy. Accordingly, the baby senses the excitement and responds to it with excitement that has no representation. But if this excitement can be contained in the body through an interdiction also emanating from the mother and does not meet with sensory stimulation provided by the mother, it can be represented by a fantasy that will eventually find a way of connecting with erogenous zones that lend themselves to autoerotic gratification through discharge.

According to Fain and Braunschweig, this autoerotic gratification is linked to fantasies about the activities of the absent couple with which the child identifies because it too has a love relation with the mother. Braunschweig and Fain call this identification with the absent couple a hysterical identification because it leads to a reaction in the child's body, creating a continuity that makes the absence bearable and avoids "fears that no courage whatsoever could contain."

According to Fain (1981b), hysterical identification with both partners in the primal scene is the result of the proper mourning of the loss of the mother during her absence. It is symbolized by the penis and leads to penis envy because the infant identifies with the sexual desire of the mother for the father, and in its search for the representation of the missing third, the child hits eventually upon the father's penis, which represents that which was not represented before. Subsequently, the child identifies his own body with this penis, and this identification leads to the organization and evolution of the narcissistic core.

Basically, Braunschweig and Fain postulate a bisexual identification with the absent couple. They think that the child identifies with the mother as well as with the father and that this double identification accounts for the active (aimed at the object) as well as the passive (aimed at the self) elements of the drive. However, their writings stress the role of penis envy and the identification with the father's penis more than the identification with the mother who is loved and desired by the father. I attribute this tendency to the remnant of Lacan's thinking which undoubtedly prompted some of these reflections.

Lacan (1966) said that the impact of the absence of the mother is symbolized by the term *Name-of-the-Father* (Nom-du-Père). Her desire for him is signified to the child by the father's name and his phallus. Lacan has rightly been criticized for this phallocentric view of the psyche, and Braunschweig and Fain have definitely made an attempt to change this with their supposition of a bisexual identification.[1]

Braunschweig and Fain's mention of the role of the father's penis and envy of this penis in the constitution of the representational world is clearly in this Lacanian tradition. They base their thinking on the idea that through the modification within the mother's body the subject has a premonition that somewhere there exists another object who is sexually attractive. They deviate from Lacan's point of view because they stress the greater importance of an identification with both parents, accounting in this way for the capacity of the instinct to undergo the double reversal from active to passive and from object to self that guarantees the irreversibility of the representation. Where the capacity of the instinct to undergo the double reversal is missing, the representation is vulnerable to disintegration.

Hysterical identification, as described by Fain, is the antithesis of projective identification. Projective identification fails in the effort to contain within a represented form an excitation that is insufficiently symbolized. Projective identification is born of disappointment and is revived at each new one.

> At the basis of *projective identification* we put the denial of the existence of the father's desire. This is a denial that is closely linked to that of a mother who does not accept her femininity. This is a portion of reality that is denied when the identification with the desire of the father does not elaborate itself. As a consequence of this, the denied piece of reality intrudes from the outside. Even though it is constantly perceived, reality is rejected as a possible source of supplies for the representational system. [Fain 1981b, p. 995]

Braunschweig and Fain link hysterical identification with the ability to acknowledge that something is missing, the ability to mourn it, and, by means of the mechanism of masochism, the ability to attach excitement to the pain of mourning. Hysterical identification, as they postulate it, brings about a process of symbolization, a genuine putting into place of the primary process with its condensations and displacements. Contrasted to this, projective identification has the emptying-out effect that they consider evidence of pathology. Thus, they say that the woman who is mentally absent thinks of a concrete sexual object that makes the present mother not only partially missing but ready to put into action censorship mechanisms that create sleep. She is also ready to sexualize the censorship functions, thereby sending the content of hysterical identification into the unconscious. It is in this conjunction that we situate the memorable dream (Fain 1971, p. 295).

Primary narcissism is built around these images, memory traces, and hallucinatory wish fulfillments. It organizes itself in relative quiet, yet it is constantly solicited through a certain level of excitation caused by the normal incompleteness of the stimulus barrier. In this way, Braunschweig and Fain postulate a primary narcissism that is born out of the ability to derive pleasure from tension, that is, primary masochism. This approach links the evolution of drive to structure that is constituted at the same time, neither existing ever without the other. Both are preceded by unrepresented excitement aiming at nothing but discharge and exhaustion, both of which are the result of the mother's return to the father.

The focus of their theory is always on the link between mental life and interruptions in gratification; they stress the gap, the latency, between the experience of the absence and the fantasies that eventually fill the gap. They postulate the same latency between excitation and fantasy as Freud assumed to exist between the day's event and the dream at night.

The excitement caused by the absent mother is connected with the paternal phallus which has a dual nature: because of the mother's unconscious wish for her own incestuous object, the sexual relationship with the father of the child is also the consummation of the oedipal wish. Braunschweig believes that every sexual act is a repressed incest (private communication). Fain (1981b) asserts that "the child is the penis that satisfies the mother's penis envy" (p. 997). This oedipal fantasy, which makes out of the baby the product of incest and represents the mother's or the mother's father's penis, creates what Braunschweig and Fain call the baby of the night. This baby duplicates the mother's incestuous object and denies the loss of the latter, as well as her own feminine sexuality. In this way, the child of the night doubles for a lost object and leads to the process of fetishization which forms part of the infant's unconscious. Infants, whose function is fetishistic, support the mother's denial of the loss of her own oedipal object. This denial can be transmitted to the infant who, instead of bearing the loss of the mother as she resumes her love relationship with the father and turning the mourning process into an erotic fantasy, does not miss nor mourn.

Braunschweig and Fain think that in normal development the baby senses a discontinuity in the mother's investment, distinguishes day from night, and eventually forms a large part of his or her identity around the relationship to the real father rather than to the mother's incestuous object. Braunschweig and Fain (1981b) say that the real father is the screen memory behind which is hidden an incestuous mother-baby fantasy pertaining to the night. Thus Braunschweig and Fain convert the image of the father of the child into a screen, perhaps the first, born of a defensive activity aimed at the representation of the incestuous loves of the mother with her baby of the night (the penis of her father). This screen, the consciousness of the father, the image of the father, covers up the fantasy of his absence. He is absent from the mother's unconscious in the night where she is with her own father or the latter's penis, symbolized by the baby. "This leads to the double pronouncement on the part of the child: I am the penis of the father of my mother. I am the child of my father" (p. 1230). This double pronouncement corresponds to what they call the baby of the night and the baby of the day.

In Braunschweig and Fain's thinking, the mother's duality consists of prompting incestuous fantasies, but she also becomes identical with the messenger of the castration threat by the child's real father. By this the authors mean that the child learns to include the third element in the love triangle and to screen out the mother's incestuous fantasies by means of the image of the real father. It is she, therefore, who helps the child in the attainment of the dominance of secondary process functioning.

As such, she is responsible for the original crude stimulus barrier, the process of censorship, the inhibition of discharge, the repressed erotic fantasies, and the transmission of the castration threat for both sexes.

As a consequence, they postulate that in addition to the first process that concerns the mother's ability to relinquish temporarily her role as a mother, there is a second one that involves the capacity of all three participants to have their proper place, which means that the image of the child's father and the mother's lover are not crushed by the image of the mother's oedipal object or the child who represents it. This last process is helped by the transmission of the castration threat which, as is usual for these two authors, is not adequately explained.

They never define the castration threat that prompts the important distinction between the baby of the night and the baby of the day. The transmission of the castration threat, which is prompted by the mother's concern for her child's body, is tied to the fantasies of the child's father. Braunschweig and Fain (1975b) say that, according to Freud, the mother is seductive until she becomes "frightened by the genital effects of her seduction; she then transmits the image of a jealous and terrible father by becoming the messenger for the castration threat, the effects of which the little boy sees on the body of the girl" (p. 91). The father's concern for his own child also works in the direction of the repression of the mother's counteroedipal cathexis of her child and strengthens the latter's instinct of self-preservation. But once more, as in the case of hysterical identification and masochism, they take a term from psychoanalytic theory, hypothesize that it has a first and a second phase, and apply it in this way to a much earlier period of life.

They think that if the real father is not considered sufficiently menacing, there ensues a pathological dependency of the child on the mother, who ipso facto becomes what they call the guarantor of the investment. When the object is lost in later life, depression sets in because the investment is possible only in the presence of the object and is given up at the time of loss. Such a development runs counter to the constitution of the drive as they see it; that is, it is based on the absence of the primary object and the role the child's father plays in this absence. The mother who denies loss by reacting to her child as if he were the stand-in for her incestuous object does not show adequate concern for the child. This absence of anxiety for the child can work against the child's adequate sense of reality.

As an illustration, a case comes to mind in which a boy carried out his mother's hostility against her boss in such a way that the latter, because of the mother's presence, was unable to retaliate. By not discouraging sufficiently the son's aggression, the mother seemed to deny that he could be hurt. The son converted this attitude into a magical belief in his immunity from retaliation provided he was within a certain geographical proximity from a woman who would protect him. Because of this fantasy, he denied the great harm he caused himself due to his provocative behavior or his inability to modulate his aggression, which he channeled against himself when all else failed. This development shielded this patient from depression because he could deny the loss of the mother with the magic of this fantasy. It is in this manner that I interpret Braunschweig and Fain's (1981a) notion of the transmission of the castration threat, especially during the preoedipal phases they are referring to. Later, and more evidently, the castration threat pertains to aggression against the father or other oedipal rivals. "The edification of the superego, the structure which carries paternal power devoid of his desire, marks the end of the denial of the castration threat, places the individual in a state of mourning for his incestuous objects with erotic aims. Latency brings a period of no return until postpuberty" (p. 217).

Castoriadis-Aulagnier (1975) expresses some of the same views. She considers the child to be the result of the mother's love for what she calls *the shadow*. Whatever of this love can be transformed into libido that is permitted and expressible comes through to the child. The danger is that the mother's libido turns away from the child and back to the shadow. But the shadow also prevents the mother from doing that because the wish preceding the one of having a child with the father would be the one of having a child with the mother, which is more threatening. Therefore the child is the one who shows the victory of the I on the repressed, but also—and here is the paradox of the situation—the child comes closest to the object of the unconscious wish whose return would make out of the child a forbidden appropriation. It is the child who becomes the buttress that protects the mother against the return of her own repression, from which derives the paradoxical and dangerous position the child occupies: whereas the child occupies the place closest to the object of an unconscious desire, it is the child that one asks to become the obstacle to this return. The mother is like a forbidden giver: she might be said to be the dispenser of the wish, a gift that is essential for psychic structure, but she refuses to be the dispenser of the object, a refusal that is equally necessary. It is the father who insures that the mother's rules are not arbitrary. (This leads back to the issue so frequently found in perversions and described in great detail by the work of Chasseguet-Smirgel.)

I am aware that these thoughts could lead to mischief in interpretations given to patients because they are based on so many unverifiable assumptions and take us further away from working with actual memories. They do serve as a reminder that a child can and does embody the relationship of the parents to their oedipal objects, a fact that helps in the understanding of certain cases.

An interesting 1981 study by Alain de Mijolla entitled *Les Visiteurs du Moi, Fantasmes d'Identification (The Visitors of the Ego, Fantasies of Identification)* is based on this theory. De Mijolla traces by means of letters and other documents, the identification patterns of Beethoven, Freud, Rimbaud, and others. He demonstrates convincingly the strong identifications with oedipal objects of the parents. I have referred in an earlier chapter to the fact that in Freud's case identification with his paternal grandfather, Schlomo, explains the origin of the image of the sage that emerges from *The Interpretation of Dreams* (1900) more convincingly than the image of the father based on his real father. In this country, this approach is embodied by those who do family therapy with the help of a genogram and involve various generations in the treatment process (*N.Y. Times*, January 21, 1986). The danger in this approach is that the analyst could use his interest in the objects of identification and introjects in order to create a demonology leading to treatment akin to exorcism.

Secondary Process and Desexualization

Braunschweig and Fain have never attempted to devise a complete developmental theory. On the contrary, Fain (1971) says that psychoanalytic theories centered on the genetic development of the child are marked by the wish to maintain the maternal instinct because it has an antierotic aspect. Thus, even in the context of discussing desexualization, which they consider part of a normal and necessary evolution, they return to their main theme, penis envy and its derivatives, and give it their main attention. Due to this tendency, which may well stem from their opposition to the notion that the ego is basically a desexualized structure, desexualization appears in their writings only tangentially. It comes up, for instance, when they say that the postulated hysterical identification of the child with the sexual wishes of the real parents, whose unconscious base is marked by the oedipal structure (therefore symbolic), can only be organized if it is countercathected and reworked. This brings us back to censorship or the censorship of the woman in love, which was discussed in the previous chapter with regard to the ability to retain the excitation caused by the absence of the mother. One of its aspects is desexualization.

Braunschweig and Fain do not refer to it in a more systematic way, and when the term comes up, it is in the context of the pathology of the totally desexualized personality organization of patients suffering from psychosomatic illnesses. Fain (1971) thinks that secondary process functioning that is desexualized and that relies on neutralized aggression for its organization borders on pathology. In addition to his rather negative view of desexualization, Fain also rejects the notion of neutralization of aggression because it would reduce maturation to a process whereby excitations feed a calming stimulus barrier that does not become attached to an image. He thinks that instead we should think of the ego's task as being the attaching of excitations to images. The ego should leave neither undifferentiated or unrepresented excitations, nor should it leave a reality that then acts as a stimulus barrier and that contains but does not become attached to exciting representations.

Braunschweig and Fain (1975b) say that total desexualization of the interplay between mother and child would generate guilt because it would involve the castration of the father, which is somewhat assuaged by idealization. They say that it becomes the question of the myth of the dead father, or on the level of the individual, of a father castrated of his desire. This is the idealized father in *Totem and Taboo*. "This ideal, imposed often unconsciously by a suggestion, tends to occupy in an abusive manner, by cutting short the possibility of reversing the impulse, the virile [active] aspects of the hysterical fantasy." They are referring to the double reversal of *Instincts and Their Vicissitudes*. They continue: "We have postulated that the induced response is depression instead of mourning, with all its possibilities of a renewed upsurge of libido" (1981a, p. 206). One of their dicta is: "Death becomes the correlate of desexualization" (Braunschweig and Fain 1975a, p. 211). They relate depression to idealization and desexualization, but they elaborate on this idea in their study of countertransference. I have therefore included their comments in the section on the analytic relationship later in this chapter.

In this way, mainly by means of omission, they appear to play down the notion that secondary process corresponds to desexualization, and fail to discuss the degree to which the repression of the Oedipus complex is necessary. Instead, they link secondary process to the censorship of the baby of the night, which is supported by the mother.

Braunschweig and Fain say that the oscillation between the baby of the night and the baby of the day corresponds to the oscillation between primary and secondary process. According to Braunschweig and Fain (1981b) secondary process maintains primary process because this is where much of the instinctual life of the person has to remain alive, whereas conscious thinking has a screen quality that renders it fairly banal and gives the impression of having nothing to hide. However, they think that it is normal for there to be somewhat of a split within the personality in order to allow the pleasure principle to dominate the reality principle.

In this way, Braunschweig and Fain's description of secondary process contains little of what we generally tend to associate with it. Their view of the baby of the day does not correspond to the usual notion of secondary process which is thought to be derived from the relation to external reality and not from a more realistic oedipal fantasy. Their view of development advocates that a more realistic fantasy underlies secondary process in contrast to the fantasy of the baby of the night which conforms to the image of the mother and her own oedipal object and with which the baby might identify.

I used the term *they advocate* advisedly because frequently their view is caused by a bias and seems to warn against other biases rather than aim at a balanced attitude. But because it counters another equally prevalent bias, in which secondary process is considered mature and desirable and the desexualizing action of idealization is ignored, it seemed worth listening to their cautions.[2]

Braunschweig and Fain link the sequence in which there is always *something* with secondary process, semantic precision, and depression in the face of a loss. They call it *fetishistic* but assume that this kind of fetishism is necessary for psychic functioning. For instance, they believe that certain fetishistic qualities are superimposed on the object in order for it to be experienced as the refound object. But I think that in choosing the term fetish, they added a certain prejudice to their theory. Fain (1962) supports this impression when he warns against the shortcomings of the process: he thinks that when thinking cannot be invaded, it is invested as an object. It can be compared to the light children need during the night.

There can be no question that by avoiding the task of a complete developmental history, these authors seem to take a very casual attitude toward the concepts they are using, and it has been an arduous task to understand their thinking and to systematize it as much as I have. I was often tempted to omit more than I did because of the ambiguity of what they say. I do not agree with them in denigrating secondary process when it comes to communication among analysts. Nevertheless I overcame my misgivings in the hope that these theories might stimulate others to think along the same lines and to benefit from them. When these writings avoid the total glorification of the obscure they mitigate against reification in psychoanalysis. When readers can keep in mind that terminology that applies to one context should be avoided in another where it is inappropriate, they can perhaps allow Braunschweig and Fain's thinking to penetrate and to stimulate some new directions. They had this effect on me, and I think that they deserve attention even though they write far too loosely for scientific communication.

What their texts lack to a deplorable extent are references to defenses or levels of regression. This is in keeping with the style of many post-Lacanians, who are not interested in stratifications of defenses or levels of regression. Laplanche (1981b, p. 50) claims that *defense* and *conflict* are not terms used by Lacan. This approach seems to be related to the glorification of the unconscious, which has played such a prominent part in the history of French psychoanalysis.

The Preoedipal Place of the Father

However, from a totally different sector within the Paris Psychoanalytic Society there are reminders that interpretations based on triangular relationships are prevalent in the thinking of most French analysts, even among those who are strongly opposed to the Lacanian heritage. For example, when Chasseguet-Smirgel (1986b) speaks about the wish to return to the maternal belly in perversion, she is emphatic about her conviction that this does not constitute an interpretation based on the mother-child dyad, rather, it is based on the destruction of the father, who stands in the way of this return to the mother's womb. In this case, she did not hypothesize that the father was absent from the psychic reality of nonpsychotic patients harboring the return to the womb fantasy. Rather, the fantasy entails a father who had to be destroyed in order to gain access to the mother's genitals. Therefore, guilt, fear of punishment, and the defenses against them play such a dominant role in the perversions.

Another theory, less daring than Braunschweig and Fain's, yet also original, aroused my interest, too. It is by Le Guen (1974), a former Lacanian, and concerns the origins of the Oedipus complex. His theory attempts to elucidate the layering of objects images and the unconscious meanings attached to them, therefore he seems less abstract and removed from actual experience than Braunschweig and Fain. Le Guen links the stranger anxiety at eight months of age to the Oedipus complex because it involves the mother, the child, and the stranger. In this *originating Oedipus*, as he calls it, the stranger, who designates the loss of the mother, acts as the precursor for the oedipal father. He only exists inasmuch as his irruption and the child's awareness of it, leads to the discovery of the object's absence, but he does not exist as an object in his own right. Despite being anonymous, his role is crucial in that he marks the loss of the mother; one might say that he forbids her, and he marks her place. As such, he is entirely negative, existing as he does through the lack of the mother: truly a *not mother*.

Marking the absence of the mother as he does, the nonmother transmits no information: the departure was known. Instead his presence arouses the child's wish for the mother. Therefore he causes the experience of dissatisfaction and frustration. Indeed, Le Guen (1974) thinks that the nonmother forbids the mother by designating her as absent; or the nonmother could be said to be the model of all future prohibitions. The desire for the mother's presence entails the refusal to accept the nonmother, his destruction, because reunion with the mother implies sending the nonmother back into the void. "It is the prefiguration of the wish for the murder of the father" (p. 23).

Le Guen thinks that Freud has never properly explained the advent of the father into the psyche of the child and that eventually Freud had to have recourse to a phylogenic explanation of the original murder of the father that is transmitted by means of heredity.

Le Guen does not believe that Klein solved the problem of the father because her theory postulates only pseudo-objects and because Klein has never properly constituted the oedipal triangle. He also takes issue with the notion of part objects and thinks that for the subject a part object is simply an index of the lability of the representation for an object. Moreover, he does not think that the triangle has been established by Lacan. The latter situates it along with the mirror stage in which the child is alone and has expelled mother and father. Lacan's references to the Other, that is, the mirror image, do not seem to Le Guen to be a proper explanation for the advent of the father in the psyche of the child.

Summarizing Lacan's view of the reasons for and the origin of a father, Le Guen suggests that in the Lacanian system there is the reference to the mother's wish for the phallus and the child's wish to be the phallus that satisfies her. It is understood that the phallus is that of the father. It is neither a fantasy nor an object (be it partial, internal, or other), still less an organ; it is a signifier (it therefore belongs to language). Le Guen is critical of the notion of the mother's desire for the father being somehow transmitted to the child in such a way that the phallus becomes equated with the place of the mirror image. He considers it too great a jump in logic. (This judgment is in sharp contrast to that made by Braunschweig and Fain, who are not deterred by this kind of criticism and base their theory on a notion of unconscious communication between the mother's erotic thoughts and the child she is handling.)

To return to Le Guen's theory, he says "the nonmother represents both the lack of the mother and the one who provokes it. The child passes progressively from trauma to danger and from danger to threat; it is that which differentiates the castration complex from the work of mourning where the subject has to face the realization of a loss and not only a simple threat" (pp. 46–47). Eventually the threat has to be differentiated from loss.

Le Guen proposes that the early image of the mother implicates what is later known as the penis. She has breasts that are the first symbol of *having* and that are later supplanted by other narcissistically valued attributes. Here again, of course, it is a matter of deferred action, and the mother in the earliest stage is phallic because she *has*, even though *phallic* is an idea that pertains to a later period of development.

Le Guen postulates that the nonmother exists only to signify the nonexistence of the mother. It is, therefore, a concept that is empty. It calls forth the notion of a hollow that only the mother's reappearance can fill. In this sense, Le Guen thinks that the nonmother reveals the underpinnings of castration fantasies. This takes into account some of Melanie Klein's ideas of an early Oedipus complex and also incorporates some of the Lacanian ideas about the gap residing at the core of being. Similarly, the image of the father as both castrated and castrating is compatible with Freud's image of the totemic meal that follows upon the original murder of the father. The father appears first as a god and then as the sacrificial animal. Le Guen thinks that his theory takes into consideration these phenomena and makes a place for what eventuates in the image of the father at the end of a complex development.

The concepts of both deferred action and *anaclesis,* which Laplanche prefers to call propping, merit a brief aside. Since none of these words are particularly good translations of the terms that Freud and now Le Guen have exploited, another attempt must be made to give them meaning. Thus, the nonmother, according to this theory, becomes the support, the underpinning, upon which the image of the father is built, perhaps in the same way as a church can be built upon an older basilica. However, since Le Guen's theory involves living images, the interaction is less static and layered. The most famous illustration is the Wolfman's dream, in which Freud explains what he means by this deferred action upon a scene that is perceived without anxiety and without being understood. Only at a later date, when the scene is understood with all its implications, is the anxiety generated and repression instituted. On the one hand, we can observe this retroactive quality time and again; on the other, it is relatively neglected in the genetic explanatory models. It is predicated on retroactive resexualization that implies a development that is neither layered nor linear. This concept helps to explain phenomena such as survivor guilt because it explains why some people can do everything in their power to survive a battle, incarceration in a concentration camp, and other traumatic events, as long as survival is in the service of self-preservation. But these same people can become overcome with guilt when, after a period of latency, there is a resumption of normal sexualized fantasies or activities that cause survival to merge with the fantasy of victory over the dead oedipal rival. This deferred resexualization is dependent on a latency between the trauma and the symptom.

Le Guen thinks that we do not have to have recourse to a preexisting scheme in the collective unconscious to explain the fantasy of the murder of the father, since stranger anxiety pertains to each person's history and can be taken as the basis for the Oedipus conflict. Le Guen has expressed his reluctance to construct a theory that attempts to account for the period that precedes ego formation, and since the birth of the ego is more contemporaneous with stranger anxiety than with the return of the mother to the bed of the father when the baby is three months old, Le Guen prefers to build his theory around the advent of the stranger. The stranger is the originator of fantasies and wishes because he signifies the loss of the mother. In Le Guen's theory, the image of the father appears later and is more reassuring than its underpinnings, that is, the stranger or the nonmother. In this way, the image of the father does not become part of the earliest triangle which, by virtue of this fact, should not be designated as oedipal.

Le Guen (1974) thinks that the game of the wooden reel described by Freud in *Beyond the Pleasure Principle* (1920) enables the child to take the place of the nonmother, who makes the mother disappear. He not only masters the mother, whom he can cause to disappear and reappear, but he also masters the nonmother by means of an identification with it. This is identification with the aggressor, according to Le Guen, who thinks that of the two phases of the game, the phase in which the toy is rejected is more important than that in which it is refound. The refinding brings the child back to the mother-child couple, whereas the disappearance of the reel concerns a threesome that is mastered here for the first time by the child's turning passive into active and initiating the disappearance. It is a defense against loss in that it is converted into a disappearance that does not require mourning. If there were a real loss of the mother, the game would be impossible.

Le Guen thinks that the discovery of the differences between the sexes reduplicates stranger anxiety. The stranger is the sex of the other. The antecedent to the distinction between the sexes is the breast, and in this differentiation the father and children are classified together and the mother stands out as the one who has. This permits a primary identification with the father, who at this stage of development belongs among the ones who do not *have*.

At a slightly later stage of development, one has to be father in order to have mother; only later still does one have to have a penis to be father (p. 123). Here Le Guen quotes Lacan: "Let us say that these relations [between the sexes] will revolve around a being and having that, while relating to a signifier, the phallus, have the thwarted effect of giving on the one hand reality to the subject in this signifier, and on the other to render unreal the relations to be signified" (Lacan 1966, p. 694). As usual, Lacan creates more obscurity than light, and Le Guen's theory is supported by the observation that within the evolution of the individual, the images of mother and father change. Therefore the meaning of the possession of breasts, especially if it is kept separate from the process of introjection of what Laplanche calls the milk, enables Le Guen to postulate a maternal attribute similar to the father's penis, that is its precursor, and hers to keep.

Le Guen thinks that Freud's idea according to which children interpret the difference between the sexes in terms of the mother is the correct one: it is the mother who gives her son a penis and denies it to her daughter. She gives it to the one whose idea of the differences between the sexes is based on the fantasy of castration.

> The revelation of the penis throws [the girl] back to her lack, sign of the mother's treason, in the same way as the irruption of the

> nonmother signified to her her absence; this originating situation is the underpinning of the new scene of the discovery of the anatomical difference between the sexes and the whole takes on meaning afterwards (by means of deferred action), according to the equation: mother implicates penis, it being understood that the penis is both the mother and that which authorizes possession of her. Thus originates penis envy. [p. 133]

Therefore, the wish to have is much more immediate than the fear of losing it. Only the castration threat can introduce that meaning into the perception of the sex of the girl for the boy. Otherwise, according to Le Guen, the sight of the female genital is a matter of indifference to the boy. He has no reason to think of loss or castration. The fate of man relates more to finding a penis that is too small than one that is missing. Le Guen thinks that the problems of the boy are more complicated than those of the girl; the discovery of the penis sends her right back to the originating triangulation, whereas the boy must not only discover the absence of the penis of women but also recognize the size (*grandeur* in French) and the force of the father's penis. According to Le Guen the father's penis is also the token of the mother's love for the father in the sense that she is considered the one who gave it to her favorite.

The wish for a child, according to Le Guen, is the wish to reproduce oneself with the mother. Since it is linked to the mother, it is also in line with the desire to obtain a penis from her. Le Guen's theory concerning subsequent development is not as clear as it should be, but he does believe that the wish for a child is not a poor substitute for the penis that cannot be and constitutes therefore a primary fulfillment in the life of the woman.

The application of Le Guen's thoughts to analysis is demonstrated in a passage in which he has recourse "to a concise and therefore false formula." He says that the analysand presents himself for treatment by proposing a maternal transference, that the analyst imposes upon him a paternal transference, and it is precisely in this difference, in this fault, that interpretation and mutation are introduced. Thus the analyst always brings back the paternal imago, but never constitutes himself as father. It is here that we find both the model of the originating Oedipus—the psychoanalyst is the nonmother who takes on meaning by signifying the absence of the mother—and the myth of mothers and sons that can only appear on the authority of the father.

Like Braunschweig and Fain, Le Guen postulates that the wish is born at the same time as the interdiction, the nonmother being the one who arouses both. In this theory, too, the object attains meaning through its absence. These are the points of similarity; otherwise there are many differences, in view of the fact that Braunschweig and Fain aim at explaining instinctual and sexual drive behavior as well as dismantling to some degree secondary process functioning. Their emphasis is therefore only secondarily on the object and only inasmuch as it can throw the individual back to his own mental and representational faculties in which the real object almost attains a screening function for the fantasized incestuous one.

Fain (1971) claims that the stranger does not exist in faulty development either because a constant stimulus-barrier-type activity may keep him inoffensive or because between the excitation and the representation there persists a gap from which springs a shattering primary reality, in which the erection of a whole edifice affirms that there is nothing and that the representation that hides the void is responsible (primary fetishism). This occurs despite the repeated affirmation of the stranger's existence, which denies the fact that the poorly differentiated excitation remains unable to represent itself. Fain (1971) says that the stranger makes it impossible to maintain the pleasure ego over the reality ego because of the influx of undifferentiated stimuli which threaten by their not being managed by the stimulus barrier. His stress is on the exciting quality of the lack of representation of the reality beyond the pleasure ego, whereas

Le Guen demonstrates the sequence of representations that are superimposed on each other.

In this way, each theorist attains an internal consistency that never quite matches that of the others. However, despite these divergencies they resemble each other more than they resemble their foreign colleagues. Their theories concerning individuation and the separation from the mother are quite different from those of the Americans because the French theories invariably involve a triangle. The French tend to think in terms that express the eventual Oedipus complex either because they postulate an earlier Oedipus complex or because they think that in the analysis of adults the pregenital layers appear to be fused with the oedipal ones. Again, in this approach, they differentiate themselves from other theorists whose interpretations pay greater attention to developmental layers and who tend to concentrate to a greater degree on the interplay of mother and child during these early phases. It is this difference in perspective that makes their views challenging and worthy of attention.

Notes

[1]Laplanche, who became interested in the study of psychosis during his Lacanian days, refers to the impact of the lack of the father in the German poet Hoelderlin's psychosis. Couched in Lacanian terminology, Laplanche (1961) suggests that the absence of the father in psychosis is not the origin of the difficulty. The difficulty is that the fault could help the psychotic, but it is the absence of this fault, the fact that nothing appears to be missing to the subject, whereas in his psyche something is missing indeed. Laplanche's assessment of Hoelderlin's breakdown was that "Hoelderlin suffered from the absence of fault" (p. 132).

[2]Laplanche (1970, 1976 ed.) traces Freud's thinking with regard to the ego. He thinks that there was a brief time when Freud accepted the ego with its desexualized energy and its binding qualities but then undid his own theoretical construct by introducing the death instinct, and stuck to it. Laplanche thinks that Freud's introduction of the death instinct saved this theory of sexuality.

14

Ideas on Reality in Human Development and the Psychoanalytic Situation

There are many reasons why the French became intrigued by the function of reality in psychic life. Lacan's anti-ego stance is only one. Another is the conclusions drawn by the *psychosomaticiens* concerning the pathology they encountered among their patients that they think is caused by a delibidinized super-reality-adaptive ego. Yet a third set of motivating factors is the discarding of the idea that there is a biologically determined drive development that is ipso facto seeking an object that is part of external reality. Lastly, there is the analytic process itself with its complex relationship to reality.

It is readily apparent that Fain and Braunschweig's approach to psychoanalysis minimizes the impact of reality and real objects. It dispenses with reality other than in the service of the pleasure principle, that is, as the source for fantasies. Braunschweig (1983) says that "the function of the real is wrong in that it makes out of reality a nonpsychic concept, that is, escaping libido theory which he (Freud) demonstrated applies to all facts of psychic life" (p. 1032).[1]

Actually, Freud's ideas about reality were complex, and there is no reason to believe that his intention was to create a kind of pansexuality, even though his work emphasized that the ego functions in the service of the pleasure principle. Braunschweig and Fain (1975b) maintain that the interest that was focused on the ego at a certain time could only establish itself to the detriment of representations constituted by erotism. They say, "Somehow, when the ego becomes the object of a psychological study, the authors of such a study become psychologists and are no longer, properly speaking, psychoanalysts" (p. 190).

In their way of thinking, external reality has a place in the constitution of the drive. What was innate and biological in Freud's theory has become environmentally determined in theirs, but once the object's role in the erogenization of the body and the internalization of a prohibition aiding in the retention of libido has been played, they pay little attention to the role of external reality.

Racamier, whose work would merit closer attention than I am paying to it in this overview only because it mostly concerns psychosis and comes close to the approaches taken by American analysts, does not share this bias. He observes, "Like all those who start to do a little cooking in Freud's pots, I thought to find in his work a psychoanalytic conception of reality that is simple and cut from one piece that I could use as a target according to my own pleasure. It was the image of reality as antagonist of pleasure" (1962, 1979 ed., p. 285). He concludes that to think of reality on one side and the unconscious on the other would mean the castration of psychoanalysis. Reality must be seen as a constituent of the psyche as well as being experienced outside of it. The reality principle is not opposed to the pleasure principle; therefore the relationship between psychosis and reality is much more complex than the simple statement to the effect that in psychosis reality is lost. Rather, there is a loss in the mediating process that screens, selects, and libidinizes the relations to the outside world. There can be both too much and too little reality in psychosis.

Reality in the Work of Castoriadis-Aulagnier

Castoriadis-Aulagnier (1975), whose main interest also concerns psychosis, has a most original way of conceptualizing early human development and its relationship to reality. She thinks that a judgment based on the reality principle underlies primary process and says that "fantasy and the unconscious result from the joint work of the constitutive assumption and a first judgment, imposed by the reality principle, on the presence of an external and separate space" (p. 84). But this reality judgment is subsequently reworked so as to conform to the pleasure principle. She thinks that it is necessary for the one who fantasizes to put into the scene being contemplated two objects and outside the scene a third who looks on, represented by the gaze. She suggests that two objects are necessary in the scenario because every fantasy also represents the relation linking the space of the subject's own body to the space of the body representing the Other. Thus, they are the metonymic representatives of these two spaces. The primary process functions according to the need to place outside this scene a gaze that supposedly experiences pleasure or unpleasure. This postulate is based on a causal relation "between the experience of pleasure, or unpleasure, and the omnipotence of the desire of the Other" (p. 87).

She thinks that primary process entails the recognition of an elsewhere, cathected by the first representative of the Other, an elsewhere by which the existence of the father is preannounced and that leads to the recognition of the parental couple. Before this elsewhere is occupied by attributes proving paternal presence, it is that by which the psyche presents to itself the existence of an enigmatic object or place which permits the

Other to satisfy a desire that no longer asks the help of the one who is watching the scene.

It is interesting that she considers the basis of primary process the recognition of a limit, which presupposes that a judgment of reality is at work at the beginning of primary process functioning. The action of the pleasure principle will be to remodel this elsewhere to make it conform to the representation of the world invented by the primary process, which paradoxically permits it to fail to recognize the reality that was necessary for it to start functioning. She defines the primary process itself as functioning according to the belief that everything that exists is the effect of the omnipotence of the wish of the Other. And with the fantasy of omnipotence, even of the Other, the concept of elsewhere is denied.

With the reference to the wish of the Other, or the desire of the Other, we have entered the Lacanian vocabulary, although Castoriadis-Aulagnier uses the expression in a totally comprehensible way, whereas when it appears in the literature of the true followers of Lacan it becomes mystifying. Her idea of the primary process is based on a fantasy involving two participants directed by the wish of a third. It is reminiscent of the fantasy of a patient who thought that he and his woman analyst would work until his resources were depleted and the treatment would end in failure. Then his father would be vindicated. The omnipotence of the wish projected onto an idealized father is clearly evident in this fantasy as well as in that of the two participants who are being directed by the wish of the third. This patient's fantasies were prompted by the need to deny an external reality over which he had no influence, a denial that became less necessary as he felt less threatened by the prospect of his own success and accomplishments.

To some degree Castoriadis-Aulagnier's study is influenced by Lacan's (1949, 1966) objection to the conception of the ego as organized by the reality principle because he finds it to be a formulation of a "scientific prejudice which is most contrary to the dialectic of knowledge" (p. 99). But Castoriadis-Aulagnier, who was trained by Lacan and is now one of the best-known members of the Fourth group, conducted a thoughtful reexamination of the problems of human development in the light of the problems of psychosis. Le Guen (1974) said that Lacan's greatest merit was to have shown the emptiness of some hollow ideas, and it seems to me that some of his disciples have put this tendency to good use. Castoriadis-Aulagnier challenged some established notions such as the layering of the processes which led her to the interesting conclusion that the primary process aims at defending against the reality that sets it in motion.

Castoriadis-Aulagnier suggests that there are three modes of functioning, or three processes of metabolization: the originating process, the primary process, and the secondary process. The representations that result from these processes are respectively the pictographic representation, fantasy, and ideational representation.[2]

The Originating Process at the Onset of Mental Life

Other than suggesting that it is a reality judgment that sets primary process in motion, Castoriadis-Aulagnier's most original ideas concern the existence of the *originating process*. It is a process that is seen as being represented as the originator of what it represents, or as she says it, everything that exists is self-engendered by the system that represents it. It is shaped according to the model of the meeting between a sense organ and an external object that can stimulate it, but it has the particularity that it ignores the duality of which it is composed. What is represented passes itself off to the psyche as a presentation of itself: "the representing agent sees in the representation the product of its autonomous work, it contemplates in it the engendering of its own image" (p. 48). It is accompanied by a prime of pleasure.

Unpleasure exists every time a new representation is required. Castoriadis-Aulagnier (1975) links this displeasure with the death instinct that only aims at abolishing excitations, or as she says, to restore the "previous sleep, an unintelligible 'before' in which all was silence" (p. 51). When the originating process combines with unpleasure, the mind sees itself as the source of the unpleasure and wishes to destroy this image of itself. "Unpleasure has as its corollary and as its synonym a desire for self-destruction" (p. 51). It evokes a radical hatred, present from the beginning, for an activity of representation that presupposes, because of its link with the body, a perception of a state of need which its function is to annul. The desire not to have to desire is an aim inherent in desire itself. "Desire of no-desire" is her formula for the death instinct. This accounts for the view of the world in which the perceiver and what is perceived as well as the activity of representing the perception are inextricably interwoven. It is a process that accounts for certain states of narcissism and psychosis, especially in its self-mutilating aspects that resemble killing of the bearer of bad news in order not to hear it.

Automutilation, or the wish for self-destruction of the representing agency, is different from the wish to make the object disappear through metabolizing it. The first derives from Thanatos, whereas the latter derives from Eros.

The originating process constitutes the representative background that gives the individual the indefinable feeling of being at home in his skin, feeling well, feeling ill at ease, carrying the world on his shoulders, and so forth. Castoriadis-Aulagnier (1975) suggests that

> in the field of psychosis this representative background can at times occupy the front of the stage. Not that the pictogram, as such, invades consciousness, but the work of secondary process thinking, which in its own way continues its fight and tries to defend itself against this breach, sees its task reversed. It will no longer be a matter of making sense out of the world and feelings that supposedly conform to the encounters from which they emerge, but the

> desperate attempt to render sensible and expressable in words experiences that stem from a representation in which the world is nothing more than the reflection of a body swallowing itself, mutilating itself, rejecting itself. [p. 29]

She also suggests that for the I, the activity of representing is synonymous with interpretation (1975). This means that in her opinion representing is not the equivalent of mirroring an external reality. If indeed this happens to be in keeping with the vocabulary and the thoughts of her previous teacher, it lacks political overtones and seems based on sound reasoning. She has rethought assumptions about the primary and secondary processes, has added an originating process to her developmental theory, and has placed the reality principle at an early stage of this evolution.

Reality in the Psychoanalytic Situation

The French also have a different view of the place of reality in the psychoanalytic process, and the second part of this chapter will be devoted to their ideas on this particular issue. They do not postulate, as some analysts in this country do, the existence of a therapeutic alliance between patient and analyst suggesting that the process is based on the working relationship between the two participants. In France this non-transferential part is just about ignored, and the theories about the analytic situation strive to go beyond the twosome.

André Green (1975a) states emphatically that there is no dual relationship; that in analysis it is the analytic framework that assumes the function of the third. This kind of thinking uses triangulation without oedipalization, just as McDougall does (1980) when she writes that psychosomatic patients create a triangle between the doctor, the patient, and the diseased organ.

Similarly, Chasseguet-Smirgel (1974b) voices her criticism of analysis that is conceived as a dual process. She stresses that there is always a missing third and that analysis does not so much consist of rules that the analyst imposes on the analysand as a set of laws to which they both must submit. She is critical of a conception of analysis that is rather current among her French colleagues and which suggests that the process is imagined and invented by the analyst. She believes this concept brings analysis back to idealism and converts the patient into a creation of the analyst. It makes knowledge impossible. She is convinced that Freud's discovery exists independently and therefore is not simply there by virtue of his imposing his ideas upon the material of the sessions with patients who consulted him. She thinks that the forms of treatment that involve the analyst as a lawgiver, such as that practiced by Lacanian analysts who determine arbitrarily the length of each session, result in a sadomasochistic relationship between analyst and patient.

Chasseguet-Smirgel (1974b) says, "The analyst who takes possession of the law and modifies to his whim the coordinates of the analytic situation imposes himself as the incarnation of reality, which can only result in the total alienation of the patient by means of a confusion between external and psychic reality. This is a return to the dual relationship that is not mediatized" (p. 190). The missing third, according to Chasseguet-Smirgel, is the analyst's superego.

Chasseguet-Smirgel uses the term *missing third* differently from the way her colleagues use it. Yet she seems to be right in the French tradition because of the emphasis on a third factor alongside the presence of the analyst, which is, it seems to me, typical of the French way of regarding the analytic situation.

In keeping with the French propensity to think of both that which is absent as well as that which is present, Pasche (1975) points out that the analytic situation entails the denial of the absence created by the analyst's invisibility. According to him, the analyst undergoes a kind of autocastration. "In thinking that it is the analyst's omnipotence which permits him to be silent and to hide, one takes the effect for the cause" (p. 566). In other words, the invisibility of the analyst leads to fantasies of his omnipotence. It is the proper appreciation by the analysand of the impotence imposed on the analyst which makes out of him the underpinning of parental omnipotence: like a fetish. Analysis creates both the negative reality of the analyst and its denial, which means the recognition and the denial of all that underlies the analyst's positive reality. This idea is stated with the love for paradox that typifies French psychoanalysts. It highlights the complexity of the analytic situation in which a person suspends, denies, scotomizes, or otherwise defends against the many clues received about reality of the analyst, and in a sense allows the analyst to become an object in the patient's personal drama. The intensity and the effectiveness with which this happens varies almost from moment to moment for each patient and determines whether the analyst, to speak with Lewin, has to wake the patient or help him to sleep.

Pasche (1975) says that psychosomatic patients see only the analysts' reality and limit their role to that of a therapist; psychotics see only the analysts' unconscious impulses; for perverts, the psychoanalyst becomes a utensil to be enjoyed, dirtied, destroyed, in order to reduce him to a state of a fetish; character neurotics use what they know in order to master; and depressives tend to introject the analysts reserve and interpret it as deficiency, as the shadow of an object. A full understanding that analysts both stimulate and frustrate these impulses leads to an appreciation of the force of resistance in analysis and counters some of the more benign views of their role.

It is evident that many French analysts avoid the idea of a psychoanalytic relationship involving two participants. Whether it is the analyst's superego, the analyst's analyst (André Green), the split between the omnipotence and the impotence of the analyst (Pasche), or the indifference of the analyst coupled with interest in the patient (Braunschweig), there exists no one-to-one correspondence between the reality of the person and the mental representations it engenders.

In the context of her extensive work on psychoanalysis and reality, Braunschweig (1971) says the neurotic, with his unhappiness and lack of satisfaction, would like psychoanalysis to cause magically the coincidence of the truth of his wish and the reality of the object. This coincidence is possible only by means of a fetish. This is why the pervert needs nothing from the psychoanalyst; but does it not also imply that the neurotic would like to pervert psychoanalysis?

Here, at its most vociferous, is the objection to coupling the person of the analyst with anything real. According to the view of many of the analysts quoted, to see the analytic relationship as a real one would rob it of its symbolism and would endow it with the functions of a fetish that helps to deny what is missing. It would be a perversion of psychoanalysis. Braunschweig (1971) points out that

> the exclusion of the third leads to an obstacle to symbolization. The *symbol can appear only at the place where something is lacking*. Too much presence inhibits capacities for displacement, condensation, symbolization; and excess of absence condenses later on with merger fantasy of the return to primary identification, the body of the mother, nonbeing and the female sex mixed with the open wound of castration. This excess will lead to fetish formation and not to primary penis envy. Penis envy conditions the birth within the individual of the phallic significant, symbol of what is desirable, narcissistic, erotic, of being and having. [p. 777]

Placing fetish and primary penis envy in opposition to each other, as Braunschweig does, highlights an important aspect of her point of view. The fetish affirms that nothing is missing, whereas penis envy involves the recognition of a lack. There is a great similarity between Braunschweig's view of what happens in analysis and Fain's ideas of the birth of fantasy life discussed in the previous chapter. Braunschweig asserts that "the sum of the external excitations emanating from the presence of the physical person of the analyst in session conjure up at the same time his absence: Here is the most powerful impetus to the instigation of a backward step of the drive seeking to represent itself and to use gradually an increasing quantity of representations repressed all along its history, and this in opposition to the resistances to verbalization" (p. 747).

Braunschweig thinks that the indifference of the analyst plays a crucial role. She told me that most of her interpretations are aimed at revealing to the patient his or her antagonism toward the analyst as the instigator of libidinal impulses experienced as a result of the dissolution of the fantasy of the narcissistic patient-analyst unit. She calls it the hatred of the ego toward the drives stemming from the fact that the patient is asked to return to the diverse identifications and to relive at each level the castration, for this is what they tend to call frustration, denied by the ego.

Taken out of the context of its overly complicated formulation, it means that the patient has to confront the denied frustrations caused by what is missing in the analytic situation, that this necessity is met with the patient's aggression, but that the frustrations have to be acknowledged for the analysis to proceed.

Braunschweig and Fain think that this leads to aggression due to the patient's inability to represent the libidinal excitement generated by the gap. Eventually it can become represented, tied to the notion of a phallus that gratified the mother's erotic longings with which the individual identifies and thereby libidinizes the patient's own body. They say that as the language in analysis becomes desexualized the body becomes resexualized. The pleasure of libidinal excitation is linked with what is missing and replaced by a fantasy. Time and again, they stress the importance of the experience of the gap followed by something that fills it. When they become totally carried away with themselves they draw an analogy between the experience of something missing in analysis and the image of the vagina. In both cases, something exciting eventually has to be allowed to penetrate, which cannot happen if the gap is not experienced first. Because they think that this passivization (the experience of a gap that has to be filled) enables the instinct to undergo the double reversal necessary for the retention of energy and structure formation, this passivization is essential for both sexes, but they are also convinced that there is a strong narcissistic defense against this because it is also associated with feminization, and therefore it represents the greatest obstacle in analysis for both sexes.

They are concerned about the need of analysts and psychoanalytic theory to gloss over that which is imprecise or missing, and they are sensitive to what Jacobson calls *screen hunger*. Braunschweig and Fain (1981b) come close to equating all memories with screen memories because they are experienced as coming from real events and from the outside, they occupy fully the perceptual conscious, and they are therefore the best example of the hidden hallucinatory wish fulfillment.

The authors say that the screen memory succeeds where the neurotic symptom fails. They ask: "Is not the haste of the neurotic undertaking a psychoanalytic treatment to find memories, the aspiration to transform symptoms into screen memories? Is not the wish of the analyst the same at times?" (p. 1225). With regard to the interpretation of dreams in psychoanalysis, they caution that by looking for hidden childhood memories, the analyst might be obscuring the possibility of the psychic reality of the dreams of the mother in which the analysand is the object of the mother's oedipal desires. Furthermore, if the analysis of the ego does not sufficiently take into consideration the derivatives of the unconscious, it can also have screening functions. Memory can aim, according to them, at banalization and resemble operational thinking. Therefore they warn against an approach to analysis that favors screen memory formation.

Fain (1971) also cautions against consensus, which he says is established according to the model of a split. It is a reality that is shared and therefore the object of a collective conscious negation, a denuded reality such as is found in the relationship between the psychosomatic patient and the environment.

They repeatedly stress the need for latent thoughts and imprecision in order to mediate between the impact of reality and the inner world of the person. Thus Braunschweig and Fain (1975b) distrust semantic precision. "Semantic precision (that is, oneness of meaning) originates at the level of the unconscious from the myth of the dead father or for the individual of the father castrated of his desire" (p. 134). The father figure who is created in the place of the murdered one is wholly loved, partly because it has become an ideal and therefore desexualized. In their 1976 study, the authors claim that as long as the analyst is idealized he or she is also desexualized, and only when there is a shift of this image as a result of gaps in the analyst's knowledge is the tender attachment resexualized. This opens the possibility to identify hysterically with "the one who was supposed to know but who can only operate in the same way toward an ideal that he cannot satisfy" (p. 486). It is the failure to be ideal that creates the missing person from the ideal.

They say that the psychoanalytic process with its taboos and restrictions signifies the absence of this ideal. Any alteration in the process itself signifies to the patient that there can be reparation in reality. It would fortify the patient's fantasies in the direction of assuming that something that has never been is indeed possible. Fain recalls Green's warning that "the analyst is there to serve the process and not to use it" (Green 1976, p. 75).

Braunschweig and Fain (1976) object to the idea that something can be introjected in analysis. They think that the notion that something can be taken comes too close to the fantasy of reparation. They distinguish between two sources of frustration in analysis. One they call the failure of the framework to satisfy; the other is the failure to substitute. The first is experienced by the hysteric, whereas the second stems from the analysis of depressives. In the first there is frustration tolerance, whereas in the second there is the search for the concrete substitute for that which has been lost. This is the mother of the depressive, whom they call the guarantor of the investment, that is, the one who has always presented herself as the sole object without whom love is abolished. The depressive mode with its attachment to the object that alone can guarantee the erotic investment of the outside world is viewed here in the line of those forms of pathology in which the impulse does not attain the flexibility to turn. Braunschweig and Fain go very far with these speculations on the inability to mourn as well as the mother's inability to help the infant develop libido sufficient to invest the body erotically independently of the presence of the object. This constitutes the epitomy of the dual relationship.

In analysis, the indifference of the analyst eventually represents the loss of the internal object and the undoing of the narcissism of the ego leading to the triangular relationship between parent and child.[3]

In this view, nothing is repaired, and nothing is introjected. We could say that it is a negative definition of the psychoanalytic process because it really does not define the action or interaction that does take place; it only emphasizes how the psychoanalytic process should not be viewed. In this respect, there is often something incomplete in these observations, and they are best viewed as cautions against this or that misconception of analysis. But as such, I consider them valuable. Analysts can become excessively concerned with the real qualities of the early objects in a patient's life or with the reparative quality of the empathic analytic environment. The French remind us that psychoanalysis is neither nursing care nor a court of law, although I am sure that they, like analysts elsewhere, have to rely on the integrity of each individual practitioner to practice the subtle art of this impossible profession, and that, in their case, they have to guard against their love of brilliant discourse so that it does not color their interactions with patients to such a degree that the treatment remains in fantasy and loses touch with reality altogether.

Notes

[1]Laplanche (1981a) also voiced his opposition to the idea that anxiety is derived from the fear of real harm in childhood. He thinks that anxiety originates in the ego as a result of pressures from the id or superego and that the question of real harm does not enter into the theory of anxiety. It is a response to an internal danger situation in which the binding forces of the ego could be overpowered by the unbinding forces, coming mostly from the id.

[2]I do not wish to say much about the third representation because it is here that the Lacanian influence makes itself felt in a way that I consider unacceptable. She calls ideational representation also the statement or the declaration, and this in turn relates to the effect of the discourse of the mother, all of which is reminiscent of the heavy reliance on language that distorts Lacanian psychoanalysis.

[3]Lacanians, according to Schneiderman (1983) link the silence of the analyst to the representation of death.

Epilogue: An Appreciation of the French Contribution

The French ability to combine the new with the old, their ability to see within the tradition the potentiality for innovation: this is what has endeared them to me. They have cultivated Freud's garden in a way that did not maintain it as a shrine or an overly restricted area. In this way they exhibit a capacity that is not as prominent in other countries. But to admire one nation's assets does not have to lead to a denigration of another's. I would not want to have to choose between the meticulous and patient research in which some of my American colleagues have engaged and the French approach; which is more speculative and intuitive. There is no reason why one cannot stimulate and enrich the other.

There is justification for the belief that scientific methodology and laboratory precision have one merit whereas brilliant intuition has another, and that the progress of science depends on a constant interplay between the two. There can be no theory without intuition, and there can be no validation without rigorous articulation and testing. I am convinced that Freud's discoveries took the route of brilliant intuition followed by repeated attempts to construct them into a well-reasoned theory.

The future of psychoanalysis clearly rests on the interaction between intuition and meticulous research that applies, confirms, and refines these discoveries. What was done by one man at the outset can be continued through the efforts of a great number of people drawing from each other's assets. The French, known for their rationality, suddenly discovered a fascination for the irrational, and as I have attempted to show, they have applied their considerable intellectual gifts to the further elucidation of the unconscious. Sometimes their pronouncements lack the meticulousness and the specificity we expect from scientific thinking, but ideally this could stimulate others to further thinking and research rather than rejection.

The French are more daring, and their audacity leads them to pronouncements that are often quite on the mark. I remember a conversation with Béla Grunberger in which he said that a prospective patient had found his name in the telephone book. "I knew immediately that he was paranoid." Later, in the quiet hours, I thought about this quick diagnosis and saw how justified it was. I realized that only a person who distrusts everyone would fail to look more closely at the qualifications of an analyst. I then remembered a patient who consulted me after she who had obtained my name from a person whom she disliked and distrusted: the treatment did not work.

Chasseguet-Smirgel once noted that the depressive has never accepted the loss of the oedipal object. When I asked her if she had ever written more extensively about this problem, she told me that she had not. It was one of those casually written statements. Throughout this book there are many of these. André Green has made some very apt and daring observations. Michel Fain outdoes almost everyone in this kind of audacity.

By comparison Americans are modest and most methodical. At best, it is a refreshing change to read a work where thoughts are spelled out in great detail and where terms are defined. At worst this approach can become tedious and uninspired, moving with a wooden quality that lacks the excitement of discovery. Both national tendencies can go to intolerable extremes, and both can be equally fruitful and appealing. My concentration on the French capacity for elegant thinking is not meant to denigrate other forms of obtaining knowledge.

By remaining in the areas in which I felt reasonably competent, I had to omit important aspects of the work being done in France. By not comparing the theories of the French with those of analysts concerned with the same problems in the United States I have restricted the scope of the text. This is a limitation I set for myself.

More than anything I wanted to arouse the curiosity of others about this fascinating world that opened for me when I started to study French psychoanalysis. I have not wanted to proselytize: I am not even always in full agreement with the views that I have conveyed. However, I have appreciated them for the vistas they open and for the inspiration they might give others to rethink some of the tenets that perhaps they might not otherwise have questioned.

The task of ending this book reminds me of a remark made by one of my professors at the end of a course: a course, like a book, is abandoned; it is never finished. Neither is a seed that has been planted. I hope to have shown that Freud's garden lends itself to continuous planting, harvesting, and cross-fertilization between people who cultivate it in their own way and that the French way of doing this can serve as a source of stimulation and inspiration. In short, I hope that the reader will want to cultivate his own garden with some of the seeds imported from France.

References

Abraham, K. A. (1924). Short study of the development of the libido. In *Selected Papers on Psychoanalysis*, pp. 418–516. London: Hogarth, 1968.

Alexandrian, S. (1972). Le rêve dans le surréalisme. *Nouvelle Revue de Psychanalyse* 5:27–50.

Altman, L. (1975). A case of narcissistic personality disorder: the problem of treatment. *International Journal of Psycho–Analysis* 56:187–197.

Anzieu, D. (1974). De la marque laissée sur la psychanalyse par ses origines. In *Les Chemins de l'Anti-Oedipe*, ed. J. Chasseguet-Smirgel, pp. 159–169. Toulouse: Privat.

____ (1975). *L'auto-analyse de Freud et la Découverte de la Psychanalyse.* Paris: Presses Universitaires de France.

____ (1977). L'image, le texte, et la pensée. *Nouvelle Revue de Psychanalyse* 16:119–134.

____ (1979). La psychanalyse au service de la psychologie. *Nouvelle Revue de Psychanalyse* 20:58–76.

____ (1986). *Une Peau pour les Pensées.* Paris: Clancier-Guenaud.

Ascher, M. (1986). Conjoint treatment of a mother and her sixteen-month-old toddler. *International Journal of Psychoanalytic Psychotherapy* 11:315–330.

Balkanyi, C. (1976). Remarques sur les rapports de la linguistique et de la psychanalyse. *Revue Française de Psychanalyse* 40:725–732.

Bär, E. S. (1974). Understanding Lacan. *Psychoanalysis and Contemporary Science* 3:473–544.

Barande, R. (1975). Quels psychanalystes et pour quel faire? *Revue Française de Psychanalyse* 39:225–246.

____ (1979). Transmission ou processus? *Revue Française de Psychanalyse* 43:211–223.

____ (1984). Une religion nouvelle. Qu'elle est belle la 'part transmise' lorsque la psychanalyse nous est contée comme roman familial. *Revue Française de Psychanalyse* 48:321–329.

Barande, I., and Barande, R. (1975). *Histoire de la Psychanalyse en France.* Toulouse: Privat.

Bertin, C. (1982). *Marie Bonaparte A Life.* New York: Harcourt Brace Jovanovich.

Besançon, A. (1974). Freud, Abraham, Laios. In *Les Chemins de l'Anti-Oedipe,* ed. J. Chasseguet-Smirgel, pp. 23–38. Toulouse: Privat.

Bourguignon, A. (1977). Mémorial d'une rencontre. *Nouvelle Revue de Psychanalyse* 15:235–250.

Bourguignon, A., and Bourguignon, O. (1983). Singularité d'une histoire. *Revue Française de Psychanalyse* 47:1259–1279.

Braunschweig, D. (1971). Psychanalyse et realité. *Revue Française de Psychanalyse* 35:655–800.

_____ (1983). Traces de Jung dans l'évolution théorique de Freud. *Revue Française de Psychanalyse* 47:1027–1044.

Braunschweig, D., and Fain, M. (1971). *Eros et Antéros*. Paris: Payot.

_____ (1975a). Le messianisme en psychanalyse. *Revue Française de Psychanalyse* 39:195–225.

_____ (1975b). *La Nuit, Le Jour*. Paris: Presses Universitaires de France.

_____ (1976). Reflexions introductives à l'étude de quelques facteurs actifs dans le contre-transfert. *Revue Française de Psychanalyse* 40:483–540.

_____ (1981a). Un aspect de la constitution de la source pulsionelle. *Revue Française de Psychanalyse* 45:205–226.

_____ (1981b). Bloc-notes et lanternes magiques. *Revue Française de Psychanalyse* 45:1221–1241.

Brenner, C. (1955). *An Elementary Textbook of Psychoanalysis*. New York: Doubleday.

Cahn, R. (1983). Le procès du cadre. *Revue Française de Psychanalyse* 47:1107–1134.

Castoriadis-Aulagnier, P. (1975). *La Violence de l'Interprétation*. Paris: Presses Universitaires de France.

Chasseguet-Smirgel, J. (1962). L'analité et les composantes anales du vécu corporel. *Canadian Psychiatric Association Journal* 7:16–24.

_____ (1964). *La Sexualité Féminine*. Paris: Payot. *Female Sexuality* Trans. Ann Arbor: University of Michigan Press, 1970.

_____ (1966). Notes cliniques sur un fantasme commun à la phobie et à la paranoia. *Revue Française de Psychanalyse* 30:121–144.

_____ (1967). Note clinique sur les rêves d'examen. In *Pour une Psychanalyse de l'Art et de la Créativité*, pp. 177–182. Paris: Payot 1971.

_____ (1971). *Pour une Psychanalyse de l'Art et de la Créativité*. Paris: Payot.

____ ed. (1974a). *Les Chemins de l'Anti-Oedipe*. Toulouse: Privat.

____ (1974b). Brêves reflexions critiques sur la construction en analyse. *Revue Française de Psychanalyse* 38:183–196.

____ (1975a). Notule sur les mots et les choses. *Revue Française de Psychanalyse* 34:599–602.

____ (1975b). *L'Idéal du Moi*. Tchou.

____ (1976). Freud and female sexuality. *International Journal of Psychoanalysis* 57:275–286.

____ (1981). Loss of reality in perversions. *Journal of the American Psychoanalytic Association* 29:511–534.

____ (1984a). L'histoire de la psychanalyse française. Unpublished manuscript.

____ (1984b). *Éthique et Esthétique de la Perversion*. Seyssel: Champ Vallon.

____ (1986a). "The Green Theater": An attempt at interpretation of group manifestations of unconscious guilt. In *Sexuality and Mind*, pp. 109–127. New York: University Press.

____ (1986b). The archaic matrix of the Oedipus complex. In *Sexuality and Mind*, pp. 74–91. New York: New York University Press.

____ (1987). Une tentative de solution perverse chez une femme et son échec. Paper presented at the International Psychoanalytic Association, 35th Congress, Montreal, July 1987.

Chiland, C. (1974). Chemins de l'Oedipe à l'anti-Oedipe. In *Les Chemins de l'Anti-Oedipe*, ed. J. Chasseguet-Smirgel, pp. 39–58. Toulouse: Privat.

____ (1981). The psychoanalytic movement in France. *French–Language Psychology* 2, pp. 55–68. North-Holland Publishing Company.

Cosnier, J. (1979). La transmission de la psychanalyse. *Revue Française de Psychanalyse* 43:227–238.

Cournut, J. (1975). Le travail associatif. *Revue Française de Psychanalyse* 39:581–589.

____ (1979). L'analyse dite dictatique. *Revue Française de Psychanalyse* 43:239–246.

Cremerius, J. (1977). Ist die "psychosomatische Struktur" der franzoesischen Schule krankheitsspezifisch? *Psyche* 31:293–317.

____ (1982). Die Bedeutung des Dissidenten fuer die Psychoanalyse. *Psyche* 36:481–514.

Cremerius, J., Hoffman, S. O., Hoffmeister, W., and Trinborn, W. (1979). Die manipulierte Objekte. *Psyche* 33:801–828.

Davis, F. B. (1973). Three letters from Sigmund Freud to André Breton. *Journal of the American Psychoanalytic Association* 21:127–134.

Donnet, J. L. (1983). L'enjeu de l'interpretation. *Revue Française de Psychanalyse* 47:1135–1150.

Fain, M. (1962). Contribution à l'étude des variations de la symptomatologie. *Revue Française de Psychanalyse* 26:353–382.

____ (1971). Prélude à la vie fantasmatique. *Revue Française de Psychanalyse* 35:291–364.

____ (1981a). Vers une conception psychosomatique de l'inconscient. *Revue Française de Psychanalyse* 45:281–292.

____ (1981b). Diachronie, structure, conflit Oedipien. *Revue Française de Psychanalyse* 45:985–997.

Fain, M., and Marty, P. (1959). Aspects fonctionnels et rôle structurant de l'investissement homosexuel au cours de traitements psychanalytiques d'adultes. *Revue Française de Psychanalyse* 23:607–617.

____ (1965). A propos du narcissisme et de sa genèse. *Revue Française de psychanalyse* 29:561–572.

Favret-Saada, J. (1977). Excusez-moi, je ne fais que passer. *Les Temps Modernes* 32:2089–2103.

Federn, E. (1975). Y a-t-il encore un mouvement psychanalytique? *Revue Française de Psychanalyse* 39:59–69.

Fenichel, O. (1945). *The Psychoanalytic Theory of Neurosis*. New York: Norton.

Ferber, R. (1985). Solve your child's sleep problems. Videotape shown on ABC-TV's "20/20." Based on R. Ferber, *Solve Your Child's Sleep Problems*. Boston: Simon & Schuster.

Ferenczi, S. (1912). *Sex in Psychoanalysis*. New York: Dover, 1956.

____ (1923). *Thalassa: A Theory of Genitality*. New York: Norton, 1968.

Ferry, L., and Renaut, R. (1985). *La Pensée 68*. Paris: Gallimard.

Freud, S. (1900). The interpretation of dreams. *Standard Edition* 4/5.

____ (1905). Three essays on the theory of sexuality. *Standard Edition* 7:125–248.

____ (1909). Analysis of a phobia in a five-year-old boy. *Standard Edition* 10:3–152.

____ (1911). Formulations on the two principles of mental functioning. *Standard Edition* 12:213–226.

____ (1913). Totem and taboo. *Standard Edition* 13:1–164.

____ (1914a). On the history of the psycho-analytic movement. *Standard Edition* 14:7–66.

____ (1914b). On narcissism. *Standard Edition* 14:67–104.

____ (1915). Instincts and their vicissitudes. *Standard Edition* 14:109–140.

____ (1920). Beyond the pleasure principle. *Standard Edition* 18:3–66.

____ (1921). Group psychology and the analysis of the ego. *Standard Edition* 18:67–144.

____ (1923). The ego and the id. *Standard Edition* 19:3–68.

____ (1925). An autobiographical study. *Standard Edition* 20:7–74.

____ (1932). Neue Folge der Vorlesungen zur Einfuehrung in die Psychoanalyse. *Gesammelte Werke* 15. Frankfurt: S. Fischer Verlag, 1944.

____ (1933). New introductory lectures on psycho-analysis. *Standard Edition* 22:3–184.

Freud, S. (1960). *Briefe 1873–1939*. Frankfurt: S. Fischer Verlag.

Freud, S., and Abraham, K. (1965). *Briefe 1907–1926*. Frankfurt: S. Fischer Verlag.

Freud, S., and Jung, C. G. (1974). *Letters*. Ed. William McGuire. Princeton: Princeton University Press.

Freud, S., and Laforgue, R. (1977). Correspondence 1923–1937. *Nouvelle Revue de Psychanalyse* 15:251–314.

Gallant, M. (1985). Limpid pessimist. *New York Review of Books* 32 (19):19–24.

Gillibert, J. (1979). Transmission, démission. *Revue Française de Psychanalyse* 43:247–260.

Girard, C. (1984). La part transmise. *Revue Française de Psychanalyse* 48:19–238.

Green, A. (1970). L'affect. *Revue Française de Psychanalyse* 34:883–1141.

____ (1975a). La psychanalyse, son objet, son avenir. *Revue Française de Psychanalyse* 39:103–134.

____ (1975b). La sexualisation et son économie. *Revue Française de Psychanalyse* 39:895–918. Trans. in *Psychoanalysis in France*, ed. S. Lebovici and D. Widlocher, pp. 111–126. New York: International Universities Press, 1980.

____ (1976). Un, autre, neutre: valeurs narcissiques du même. *Nouvelle Revue de Psychanalyse* 9:37–80.

____ (1977). Conceptions of affect. *International Journal of Psycho-Analysis* 58:129–156.

____ (1983). *Narcissisme de Vie, Narcissisme de Mort.* Paris: Editions de Minuit.

Gressot, M. (1975). A propos d'avenir de la psychanalyse. *Revue Française de Psychanalyse* 39:5–26.

Grunberger, B. (1954). Interprétation prégénitale. *Revue Française de Psychanalyse* 18:428–495.

____ (1964). Jalons pour l'étude du narcissisme dans la sexualité féminine. In *La Sexualité Feminine*, ed. J. Chasseguet-Smirgel, pp. 101–126. Paris: Payot. *Female Sexuality*, pp. 68–83. Ann Arbor: University of Michigan Press, 1970.

____ (1971). *Le Narcissisme.* Paris: Payot. *Narcissism.* Trans. by Joyce S. Diamanti. New York: International Universities Press, 1979.

____ (1974). De la technique active à la confusion de langues. *Revue Française de Psychanalyse* 38:521–546.

____ (1980). The oedipal conflicts of the analyst. *Psychoanalytic Quarterly* 49:606–630.

Grunberger, B., and Chasseguet-Smirgel, J. (1976). *Freud ou Reich.* Tchou.

Guillaumin, J. (1979). Transmettre, dit-elle; ou du principe de mort dans le discours institutionel. *Revue Française de Psychanalyse* 43:261–270.

Herzberg-Poloniecka, R. (1984). Périple en psychosomatique à la lumière des symptomes ou du passage du corps malade au corps érogène. In *Corps Malade et Corps Érotique*, pp. 88–99. Paris: Masson.

Jacobson, E. (1957). Denial and repression. In *Depression*, pp. 107–136. New York: International Universities Press, 1971.

Jones, E. (1957). *The Life and Work of Sigmund Freud.* New York: Basic Books.

Kaplan, D. B. (1984). Some conceptual and technical aspects of the actual neurosis. *International Journal of Psycho-Analysis* 65:295–306.

Krystal, H. (1978). Trauma and affects. *Psychoanalytic Study of the Child* 33:81–116.

____ (1981). Paper presented at the midwinter meeting of the American Psychoanalytic Association, New York, December.

Kurzweil, E. (1980). *The Age of Structuralism.* New York: Columbia University Press.

Lacan, J. (1966). *Écrits.* Paris: Éditions du Seuil.

Laplanche, J. (1961). *Hoelderlin et la Question du Père.* Paris: Presses Universitaires de France.

____ (1970). *Life and Death in Psychoanalysis.* Baltimore: Johns Hopkins University Press, 1976.

____ (1981a). A metapsychology put to the test of anxiety. *International Journal of Psycho-Analysis* 62:81–90.

____ (1981b). *Problematiques IV L'inconscient et le ça.* Paris: Presses Universitaires de France.

____ (1987). Paper presented at the 35th Congress of the International Psychoanalytic Association, special discussion group problems in translating Freud. Montreal, July 1987.

Laplanche, J., and Pontalis, J.-B. (1964). Fantasy and sexuality. *International Journal of Psycho-Analysis* 49:1–18, 1968.

____ (1967). *The Language of Psychoanalysis.* New York: Norton, 1973.

Lebovici, S. (1982). The origins and development of the Oedipus complex. *International Journal of Psycho-Analysis* 53:201–216.

Le Guen, C. (1972a). Bornage du champ psychanalytique. *Études Freudiennes* 5–6:27–41.

____ (1972b). Quand le père a peur ou comment Freud, résistant à son fantasme, a institué les Sociétés psychanalytiques. *Études Freudiennes* 5–6:41–50.

____ (1974). *L'Oedipe Originaire.* Paris: Payot.

____ (1981). Quand je me méfie de ma mémoire. *Revue Française de Psychanalyse* 45:1111–1140.

Lewin, B. (1950). Addenda to the theory of oral erotism. In *Selected Writings of Bertram D. Lewin*, ed. J. Arlow. New York: Psychoanalytic Quarterly, 1973, pp. 129–146.

Loewald, H. (1972). On motivation and instinct theory. *Psychoanalytic Study of the Child* 26:91–128.

Luquet, P. (1962). Les identifications précoces dans la structuration. *Revue Française de Psychanalyse* 26:117–247, 304–315.

Luquet-Parat, C. (1964). Le changement d'object. In *La Sexualité Féminine*, ed. J. Chasseguet-Smirgel, pp. 127–142. Paris: Payot. (Eng. trans. *Female Sexuality*, pp. 84–93. Ann Arbor: Michigan Press, 1970.)

Mackay, N. (1981). Melanie Klein's metapsychology. *International Journal of Psycho-Analysis* 62:187–198.

Malcolm, J. (1983). Review of Schneiderman's book of Jacques Lacan. *N. Y. Times Book Review*, April 3, 1983, p. 1.

Marty, P. (1952). Les difficultés narcissiques de l'observateur devant le problème psychosomatique. *Revue Française de Psychanalyse* 16:339–357.

____ (1968). La dépression essentielle. *Revue Française de Psychanalyse* 32:595–598.

____ (1980). *L'Ordre Psychosomatique*. Paris: Payot.

Marty, P., and de M'Uzan, M. (1963). La pensée opératoire. *Revue Française de Psychanalyse*, 27:345–356.

Marty, P., de M'Uzan, M., and David, C. (1963). *L'Investigation Psychosomatique*. Paris: Presses Universitaires de France.

McDougall, J. (1964). De l'homosexualité féminine. In *La Sexualité Féminine*, ed. J. Chasseguet-Smirgel, pp. 247–305. Paris: Payot. (Eng. trans. *Female Sexuality*, pp. 171–212. Ann Arbor, University of Michigan Press, 1970.)

____ (1974a). The anonymous spectator. *Contemporary Psychoanalysis* 10:289–310.

____ (1974b). The psyche-soma and the analytic process. *International Review of Psycho-Analysis* 1:437–459.

____ (1978). *Plaidoyer Pour Une Certaine Anomalie.* Paris: Gallimard.

____ (1980). A child is being eaten. *Contemporary Psychoanalysis* 16:417–459.

____ (1982). *Théâtres du Je.* Paris: Gallimard. *Theaters of the Mind.* Trans. New York: Basic Books, 1985.

de Mijolla, A. (1981). *Les Visiteurs du Moi.* Paris: Les Belles Lettres.

____ (1982). La psychanalyse en France. In *Histoire de la Psychanalyse*, ed. R. Jaccard, 2:5–118. Hachette.

Miller, J.-A., ed. (1976). La scission de 1953. *Ornicar?* 7 (suppl.).

Moore, B. (1984). Review of *Psychoanalysis in France. Journal of the American Psychoanalytic Association* 32:195–199.

Nora, P. (1978). America and the French intellectuals. *Daedalus* Winter: pp. 325–335.

Oliner, M. M. (1958). Perceived similarity to the parent of the same sex and sex role acceptance. Unpublished doctoral dissertation, Columbia University.

____ (1982a). Hysterical features among children of survivors. In *Generations of the Holocaust*, ed. M. Bergmann and M. Jucovy, pp. 267–286. New York: Basic Books.

____ (1982b). The anal phase. In *Early Female Development*, ed. D. Mendell, pp. 25–60. New York: Spectrum Publications.

____ (1988). Anal components of overeating. In *Bulimia: Psychoanalytic Treatment and Theory*, ed. H. J. Schwartz, pp. 215–240. Madison: International Universities Press.

Pasche, F. (1960). Le symbole personnel. In *À Partir de Freud*, pp. 157–179. Paris: Payot.

_____ (1969). *A Partir de Freud*. Paris: Payot.

_____ (1975). Perception et déni dans la relation analytique. *Revue Française de Psychanalyse* 39:565–568.

Pasche, F., and Renard, M. (1984). Sur les critères d'admission aux cures controlées. *Revue Française de Psychanalyse* 48:451–454.

Pichon, E. (1938). La réalité devant M. Laforgue. *Revue Française de Psychanalyse* 10:669–691.

Pontalis, J.-B. (1977). *Entre le Rêve et la Douleur*. Paris: Gallimard.

_____ (1979). Le métier à tisser. *Nouvelle Revue de Psychanalyse* 20:5–12.

Racamier, P.-C. (1973). *Le Psychanalyste Sans Divan*. Paris: Payot.

_____ (1979). *De Psychanalyse en Psychiatrie*. Paris: Payot.

Reich, A. (1940). Contribution to the analysis of extreme submissiveness in women. In *Psychoanalytic Contributions*, pp. 85–94. New York: International Universities Press, 1973.

_____ (1954). Early identifications as archaic elements in the superego. In *Psychoanalytic Contributions*, pp. 209–236. New York: International Universities Press, 1973.

Richards, A. (1984). Review of Grunberger's *Narcissism*. *Journal of the American Psychoanalytic Association* 32:199–204.

Robert, M. (1974). *D'Oedipe à Moise, Freud et la Conscience Juive*. Calmann-Levy.

Roudinesco, E. (1982). *La Bataille de Cent Ans*. Vol. 1. Paris: Editions Ramsay.

_____ (1986). *Histoire de la Psychanalyse en France.2*. Paris: Seuil.

Roustang, F. (1976). *Un Destin Si Funeste*. Paris: Éditions de Minuit.

_____ (1986). *Lacan de l'Équivoque à l'Impasse*. Paris: Éditions de Minuit.

Sandler, A. M. (1982). The selection and function of the training analyst in Europe. *International Revue of Psychoanalysis* 9:386–397.

Schneiderman, S. (1983). *Jacques Lacan*. Boston: Harvard University Press.

Schur, M. (1955). Comments on the metapsychology of somatization. *Psychoanalytic Study of the Child* 10:119–164.

____ (1972). *Freud: Living and Dying*. New York: International Universities Press.

Smirnoff, V. N. (1979). De Vienne à Paris. *Nouvelle Revue de Psychanalyse* 20:13–58.

Spitz, R. A., and Wolf, K. M. (1946). Anaclitic depression. An inquiry into the genesis of psychiatric condition in early childhood. *Psychoanalytic Study of the Child* 2:313–342.

Stéphane, A. (pseud.) (1969). *L'Univers Contestationnaire*. Paris: Payot.

Stein, M. (1966). Self observation, reality, and the superego. In: *Psychoanalysis: A General Psychology*, ed. R. M. Loewenstein, L. M. Newman, M. Schur, and A. J. Solnit, pp. 275–297. New York: International Universities Press.

Stern, M. M. (1951). Anxiety, trauma, and shock. *Psychoanalytic Quarterly* 20:2 179–203.

Turkle, S. (1978). *Psychoanalytic Politics, Freud's French Revolution*. New York: Basic Books.

Index